Groups

	8. Communication	9. Motives & Expectations	10. Playing Well Together
Trouble Signs	• Discomfort is hindering communication • Information is not disclosed • Assumptions replace communications • Difficulties erode trust among team members • Team members "go dark"	• Behavior of others elicits anger or surprise • Projects are driven with unreasonable expectations • Conflicts erode team morale	• There is a strong dependence on heroes • Individuals hide information • Estimates are slashed to meet constraints • People are taken for granted
Success Indicators	• Feedback is used to ensure communication is complete • Strong trust exists among the team • Paraphrasing is used to clarify understanding	• Motives of others are known and respected • The team is positively motivated to perform • Bad news is provided proactively	• Team performance is rewarded • There are few disruptions to planned work • Expression of interests is acceptable
Questions to Ask	• Am I using the right medium for this message? • Are communications based on mutual respect?	• Do we all understand the project's goals? • Can I leverage knowledge of other's emotions? • Do I actually understand my product?	• What are the games being played here? • Is this information rumor or fact? • Am I comfortable with this situation?
Tools for Support	• Understand the recipient's needs • Communicate face-to-face • Improve communication skills • Take responsibility for your part of trust in relationships • Use active listening and feedback	• Use the SDI as a mechanism to explore motivations • Understand weaknesses as overdone strengths • Take responsibility for change • Reduce the intangible through analysis	• Share all relevant information • Seek common ground in negotiations • Ensure you are working from the facts • Plan in order to avoid disruptions • Work together to solve problems

FINDING YOUR WAY

To navigate around this book, we have combined shapes for the four stages of teamwork:

◆ **Individuals**

■ **Groups**

◀ **Teams**

● **Stakeholders**

…with symbols representing the four types of notes:

✚ **Trouble Signs**

ⵖ **Success Indicators**

? **Questions to Ask**

🔧 **Tools for Support**

…to provide 16 icons into the key concepts in the book.

For example, provides us Success Indicators for Teams.

The points for each type of note are sequential within each chapter.

Software Teamwork:
Taking Ownership
for Success

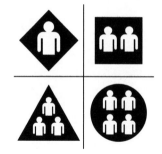

Software Teamwork: Taking Ownership for Success

Jim Brosseau

～

＾Addison-Wesley

Upper Saddle River, NJ • Boston • Indianapolis • San Francisco
New York • Toronto • Montreal • London • Munich • Paris • Madrid
Cape Town • Sydney • Tokyo • Singapore • Mexico City

Many of the designations used by manufacturers and sellers to distinguish their products are claimed as trademarks. Where those designations appear in this book, and the publisher was aware of a trademark claim, the designations have been printed with initial capital letters or in all capitals.

The author and publisher have taken care in the preparation of this book, but make no expressed or implied warranty of any kind and assume no responsibility for errors or omissions. No liability is assumed for incidental or consequential damages in connection with or arising out of the use of the information or programs contained herein.

The publisher offers excellent discounts on this book when ordered in quantity for bulk purchases or special sales, which may include electronic versions and/or custom covers and content particular to your business, training goals, marketing focus, and branding interests. For more information, please contact:

U.S. Corporate and Government Sales
(800) 382-3419
corpsales@pearsontechgroup.com

For sales outside the United States, please contact:

International Sales
international@pearsoned.com

This Book Is Safari Enabled

The Safari® Enabled icon on the cover of your favorite technology book means the book is available through Safari Bookshelf. When you buy this book, you get free access to the online edition for 45 days.

Safari Bookshelf is an electronic reference library that lets you easily search thousands of technical books, find code samples, download chapters, and access technical information whenever and wherever you need it.

To gain 45-day Safari Enabled access to this book:

- Go to www.awprofessional.com/safarienabled.
- Complete the brief registration form.
- Enter the coupon code 3DQ1-6UYQ-1XLC-S5P1-4CAN.

If you have difficulty registering on Safari Bookshelf or accessing the online edition, please e-mail customer-service@safaribooksonline.com.

Visit us on the Web: www.awprofessional.com

Library of Congress Cataloging-in-Publication Data:
Library of Congress Cataloging-in-Publication Data
Brosseau, Jim, 1960-
    Software teamwork : taking ownership for success / Jim Brosseau.
        p. cm.
    Includes bibliographical references and index.
    ISBN 0-321-48890-3 (pbk. : alk. paper)
        1. Computer software--Development--Management. I. Title.

QA76.76.D47B757 2007
005.1068--dc22

                                                                              2007034655

ISBN-13: 978-0-321-48890-9
ISBN-10: 0-321-48890-3
Text printed in the United States on recycled paper at RR Donnelley in Crawfordsville, Indiana.
First printing October 2007

Editor-in-Chief

Karen Gettman

Executive Editor

Chris Guzikowski

Senior Development Editor

Chris Zahn

Managing Editor

Gina Kanouse

Project Editor

Jovana San Nicolas-Shirley

Copy Editor

Keith Cline

Indexer

Lisa Stumpf

Proofreader

Water Crest Publishing

Editorial Assistant

Raina Chrobak

Cover Designer

Warren Oneschuk, OnDesign Creative Resources

Cover Coordination

Gary Adair

Composition

codeMantra

Contents

PART TWO

Individuals

PART FOUR

Teams

PART FIVE

Stakeholders

PART SIX

Putting It All Together

PART SEVEN

Appendix

Preface

Books such as Tom Demarco and Tim Lister's *Peopleware* and Fred Brooks's *Mythical Man-Month* are timeless. This is both because the advice provided is practical and because this advice is still rarely adopted. We all read these calls to action and imagine a better work environment, and then we lament that our managers aren't taking charge of change.

Tagging along for the ride is easy, but to be effective you need to be an active, proactive, and intentional team member. We must each take active responsibility for making things happen, for committing to and fostering a healthy environment in which great products can be built.

This is a book for everyone involved in software development, not just the managers or anointed change agents who are deemed as the point people to drive change. We all need to actively drive our work environment—it is not just a management concern. As individuals, we can all significantly improve our productivity. Practitioners are the ones best suited to propose and contribute to changes to our overall team performance.

"Leadership" here is cooperatively participating with others to most effectively achieve a common goal. A team of effective leaders can work miracles. We all need to take ownership and convert these miracles into reality on our teams.

Many of the subjects discussed in this book aren't necessarily about software development and could readily apply to almost any team environment. Indeed, many of the principles and practices discussed here are common across disciplines outside of software development. This book, however, was developed based on my experience in and with software teams, and a few factors seem to make software development experiences different:

- Because software is seen as abstract and intangible, there is generally little common understanding of the expected outcome or the scope of work.
- Because training for this field is primarily technical, there is rarely explicit focus on the management of individual attitudes or team dynamics.
- Because of these factors, teams often experience pain on projects, sometimes failing outright.
- Even so, team sustainability is rarely considered as a key success factor.

So, in one way, this book is all about software development. This is the domain in which dysfunction is most rampant, more so than in other fields I know anything about. Best practices are always discussed but rarely successfully applied. The typical approach for fixing problems is through a technical solution, by specifying more practices that end up further constraining the team. There has to be a better way.

It Is Time We Get Started

There really is not, and never will be, a "silver bullet," that magical solution to our woes. It's one thing to have Fred Brooks suggest that there were no silver bullets in 1986, and another thing altogether to have hopes dashed through trial and error of personal experience. We can't expect a hero to come along to save the day. It is up to all of us to contribute in a positive way to improving the experience of software development any way we can.

Having worked with a number of those who believe themselves to be part of the solution for this industry, I've come to the conclusion that we are all similarly challenged to some degree. Most consultants suffer from many of the same issues as the clients they are proposing to help. We all live in our own box, and we all find it difficult to see things from outside our box.

So, if there is no silver bullet on the horizon, no real heroes, and we are all in our own box, what are we to do? The solution to our problem is a *coordinated team* effort to make our life better. We all need to contribute to this solution, and these contributions need to work together for the common good.

We need to drive change ourselves. We can't blame external circumstances forever, and we can no longer rest on the relative youth of the software industry as an excuse. Although medicine has been called the youngest science, with a vast amount of information to absorb and a high rate of change, practitioners dare not use these challenges as excuses for failure. Here in the software industry, we also have much to learn and experience a high rate of change, but we have been much less proactive in managing our challenges.

We are the solution that we have been waiting for all this time. We are the ones who have the responsibility to make our software development experiences stronger. We need to start today.

We all have something to contribute, even if it is just a new set of eyes to look at a problem from a different angle. Smooth running teams build on each other's strengths to form a stronger whole.

Change is made one step at a time. Although it's nice to have an overall context or strategic goal to work toward, the problems in most software teams are so extreme, so rampant, so fundamental that even a few minor tweaks can do wonders. I've seen more than one organization turn things around with one or two well-selected adjustments.

Indeed, even with major dysfunction, massive changes will often bring more negative culture shock than positive benefits. There are companies that no longer exist today, at least partially because of the impact of a major improvement initiative.

You won't find a methodology in this book. There are plenty of them to go around, either too narrow to be widely applicable or too broad to be easily applied to a specific situation.

You won't find prescriptions or checklists here either. These are best when tuned to your specific culture, even if they are based on some of the excellent sources available in the software literature.

What you will find is an exploration of the problems that we need to consider, a reasonable order by which we should tackle those problems, and recommendations about how to deal with each stage. All points to consider, but no book will give you *the* answer.

This book is about making changes palatable to the people on our teams. Small, focused changes, with consideration to the existing culture.

The Lay of the Land

This book is divided into six major parts.

Part 1 focuses on the state of the industry today. For all the efforts spent on improvement, we are not significantly better off than we were 30 years ago. We explore the issues with both anecdotes and hard data, and I suggest a sequence of stages that can lead to a stronger overall solution.

We start through these stages in Part 2, and consider how everyone has a different view of any situation, and brings to the table unique viewpoints and emotions shaped by past preconceptions and experiences. All of these are important to consider, and should be dealt with in a conscious, objective fashion.

A range of interactions and forces will govern any group, in the workplace or elsewhere. These will strongly influence the overall nature of the relationships and the resultant quality of the work produced. Just as Part 2 explored individuals, Part 3 looks at the issues around group dynamics and relating with others.

Part 4 explores what happens as this group starts to organize into a team. The core issues here are how to effectively organize, align, guide, and coordinate the team toward a common goal.

After the team has dealt with the issues of coordination, they can look at the issues around stakeholders in Part 5. Here, the deepest challenges are in shared communication and management of change as work progresses toward successfully solving problems.

Finally, Part 6 deals with the issues of introducing change. Doing this in any form is difficult, and driving change within a comprehensive model while minimizing the negative impact can be even more so. This section identifies several guiding principles to use while fostering change in your organization.

Although the book proceeds logically, you could easily dive into each section independently. Each chapter is self-contained, but the topics are arranged in a progression that explores the range of issues from problem to solution. Icons in the margins highlight symptoms of trouble, success indicators, questions to ask, and tools to use, and are explained inside the front cover.

These reference points are thoroughly captured on the four inside covers of the book, providing a navigation guide for Parts 2 through 5.

Origins

The vast majority of the topics covered in this book have come directly from my 10 years of consulting experience, and from my direct software development experience over the 20 years before that. A problem would arise. We would work to distill the essence of the problem and identify an approach, and then resolve that problem. I've personally worked on embedded systems, air traffic control systems, and shrink-wrap products, and consulted to companies in a broad range of sectors. No one sector has yet solved the challenge of growing a sustainable team without pain, but there have been hints of success everywhere.

I published much of this material in weekly newsletters over the past five years. Initially, it seemed aggressive to launch a newsletter on a weekly basis. Over the years, however, it has been easy to consistently find new situations to write about. There is no shortage of challenges facing today's software teams. Many of those who believe it is a smooth ride are either deluding themselves or are being deluded by others.

The issues discussed herein occur in teams ranging from very early-stage start-ups (and even situations that could easily be described as pre-start-up, where they don't even realize they are trying to solve a problem with software) to very large, mature, safety-critical applications.

Many of the groups discussed in this book are only marginally aware that software development frameworks and maturity models exist, but others have been assessed at high maturity levels based on these models. Some have used established frameworks to varying degrees of success and even contributed to best practice content over the years.

The views here are not intended to replace existing approaches to resolving challenges in the software industry, but are seen more as a complementary but neglected space. We are all humans interacting to build novel systems, and to do so effectively, we need to be engaged, working in an environment that effectively channels our creativity. To some degree, what is discussed in this book is a precursor to allowing you to effectively use the more commonly discussed engineering solutions.

Anecdotes in this book reflect actual situations and events that have taken place, from a wide variety of situations. These have intentionally not been tweaked to appear as a single team throughout the book. Some readers might recognize themselves in these pages; I hope this recognition will be taken as positive.

Acknowledgments

As with any venture that spans a number of years, many people contributed significantly to make this a better product than it would have been otherwise.

Geoff Flamank, Patrick Conroy, Robert Goatham, and countless others have been my sounding board for a number of years. Thanks for ongoing discussion and rants about the state of the software industry and what to do about it.

Thanks to David Forrest, Sharon Habib, Marina Ma, and Simon Mok, of our Change Collaborative Group. You have clarified for me that the issues we face for change in software teams are truly universal issues.

Steve Tockey got me involved with book reviews for Addison-Wesley, starting with a discussion over home brews and a foray into reviewing his superb book, *Return on Software*. Karl Wiegers has provided great support and guidance over the years, including an introduction to Addison-Wesley. Both Steve and Karl provided detailed, constructive feedback on earlier drafts of this material.

Putting a book together is much more than tossing 125,000 words into a bag. More than anything else, the critical feedback of the technical reviewers keeps the author of a book like this honest. Thanks to the technical reviewers of the book: Matt Heusser provided several rounds of deep feedback, which in turn generated some rich debate on the side; Ethan Roberts, Dmitri Zimine, and Karl Wiegers also provided important feedback and advice along the way.

Thanks go out to Tim Scudder at Personal Strengths Publishing for keeping me honest about the work of Elias H. Porter and his Relationship Awareness theory.

Thanks again to Chris Guzikowski, Kim Boedigheimer, Chris Zahn, and the rest of the staff at Addison-Wesley, for all the advice and support and making the writing of this book such an enjoyable experience. The challenging moments I brought on myself.

Thanks to the readers of my newsletter for putting up with my rants on a weekly basis. I'm sure they might have seemed incoherent at times, but I hope you have managed to find nuggets in some of them.

Thanks to all the pointy-haired bosses I've had over the years who have shown me how not to run successful teams. The most painful experiences are indeed the source of our greatest learning opportunities. Not all of my bosses fall into this category, but there have been enough to keep me moving in this industry, and to see that the challenges we face truly are endemic.

To my children, Lauren and Owen, thanks for respecting the boundaries of a home-based office, at least most of the time. It was fun to try some of these ideas out on you before bringing them to a wider audience, and for that I apologize.

The biggest thanks go to my wife, Winney, for her early review of material, cleaning up many of my grammatical foibles before passing it around to be beat up by my peers, and confirming that the topics actually make sense. Additional thanks for picking up the slack at home as I dove into a cave to give birth to this thing, and my deepest thanks for supporting me as I headed out to start my own business. Nobody else would have stuck with me through the past five years like you did.

This book's for you.

About the Author

Jim Brosseau has been in the software industry since 1980, in a range of roles from tester and developer to manager and director. He has developed software and managed teams in embedded avionics, ATC systems, and commercial software packages. A common thread through his experience has been a search for more effective collaboration across teams. Jim is principal of the Clarrus Consulting Group, and since 1998 he has consulted with organizations worldwide to improve their approaches for successfully delivering software. He publishes the Clarrus Compendium, a weekly newsletter with a unique perspective on the software industry (www.clarrus.com/resources.htm). He has published numerous technical articles, and has presented at major conferences and local professional associations. Jim lives with his wife and two children in Vancouver.

PART ONE

The Problem Space

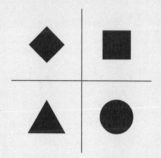

Despite technology advances that allow us to develop more functionality with less effort, many teams are not significantly more successful than their counterparts from decades earlier. Although specific practices such as version control and defect tracking have become more commonplace, major gaps in communication and coordination still exist in many teams.

We have a clear, quantified understanding of the gap between typical practices and best practices, but few organizations can string these best practices together consistently or predictably.

A piece is missing from the puzzle. Too often, teams fail to consider the soft side of collaboration. We need to deal with the human dimension.

CHAPTER ONE

Why Are We So Challenged?

There is no shortage of suggested approaches to developing software, and new ones will continue to appear, and then fall out of favor. Most improvement initiatives disappoint, and often the entire organization is not even working toward the same objectives.

Although a strong body of evidence indicates that there are better ways to develop software, adoption of these practices remains relatively low.

In this chapter, we walk through some of the ongoing attempts at resolving challenges in software development through engineering approaches. Then, we consider some of the human conditions that seem to stand in the way of progress. Finally, we look at why best practices are important, but insufficient as a solution.

Difficultware

Why is software development difficult?

Today, we still build something new almost every time, sometimes just new features and fixes for the same tired old program, or perhaps the same old features with a new framework or language. Reuse has not lived up to its promise. We rarely get past the code reuse level, which often creates more difficulties than starting anew.

In manufacturing, the approach is to rigorously analyze and design up front, and then mass produce the same product over and over again. In software development, we try to act like we're on an assembly line, but we are not. The manufacturing element of software, cutting CDs or electronic deployment, is relatively trivial (assuming we have a handle on our configurations). We often fail to give the analysis and design stages the effort and respect they deserve. Without adequate up-front diligence, simply testing the resulting product is rarely sufficient.

There is the age-old argument that software is ethereal, that its lack of substance makes it difficult to control. To some extent this is true, as the abstractions we use that allow us to worry less about the details also take us further and further from the binary representation.

In most software projects, the real lack of substance remains the lack of clear common understanding of what the product should be, and the management of that information throughout the project life cycle.

Strong Teams Always Watch for Challenges

I sat down for lunch with two of the three people from one of the strongest small software teams I've ever interacted with. They are not assessed as a high-maturity group; they will readily admit their skills and practices are not scalable. Instead, they know their science, practice their art, communicate constantly, and are fully committed to client satisfaction. They do good work. This is why I was surprised when, before they even ordered their triple espressos, they hit me with a barrage of concerns about their current gig.

I walked through some of the usual suspects.

I asked whether they had misunderstandings with the client. No, actually they seem to be getting along well. Both sides had made mid-course adjustments and were being quite reasonable.

Well, then, was it change management issues? Not really. Although there were a large number of changes, they were staying on top of them and not letting the quality of the system slip away, even with a light change management approach (perhaps this was *because* their approach to change wasn't overly rigorous).

With only a couple of people handling all the tasks, from development through management and in-between, they had some challenges in context switching: They would dive deep into an intense coding session, and then come up for air to see the overall schedule challenges.

There are often so many diverse functions to juggle in a small team that the gang from the Cirque du Soleil would be impressed, and this team was performing admirably. Even though successful by most traditional measures, they still had healthy concerns.

At the end of it all, they scheduled aggressively to drive the project forward, and their concern was that the client relationship could go sour if they didn't keep a handle on things.

They recognized the need for constant diligence to continue to keep the project on track, despite current success.

Shortsighted Solutions

When I work with groups to explore the key success factors in effective software projects, they consistently note that the team enjoyed the experience, reasonable planning took place, and communication was open and forthright.

Groups rarely suggest that strong adoption of technology is a key element for success.

Technology can indeed be a good thing, but balance is required. If most groups agree that clear communication is a must for successful teams, this can become one of the key criteria to determine whether more technology is useful.

We're best served by carefully leveraging technology when it can improve our likelihood of success, not by just adding technology to a project. Tools can provide semantic and syntactic checks to eliminate one class of issues, for example, but they are certainly no replacement for gray matter and collaboration.

Here are some of the approaches we continue to try to use to solve our problems.

Purchasing Tools, Building Documents

Technology for its own sake rarely works. Most apparent advances need some shaking out and careful fostering by early adopters before they are effective for the masses.

As an example, recall the hype of generated code from the object-based design models. Although successful for a few disciplined teams that thoroughly understand their design and are comfortable working in that space, this requires vigilance to work within the design even during integration. Despite the promise of Computer Aided Software Engineering (CASE) that has been around for decades, the full benefits will never become mainstream until the general population is as comfortable in the design phase as they are in the implementation phase. As it stands, too few teams even explicitly emphasize design in their products.

Polished reports and clean drawings can easily provide the façade of professionalism and defendability. We can so easily get caught up in superficial issues that we miss glaring holes in the information that we are actually presenting. This cosmetic view of the information is often emphasized at the expense of the content itself.

As we condense more and more information into digestible form (especially for higher levels of management), it becomes too easy to focus on style rather than function. These summaries can highlight important information or can obfuscate what is really happening—just ask any "victim" of a worthless management dashboard.

The document has always been the preferred medium for capturing and disseminating information. Unfortunately, we usually focus on the *document* as the key deliverable, where larger is perceived as better. Instead, we should work to build a *shared understanding* of the interconnected ideas that forms our product.

If we look at the quality of the communication approach for the problem we are trying to solve, we might perceive technology in an entirely different light.

We can clarify by using more, smaller pieces of information instead of building up huge, indigestible documents. We can ensure that key points are commonly understood through the use of feedback, which requires listening from both sides. We can use tools to build common understanding and to automate the mundane tasks, but we must ensure we get our points across. The document can convey information, but it is not a replacement for conversation. It is not the plan, but the planning that provides the real value. We need to communicate.

Be careful when trying to solve a problem with technology or exhaustive documentation; you may be muddying the waters rather than clarifying them.

Debating the Solution Without Consideration of the Problem

There will never be "the right approach" for all projects. Software projects come in too many shapes and sizes. There are too many cultures, and just too many reasons for developing software, even within individual organizations. There is no Holy Grail, but many approaches can be "a reasonable approach," depending on the situation.

Any approach that has survived to the point where it is defined, enjoys a name, and has a following has likely been applied with some degree of success on real projects. These approaches are made up of components that hold together to form a complete system. The buffers in critical chain management, the pair programming in Extreme Programming, the Earned Value approach in "traditional" management circles—all are pieces of well-rounded paths to success.

The problem is that as soon as any approach gathers a following, there will be those with only superficial understanding of what holds the system together who try to apply it to their situation. The results can be disastrous.[1] Just as many of us will try to build a piece of modular furniture without reading the instructions, then find a few extra bolts, take three steps back, finish late, and declare success anyway, we often take shortcuts on our "real" projects because we don't appreciate the value that these neglected tasks provide. Big or small, old or new, all established approaches have successes and failures.

The intent of any approach is to achieve project success, but they take distinctly different approaches toward that end. Matching the approach to the project is a key decision that is often missed, with far-reaching implications. With a successful match, the name of the approach can become a convenient rallying point, and the wisdom embodied in the established details and history of the approach will give us confidence that we will achieve our goals.

Insert the name of your pet approach here: Like Jessica Rabbit, these approaches are not bad; they're just implemented that way on many projects. Project success is more a function of how well the approach is selected, understood, and implemented than any other factor. Best intentions go to waste because of a poor understanding of both the project and approach needed, resulting in weak implementations of the approach and disappointing results for the project.

The "right approach," in every case, is to carefully select an approach that is a reasonable fit to your specific project's various needs, and then remain diligent every step along the way. Even with this, however, there is never a guarantee.

The Frailty of the Human Condition

A number of the challenges we face in software development result from our own shortcomings. Whether these are short attention spans, interpersonal issues, or expectations based on our position within hierarchical structures, we often artificially limit our potential for success.

Cause...Long Pause...Effect

In any discipline, we improve by making observations, distilling the problems to the root causes, identifying change elements to resolve the primary root causes, and implementing these changes. If it seems straightforward, why is it so tough for software organizations to improve over time?

The challenge starts right up front. Jacob Bigelow, a U.S. botanist and author of the first American textbook on botany, wrote, "It is common error to infer that things which are consecutive in order of time have necessarily *the relation of cause and effect.*" You need to understand this relationship to determine what to do better next time around. The greater the gap, the more difficult this is.

When we take shortcuts in software development, the effects often do not appear for quite some time. We fail to correlate the two events and hence fail to take corrective actions for next time. We might forge ahead with a back-of-the-envelope design, confident that we are progressing rapidly, only to find months later that we neglected to include a critical design component. We don't recognize that many of the defects we find have their basis in requirements, because we find them while executing the code. We fail to effectively regression test, and a defect we inject in one change will get lost in the myriad other changes we've made. When the defect bites us later, we've lost our context. In our headlong rush to sprint toward the finish line (despite the line being so far away that a sprint is unreasonable), we make decisions that are perceived to speed progress but often slow us down instead.

We often have challenges identifying root causes, but the problem is more our failure to make timely observations. Project retrospectives are a great approach for gathering up loose ends and identifying juicy elements to improve on. If we only look back at the end of a project, however, it can be months or years between the root-cause event and the discovery.

What to do then? Careful analysis of issues provides rich insight that many teams overlook. Analysis will allow you to better understand the true root causes of the problems that will inevitably be generated in any software project. This, in turn, will simplify the process of getting better. Retrospectives are effective after the fact, but nothing beats good old-fashioned diligence along the way to narrow the gap between cause and effect.

Real-World Results—in Fast-Forward

I had the opportunity to participate in an excellent project management simulation, my second time doing so. The first time I flew solo; this time we ran the exercise in groups, and I sat back and observed.

In the simulation, you (as project manager) get to decide on a monthly basis how to allocate your time on a ten-month project. You are given an expectation of resources and constraints. Each month you get an opportunity to observe how your choices have affected that month's results in terms of scope, cost, time, and quality. Real time gets compressed by a factor of a thousand or so, and significant implications are revealed quickly.

As you might expect, it is better to spend more time in defining scope and putting together a reasonable schedule, setting expectations, and managing communications up front. This sets the stage for a straightforward, predictable project that completes successfully. In the simulation, as with any real-life ten-month project, everything apparently goes well for the first couple of months. All indicators are still within acceptable norms, and there are plenty of thumbs up and pats on the back for a job well done.

Then we start to see some problems creeping in. Quality issues arise as a result of failing to deal with issues up front. Scope creep may begin to rear its ugly head. Even though we thought we had nailed the specifications, we start discovering issues that were not as clear as we thought. If we observe closely enough, we can even start to see the schedule slipping.

Everyone attempts to compensate at this point. If we see scope creep, we'll throw more effort at change management. If we fall behind schedule, we may throw more people at the problem or reallocate existing resources. Some of our actions have immediate impacts, such as a change in direct costs, but others won't show up until later. If we throw more people at the problem, we introduce communications inefficiencies that will likely be felt downstream.

Soon the project begins to spiral out of control (the simulation is frighteningly reminiscent of real-life projects). Our actions become extreme (along with our emotions), and the latency of our compensations starts to affect the project in a way we cannot possibly predict. We have a black box full of springs and pulleys and damping devices that we cannot see into, and the few strings we can pull are difficult to correlate with the outcomes we see. Our constraints frustrate our efforts to manage what we believe is the required emphasis on quality, change, scope, or other areas. As in the real world, in many cases these constraints actually serve us well and prevent us from really making a mess of things.

Almost all attempts at the simulation apparently start off fine for the first couple of months, but most end up with significant time and cost overruns, with huge quality issues, too. The beauty of this simulation is that we see the cause and effect of a ten-month project in the span of a couple of hours, and thus we can more easily make the connection between cause and effect.

The Inertia Against Taking the Proper Steps

We have all taken shortcuts that in hindsight weren't so short after all. Sometimes we dive right into the code rather than take the time to design a reasonable approach. Sometimes we forge ahead to the finish without even a clear list of what is left to do, only to find that there were a couple of "oh yeah, forgot that" items that extended that finish line.

Unless we are aware of a reason to hold back, it is human nature to rush to the endpoint. We're coding, and that's closer to the end of the life cycle than design, so we are further along than if we were designing, right? We need (often driven by management, unfortunately) to feel positive about progress, even if that progress is artificial.

Software development is described as abstract in many organizations. Part of this comes from a lack of appreciation of the value a practical approach can provide. We have all experienced the results of projects without clearly defined scope, or with an unmanaged schedule, deficient design, or inadequate testing, but we fail to make the connection back to the approach taken.

Inexperienced homeowners tackle small (or large) improvements on their own, and the results are as you would expect. Although some teams recognize reasonable software development practices, the vast majority of the industry continues to plod along with the same undisciplined home-improvement mentality. There remains little focus on the life cycle of software development in the schools, and little continuing education in the industry. Most teams are not aware of the right steps to take, and neither is there an appreciation that these steps will save them time, money, and grief. The challenge is that the "right steps" change from project to project, and there is little focus on how to select those right steps.

Human nature compels us to see artificial progress, when instead we need to select an appropriate approach for the task. Until we get better at stepping back and selecting the reasonable approach for our projects, we will continue to stumble through our projects, with corresponding results.

External Support?

Unions and guilds have long been effective in allowing workers to bond together to support their common objectives, with working conditions being a long-standing struggle between the unions and management. On balance, it seems that the labor movement has made great strides for the workplace, although at times it would appear that the power of unions has been taken too far.

Governments play a part in this social fabric, too, and in British Columbia we have the Employment Standards Act. With very clear standards regarding working conditions, it establishes requirements that corporations must comply with to ensure that their employees are treated fairly. So far, so good.

For all fields except high tech, the act provides exceptions to protect the worker based on the circumstances of the field: children in entertainment, seasonal work in agriculture, domestics within the home. For high tech, the act explicitly removes many of the elements that safeguard reasonable work conditions. I would expect that there are similar provisions in many, if not all other provinces in Canada and in other areas worldwide.

The perception is that in the tech sector, it is necessary to work under insane conditions to get our products built. The protections afforded to other industries to ensure fair treatment have largely been removed, or at least significantly eroded. I'm sure many of us have experienced the result of this to some degree.

I've been involved in a death march for a safety-critical project, working 6 or 7 days a week, 12 hours each day. The free meals and flowers to spouses got tired in a hurry. (In fact, when reviewing this chapter, my wife couldn't even recall receiving those flowers.) The conditions wore us down, caused us to make mistakes, and frayed the nerves of the whole team. Turnover was high, and divorces were not uncommon. I left with stress-related illnesses after six years.

The management culture of pushing tech employees hard to get things done is ludicrous, but remains far too common. Attempts to modify the culture are often met with cries of "Get a spine" or "There's a lineup of people waiting to work here," and to some degree, that demand simply fuels the fire. The problem spans the range from safety-critical systems to games development and all projects in between. I was recently speaking with someone from a large global consulting firm and he indicated that there is explicit pressure to put in more hours beyond the standard 40-hour workweek—it is an unwritten standard.

To my knowledge, no quantitative study indicates that running the team hard for extended periods results in higher productivity. Indeed, data from my own clients strongly indicates that longer hours result in a decrease in organizational performance. There is a huge fiscal and human cost in employee burnout and turnover, but corporations press on, aided and abetted by ludicrous exemptions to employment standards.

A few astute corporations recognize that their human resources are not easily interchangeable, and they carefully maintain an attractive working environment. In other companies, as individuals we need to take a more proactive role to advocate the changes that we want and to choose the types of companies we work with. We cannot depend on the support of others.

The Truth About Best Practices

It is possible that *best practices* is the most overused term in software development today. Anyone discussing what needs to be done to improve the situation on projects will use the term. It is the basis for almost any consultant's pitch. We train in best practices, we study and promote best practices, and we still face challenges. What is it about these best practices that makes them so compelling, and why don't they seem to work as well as consultants would suggest?

The term *best practices* is not new. The idea of activities or techniques that are the most effective at solving problems was bantered around in the early 1900s. There are best practices in manufacturing and agriculture, among others. There are Generally Accepted Accounting Practices (GAAP); although not quite best practices, they are an expression of the way things are done for accounting.

For any practice to become a good practice, it needs to be shown to be effective in the real world. To become a best practice, it needs to be seen as the most effective approach to accomplishing a goal, in a repeatable fashion over a large sample space. Let's consider each of these achievements, good and best, in turn.

Many practices have been shown to be effective in the real world, with truly amazing results. Studies in formal inspections, for example, often show a return on investment as high as 10:1, a dramatic reduction in life cycle costs, and improved delivered quality. Most other practices demonstrate less-compelling results in studies, but many are still seen as worthwhile investments: iterative life cycles, change management, software reuse, prototyping, metrics programs. They are all good practices, far too many to list here.

All of these practices have been shown to work on real projects. With appropriate practices, you can deliver a consistent and predictably repeatable product. Fewer surprises arise when there is a clear direction to move in and when it has been decided up front what steps need to be taken, where the checks and balances lie, and so on.

Certainly the literature leans toward publishing the results of successes in applying these practices. I'll throw some of my own data into the fray. I've collected demographic and performance data, as well as data related to the application of a variety of practices, from close to 700 respondents across almost 75 groups. With all that data, we compared demographics and practices against performance for all the groups, to discern any observable correlation.

Figure 1-1 shows the results. In the chart, the further to the right the bar extends for a given practice or demographic factor, the more positive the correlation to performance. The numbers represent an *average* of the correlations across four performance factors (overall issues, feature creep, rework, and on-time delivery). Although the thresholds vary from factor to factor, those with a numeric value of roughly 0.2 or more represent a variance that is greater than two standard deviations.

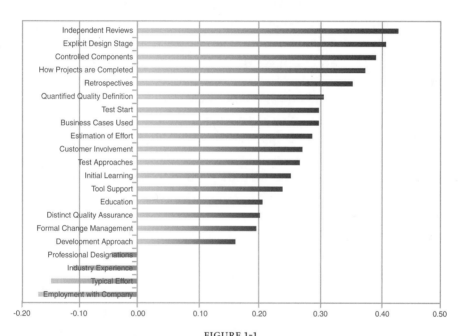

FIGURE 1-1
Correlation of demographics and practices to overall performance

Astonishingly, although perhaps not so in hindsight, there was weakly negative correlation between most demographic factors (professional designations, industry experience, typical effort, and tenure with the company) and performance. Duration of employment with the company and industry experience seemed at first counterintuitive, but actually make sense. Some people tend to stick with a company because it provides them with a steady job, and once comfortable there is no pressure to excel. For those who have been in the industry for a while, we often see similar situations where there is no incentive to remain current with changing technology.

The most negative correlation became apparent in groups that had long-established teams. It appears that inertia develops in organizations, and without the injection of new blood in the mix an organization's performance can stagnate: "That's just the way we've always done things around here."

Where is the positive correlation with performance strongest? All the strongest elements were these "best practices," most of which have been traditionally recognized as good things to do on projects. They included independent reviews, retrospectives, a quantified definition of quality, an explicit design stage, and so on.

Organizations that reasonably apply the appropriate practices are at the top of these performance charts. These practices are explicitly identified as important things to do. Rather than the lip service that falls away when schedule pressures mount, management provides the actual support and time for these practices to do what they are supposed to do: facilitate the delivery of great software on time.

But are these *best* practices? Because projects and project teams come in all shapes and sizes, it is never safe to say a priori that any practice is the most effective approach a team can take on. Although formal inspections can provide tremendous value for some projects, cultural considerations might make this practice difficult to implement, or even counterproductive with some teams. You could easily make a similar argument for any practice discussed. From that point of view, when we are talking about software development in general, the term *best practices* is hyperbole.

Under the right conditions, however, many of these practices can be very effective. This is the key point, that any practice is only situationally valuable. Short agile iterations may make sense for some projects, whereas deep analysis and design better serve other projects. Some cultures may easily embrace a flattened, distributed decision structure, whereas others thrive under a stronger hierarchy.

The fact that "it depends" whether a practice makes sense to apply is generally lost in software development. Consultants pitch their specific flavor of practices as the solution without regard for the client situation, and sometimes the results disappoint (and how often is the consultant held accountable?). On teams, we tend to accept the advice of consultants without deeper study of the ramifications of our actions. We try to apply best practices, and find we are often disappointed with the results. We conclude that this process improvement stuff doesn't work.

One of the most widely exposed catalogs of best practices is in Steve McConnell's *Rapid Development*.[2] The last third of that book consists of 27 best practice chapters, each one selected as an effective way to optimize speed on projects (indicating that there are other practices that optimize other factors). A critical part of each of these chapters is an identification of the situations in which the practice is effective, the major risks associated with the practice, and the major interactions and trade-offs. Again, this information is often overlooked during the consultant's sales cycle and neglected by many practitioners.

This might be one reason why Fred Brooks asserted, in his "No Silver Bullet" essay, "The gap between the best software engineering practice and the average practice is very wide—perhaps wider than in any other engineering discipline."[3] This assertion was made in the context of expert systems that could someday disseminate the "experience and accumulated wisdom of the best programmers" to inexperienced programmers. We're still not there more than 30 years later, and the gap remains wider than it should be.

So, there are many good practices, each having merit in some situations, but the insight of how to select and apply them is not generally exposed or recognized. Schools tend to emphasize technical skills because that is what the industry demands, and many of the practices we talk about are largely ignored or simply covered in a survey course. Many development teams rely on technical skills and heroic efforts to complete their projects. For many of the good practices that have been identified, in my experience there remains an alarmingly low rate of adoption. There are very few teams with disciplined estimation techniques, there are generally glaring omissions in analysis and design on projects, and there is little conscious selection of project life cycles. Similar gaps exist for any practice I can think of.

On top of all this, it is important to recognize that other factors contribute to project success. We can't just build a product and automatically be successful. The product needs a market, and the message needs to find that market. There is as much science in all the other disciplines as there is in product development, and any aspect of the business can make or break product adoption. Some would suggest that luck and timing play a major role, too.

With all the factors outside of software development, the apparent cost required to select and implement practices that improve product development, and the experience of poorly managed change, it is no wonder that best practice discussion quickly fades in most shops.

There are no best practices, only situationally good practices. You need to be aware of the practices, understand whether it makes sense to apply them, and then apply them correctly. This entails a great deal of effort and discovery, but done right, the payoff is enormous. With all this, there are no guarantees of success; after all, the most effective practices for your situation might be wholly outside the software development discipline.

A strategy of simply hiring the best and brightest will not, in itself, give you any advantage in the marketplace. You need to consciously determine which practices will best support your needs on a project and ensure the team has the skills and time available to actually leverage them.

Not the Only Factor

Often, when chatting with peers, the topic turns to a discussion of drivers that affect overall company performance. Generally, the anecdotal conclusion is that at best a weak correlation exists between the following of specific best practices and how a company performs. This can be frightening for someone in the business of helping companies apply best practices.

A couple of observations drive this conclusion. First, if you go to almost any presentation made by leaders of "successful companies," their stories usually revolve around being very close to broke, scrambling and scraping to survive, and then some miracle occurred to rescue them. Only rarely will you hear a tale of making it to the top through a disciplined approach of best practices (although it does occur, such as at the end of Chapter 25, "Constant Vigilance"). Best practices are rarely focused on at the business level, where it does not make for a dramatic story.

The second observation is that more than a few companies have been around for a while and are getting along with absolutely abysmal practices. If it weren't that they are still around and (in some cases) making money, they could be the poster children for why best practices are important. Huge amounts of waste, brutal product quality, and plunging employee morale are the norm in many shops that are seen as successful from a business perspective. They continue to plod along, setting a low standard for the term *good enough,* oblivious to the potential increased effectiveness that is within their grasp.

The first observation above clearly indicates that doing things right is not enough. Doing the right things is very important, too. Your product has to have a market, and you have to expose that product to the potential market. Often, with many entrepreneurs focusing on the technical solution, the disciplines of marketing and sales have a strong element of timing and luck for many success stories.

The second observation demonstrates that inertia is a strong force in business. Companies that burst onto the scene with what may appear to be luck or timing can continue to move along for quite some time with their existing momentum. Those that never make that leap will constantly struggle along, or silently fade away. In the former case, initial prominence in their sector can sustain them through many setbacks, which can slow or reverse their forward motion. In the latter case, a single bump in the road can derail them permanently.

So, does strong execution really matter if there is so much evidence of companies progressing without it?

In the first case, if luck and timing are indeed key components of what it takes to burst onto the scene, doing things right will take you further with your available cash, and will also reduce the number of bumps you will face until your time indeed arrives. For every success story that you hear, a dozen good ideas have been scuttled early because of poor execution.

In the second case, strong execution will allow you to retain that initial prominence that you had as you burst onto the scene. After you carve out your niche, you instantly become the target for competition as others learn from your mistakes and apply their own insights to the issues. Staying on top of the heap isn't easy. As you continue in your niche, margins drop, competition rises, and commoditization forces you to continuously optimize. Eroding momentum is difficult to see if you are not watching closely, and there is the danger that one day you will wake up to find that you, too, are slowly fading away.

Although application of appropriate software best practices is not a panacea, it has a key supporting role for companies struggling to burst onto the scene (and for those struggling to stay there).

Best practices rarely take a starring role in a success story, but look behind the curtain of many failures and you are likely to see a glaring absence of this critical bit player.

Summary

As a whole, the software industry is fraught with significant challenges. We tend to focus only on technology to solve our problems, while we completely gloss over the human foibles that are really at the root of most of our challenges.

Common understanding tends to drop as the size of the team grows, as communication is not adequately managed. Part of this communication needs to be an ongoing effort to drive understanding and to apply best practices.

Every organization I have encountered has room for improvement in this area, and the ones that are more effective in communicating demonstrate stronger results. The range across different teams remains very wide, and success does not come accidentally.

We need to consciously manage a shared understanding of our actions and measure their impact accordingly. To do this, we need to build an appreciation for teams and individuals as a critical component of successful software development. We are missing an appropriate focus on the human element.

How Is This Relevant?

Improvement initiatives. Think of current initiatives for improvement in your organization that affect you, or that you might even be contributing to or leading. Do they fall into the ongoing trap of dogmatically following approaches recommended by others? Do they include the blind adoption of tools?

Focus on the real goal. The technologies and the approaches we use are simply a means to an end, not the end in itself. Does your organization promote itself as "We're Approach A" or "We're Technology B?" Wouldn't it make more sense to brand yourself with "We deliver great products, and we do it in a way that is most effective?" Although it is nice to have focused expertise, it can be dangerous to pigeonhole yourself. Focus at the appropriate level.

Your performance. How do you know whether your current practices are contributing to your success or dragging you down? What measures could you put in place to help answer that question?

Quantification. Are the decisions being made in your organization based on numbers, or are decisions based on instinct or guesses? What is the success rate of these decisions that are being made?

Objectivity. Are the numbers being used within your organization free from biases? Are they collected to answer a question or to defend a position?

References

1. Jim Brosseau, "Beyond the Hype of a New Approach," *Cutter IT Journal*, July 2004.

2. Steve McConnell, *Rapid Development: Taming Wild Software Schedules* (Microsoft Press, 1996).

3. Frederick P. Brooks Jr., *The Mythical Man-Month: Essays on Software Engineering, Anniversary Edition* (Addison-Wesley, 1995).

CHAPTER TWO

Do the Right Thing

To genuinely improve our collective ability to create great software products, we need to recognize that the critical components of getting better have been largely ignored. A sustainable solution begins within each of us.

In this chapter, we make a distinction here between the approaches we normally take for getting things done and a different approach where we all proactively drive teamwork and cooperation. If we all step up and work together toward a common goal, we are much further ahead.

Doing Things Right vs. Doing the Right Thing

A distinction needs to be made in the software world, one that can generate much more effective use of our valuable time and resources.

Often, improvement initiatives are based on the desire to become more technically efficient. This is the "silver-bullet" solution and is often tools based in nature. If effectively managed, these approaches can indeed generate productivity gains or higher predictability in getting the project completed as expected. This approach is the *doing things right* method. We ensure that, given a task, we do it in the most expedient manner at our disposal. Doing things right is always apparently urgent, but rarely critical. This approach generates relatively easy solutions with relatively small gains.

However, to truly maximize the value of improvement initiatives, you need to *do the right things*. This means working on the root issues that result in the greatest benefit.

At the business level, it is important to ensure that you meet the client needs, not just get the current project done. It has to be the right project. There has to be a strong business case for proceeding with any project; and as the shape of the project changes over time, the case driving that project needs to be revisited, too. To stop a project that no longer has a viable business case is not failure. It makes good business sense to divert those resources elsewhere.

At the development level, there are an overwhelming number of tasks that you could do right. If you try to do them all with your limited resources, you are sure to fail on both time and cost factors. A key part of managing development activities is the appropriate selection of the right activities that will most likely lead to overall success. Focus must be placed on the work that provides the best value for reducing uncertainty or generating part of the final product.

We need to strive for effectiveness over mere efficiency. At all levels, it is often a safe bet that the appropriate tasks to tackle are the ones that are closest to the root cause of the problem. They will have the greatest positive impact on success.

Sustainability

When we talk about sustainability for software businesses, everyone brings a very different perspective to the table.

There are those who would be happy to make it through the day without significant grief and disruption. These individuals often work in an environment where each new day brings a different set of surprises and challenges, often negative. For these people, sustainability means reactive survival, and there's no point even looking at a more distant horizon.

Others can see past the daily grind. Sustainability for them is measured by project completion, which may be weeks or months out, and drives daily activities. This longer context brings greater meaning to their daily work.

We start thinking strategically when we consider the parade of projects that will sustain the organization over a longer term, but even here there are shades of gray. There are times when what has to be cut from the current release drives projects, a tactical rather than strategic approach. For companies accountable to shareholders, strategy might mean only planning as far out as the next quarter, or planning for the anticipated IPO or acquisition.

None of these appear to be sustainable models. With new companies sprouting up whose objective is to be acquired as soon as possible (ruthlessly driving for higher sales figures rather than sound financials), with CEOs specializing in quick turnarounds that reflect positively on the current quarter at the expense of downstream results, with VCs focusing on their own IRR and liquidity events, identifying the companies that truly emphasize long-term sustainability becomes even more difficult.

At the executive level, it is rare to see an appreciation for true sustainability that goes beyond fiscal reward. Success is measured primarily in the packages negotiated and the toys accumulated, driven almost exclusively by tactical approaches. Indeed, those driving a sustainable business (insert your truly visionary executive here) stand out because they are so rare in today's world. It is difficult to focus past the tactical milestones. It requires a concerted effort from a well-coordinated team. Unfortunately, single-mindedness is often interpreted as "it's my way or the highway."

Below the executive level, most people aren't normally expected to consider long-term sustainability. They're the worker bees who get the job done. Although many at this level appear to be comfortable with such an Orwellian approach (at least initially in their careers), there is significant value and reward in contemplating and focusing on the bigger picture. Indeed, many of us need to understand the role we play in the larger context to become a true stakeholder in the shared success with the company. As we grow, we gain an appreciation for alignment with the overall vision. Those who are unable to gain that perspective in their current organization will eventually move on, and in doing so, impact the sustainability of the organization they are leaving.

At all levels, the key ingredient for sustainability is active involvement from the people who make up the organization. Although participation does not necessarily mean consensus (this appears to work only with a relatively small group), it does mean that there is honest and open engagement at all levels within the organization. There needs to be an appreciation that this investment in human capital is essential, rather than perceiving human resources as a manageable expense. With a truly long-term vision of what the business intends to provide to its clients, the entire group can align themselves and work miracles.

Goals are better achieved when everyone is synchronized and willing to collaborate on a strategic approach.

The funny thing is, a focus on building a truly sustainable business is not necessarily at odds with any of the more tactical goals driving many of today's companies, even if it may be perceived that way. This might be more difficult, but it is also much more rewarding, especially if success is measured in terms beyond a paycheck.

The Way Things Are Done

Rear Admiral Grace Hopper said, "The most damaging phrase in the English language is 'It's always been done that way,'" and I tend to agree.

We all resist change, even if we know deep down inside that it would be for the best, and no shortage of rationalization takes place to help us maintain the status quo. We invent all manner of excuses for preferring the current situation to any change, and when all else fails, we fall back on the old standard.

It is important to recognize that change comes in many shapes and sizes, from those changes that are essential for our survival to the changes that will set us back several steps, from trivial tweaks to overwhelming disruptions. We need to train our minds to recognize opportunities where a change can add value, instead of simply refusing to take on any changes at all.

If you ever run into a situation where you can't possibly comprehend the value of the task you are being asked to do, ask around. There may be a chance that the rationale for performing a task is truly valid, but just not clear on the surface. If nobody can give you a valid justification for doing the work, there is a significant problem here that needs to be addressed. In most cases, it makes sense to focus your efforts on tasks that more clearly contribute to the organization's goals.

Part of the Standard Agreement

I was involved in a discussion with a potential referral partner a few weeks ago and had some concerns with the restrictions in their "standard" agreement.

They indicated they couldn't drop these restrictions, despite my suggestion that they were not in the best interest of our collective clients. Their only argument for their case was that they've always done it that way.

Their argument made no sense to me, and certainly provided me with no benefit. They are now an "ex-potential referral partner." I would rather be able to do what I need to so that I can serve the needs of my clients in an unfettered manner.

If the organization refuses to act on evidence of dysfunction—if you can't find out why you are being asked to do something—perhaps the problem runs deeper. At some places, all manner of tasks are performed simply because people have been told to do them, with no regard to the bigger picture. The internal cost of this overhead can be huge, and the human cost of not knowing where you contribute to the overall perspective can be just as devastating.

Questioning activities needs to be balanced against the potential for inflicting too much change too quickly in an organization. When a significant amount of effort is wasted on activities that don't clearly contribute to the overall vision, be careful not to introduce too much change. The associated hysteresis (and resulting hysteria) can be as strongly negative as the original undirected activities. Pick a few key changes, make the adjustments, assess the results, and then pick the next key areas. There will always be areas to tweak. Change is not a one-stop proposition.

When developing or adjusting a defined approach for your organization, always consider why you are taking the approach you have chosen. There should be sound rationale for each step of the process, beyond rationalizations such as "that's what we've always done," or "that's the standard for this process," or "it was easy to do it this way."

A significant part of any defined approach should be to provide clear justification of the rationale for each of the steps, to identify the situations where the suggested approach will and won't work, and which issues may arise. Even if you aren't in an organization where people will ask these very important questions, how could you possibly justify deploying something that hasn't been validated against these benchmarks?

Learn to be comfortable with an appropriate amount of ongoing change. Accept this change, seek to continuously renew, and avoid the standard rationalizations for maintaining the status quo.

We Need to Take Ownership for Success

We've all worked in situations that are less than optimal in this industry: projects that seem to go on forever, difficult people, long hours, constant surprises and fires to put out, the feeling that nothing will ever get done. In many organizations, the situation degrades to a point where those who could potentially see the big picture get their feet swept out from under them. The problems that appear to be endemic to your company are actually epidemic throughout the field.

In a culture in which missed commitments are the norm, it is easy for those with even the best intentions to ease into a comfort zone of blame. Sales and marketing seem to promise the world. The development group can't seem to meet expectations that were set elsewhere. That test team just can't be satisfied. Management wonders whether they will ever be able to herd all these groups to closure, and the customer can't seem to make up his mind. It's easy to place blame on one or more of the other groups, because you can then absolve yourself of any responsibility for change— it's outside your sphere of influence.

That view is shortsighted. All these groups with different responsibilities need to coordinate their efforts to bring the project to closure. This coordination is a combination of individual efforts toward a common goal. Realistic commitments need to be agreed upon and achieved. When they are not achieved, the root cause needs to be resolved by the group without resorting to blame. If the system is looked on as a whole rather than as a collection of separate teams, it is rare for external causes to be the cause of failure. The problems lie within, and are more often within our sphere of influence than we care to admit.

Software development is done by people, and is driven by relationships and communication. For any endeavor, effective communication is the primary asset that differentiates the successful team from the challenged group. To succeed, there needs to be an acknowledgement of individual contributions and clear intent to communicate from all individuals. We are all stakeholders with significant influence.

Owning Our Future

Whether we are officially in a recession or a full-blown depression, whether or not the improving economic indicators are real in the face of continuing challenges in the world, it is unnerving to observe how many executives will abdicate responsibility for their company's performance.

Tossing Ownership Aside

A survey across one entire organization revealed a fascinating indicator of ownership in action.

One question asked the entire group to identify their key sources of pain. Although there were a few canned elements they could select, there was also an "other" category where they could enter free-form text.

All the technical staff placed responsibility for their woes on internal issues, such as inadequate requirements analysis or insufficient testing.

Every response from the management team suggested external issues contributed to their pains. The downturn in the economy, the weakening exchange rate, and the recent war were all cited as major issues.

This was a management team in serious trouble but unwilling to step up and acknowledge there were elements within their control to drive change.

We seem to be facing a growing range of external threats such as wars, diseases, and severe weather, keeping uncertainty high and the economy challenged. With all this happening, it is unnerving to see how many companies just lay low in these tough times, waiting for external circumstances to change so that they can come out of their bunkers and flourish again. A couple of years after the dotcom implosion, we started to ask, "So, do you think things are turning around?" as an icebreaker at networking events. Usually, the response was "Things are looking better…," but the inflection was that of another question rather than an indicator of confidence.

My bet is that the external pressures driving uncertainty will not fade. There will always be conditions and events that make it difficult for businesses to easily thrive. After the dotcom bubble of huge returns and short-lived successes, when we finally realized that the "new business model" was unsustainable, we now remember that driving a successful business is not a walk in the park. The new business reality is that there *is* no new business reality, and likely will not be anytime soon. The fundamentals remain the same.

> The best way to gain security for your future is to take responsibility. You need to acknowledge that the results you reap will be primarily influenced by your own actions. To look elsewhere is to search for excuses or blame, not solutions.

Carpe Diem

Seize the day. A literal translation from Latin is "to grab the current opportunity with gusto, without regard to the downstream ramifications." We can be more proactive at making these opportunities occur, instead of waiting for them to come up and bite us on the backside.

You can follow a few steps to take control of this day. First, you need to know what you are looking for in that day. Having clear, specific goals is critical in software projects and in life. Although I usually despise corny acronyms, SMART (specific, measurable, achievable, realistic, and tangible) characteristics are critical attributes of good goals. These are the strategic targets that describe the positive future that you are working toward. "Begin with the end in mind," as Stephen Covey counsels.

When you understand your goals, you can then identify what these opportunities look like so that you can recognize them when they appear. Is it a new technology that you can leverage to your advantage? Maybe an unexpected opportunity for reuse arises that may cost you a little time now but save a bundle later. Perhaps an unlucky break somewhere else takes some of the pressure off of your deadlines. That one satisfied customer might be able to point you toward two more.

What seem to be just positive events can induce more strategic consequences, assuming that you understand where you want to go. The first one to jump on that new technology can become an industry leader. That extra time saved can allow you to focus on a new initiative that turns you in a bright new direction. One of those new prospects can turn into a strategic partner. Things start to happen.

You can also take this one step further, by proactively seeking these opportunities. With the recognition that each of these leads has the potential to become much more than just a nice event, the motivation to take charge of your own future increases dramatically. What happens is that you are always on your toes, watching for the opportunities, making these opportunities, and ready to run with them as soon as they arise.

When taking a planned, strategic approach, we need to go beyond *carpe diem*. We do not just seize the day opportunistically, we do not rely on luck or circumstance, we are in control. It is more a matter of *procreo diem*. We create our days and thus the outcomes we desire.

A Solution Framework

The solution space we have traditionally inhabited is too narrow. Tools, frameworks, and methodologies are insufficient. We need to add the elements of alternative perspectives and respect for the human condition, along with transparent communication, to the mix to identify lasting solutions that work for everyone.

Figure 2-1 presents one way to look at the range of issues of the software development space.

As with any human endeavor, software development starts with individuals. Each has his or her own unique set of values, motives, attitudes, and skills based on experience, training, and aptitude. Everyone else's personal environment is just as real as yours. Any affront to that environment, any lack of appreciation for "where you are coming from," is not taken well. Emotions are far more tactical, but just as real and important to consider as the longer-range motives and attitudes.

When these individuals gather into groups, we start to deal with interaction and the formation of relationships. We've all been involved with relationships that have been effective and with those that could stand improvement. The goal is to move into relationships that are positive, that embody mutual respect and a sense of belonging.

When organized into teams, we then are dealing with the coordination of a diverse set of individuals. Teams lean on systems and guidance to help

Overall success for stakeholders is dependent upon successful management of individuals into groups and groups into teams – this should not be left to chance.

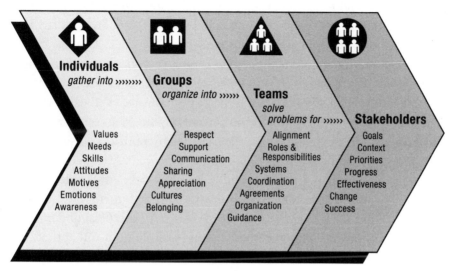

FIGURE 2-1

The range of issues in software development

them align toward a common vision. This is the first step teams take to solve a problem.

With appropriate direction, these teams will work together to solve problems for stakeholders. Not only have they evolved systems for interaction, but they are now working toward a specific common goal. The intent is to progress toward that goal and eventually an ability to determine whether the endeavor was a success or a failure.

This progression is most effective when taken in order, with nothing implicitly left to chance. Each piece taken for granted is an invitation to failure, particularly if success and failure is measured in dimensions beyond having shipped on the target date.

When looking at the breadth of issues across this range, from individuals through to stakeholders, typical approaches such as the incorporation of a packaged process framework or the purchase of a tool tend to provide superficial support at best. Although they can be seen as critical for structuring and managing huge amounts of data on large projects, all tools depend on appropriate and accurate data for good results. For requirements or design tools and for packaged processes, the overall results will be no better than the quality of the information used as input. This data and information comes from interactions across the team.

Tools, frameworks, and methodologies tend to emphasize those aspects of organization that are in the Teams area in this figure. These are necessary, to be sure, but hardly sufficient. Have you ever been involved in the deployment of a tool or methodology without 100 percent buy-in? Many purchased solutions of this type are no longer used even a year after purchase. It is the team that chooses whether to use the tool, or to learn how to use it effectively.

Our ongoing reliance on tools and methodologies is misguided in that it is largely prescriptive. The issue is not the original intent, but how this intent is translated into practice by most teams. A superficial understanding of the rationale and applicability behind well thought-out approaches drives most teams to implement these changes in a dysfunctional manner.

It is all about the people.

Software Is a Team Sport

Our motives, attitudes, skills, and team relationships are all fair game to explore and leverage as opportunities for change. We need to take personal ownership and responsibility for the results of our behaviors.

Effective software teams are more than a management issue. We cannot equate software development to the assembly-line floor, despite attempts to do so.

Procedures can serve as a guideline for what to do and provide structure for managing our information. However, they are insufficient to guarantee success in all but the most trivial cases. Projects and tactical situations are all different. A key component of these differences is the evolution of relationships as teams work together. If not carefully managed and nurtured, these relationships will almost surely erode over time.

Software is a creative endeavor done with real humans (with emotions, feelings, needs, and concerns that are both diverse and important). As Maslow suggests in his hierarchy of needs, we cannot rise into the ranks of optimized teams until our physiological and safety needs have been properly dealt with.

We need to take responsibility for explicitly and consciously managing our relationships in our teams, and to proactively design the approach we use as a team to develop software. This demands participation from all stakeholders involved and appreciation from all parties of the contribution (technically and emotionally) from everyone at the table.

Communication needs to be precise, open, and transparent. Hidden agendas cannot be tolerated, and we all need to be more effective with the skill of active listening. We need to be capable of empathizing with the positions of others before we pitch our case in discussions. Listening needs to be more than biding time to formulate our counterargument, more than waiting for an opportune moment to blurt out our perspective, and more than tolerating that noise from the other person's mouth.

Each person needs to respect differences within the group and be sure to address concerns from these different perspectives. *Vive la difference.* These differences make for unique and innovative solutions, long-lasting and strong relationships, and teams that will succeed now and in the future.

We all need to be able to consider the ramifications of our actions and understand the rationale behind what we are being asked to do. If something does not fit well with our mental model of appropriateness, we need to be able to speak up. Silence is not golden, and the absence of conflict is too often apathy. If the fit cannot be made, we need to be prepared to talk with our feet.

Although this approach is a tougher and deeper commitment to change, the solution is much longer lasting and significantly more rewarding. We need to stop playing with the symptoms. There really never will be a silver bullet.

Communication is a two-way street. Communication builds trust, and trust is essential in a team environment. We need to take charge, work together to build an effective team, and finally take ownership for software development.

Summary

For effective change in the workplace, we need to respect the distinction between doing things right and doing the right things.

We need to overcome the inertia of behaving in a certain way simply because that's the way it has been done, and we must recognize that we are responsible for ensuring that our actions lead us in the right direction.

To do this properly, we must first accept that we have a stake in the results and that we need to manage how we interact as a group. Then, we can apply the appropriate best practices that are reasonable for our culture and situation so that we have the best chances at success on our projects.

How Is This Relevant?

Sustainability. Try to identify the companies in your city that demonstrate true sustainability. What percentage of the overall population do they cover? How do they show that they are interested in success beyond the next quarter, or product cycle, or buyout? Do you consider them successful?

Small, personal steps. Achieving the big goals starts with achieving the small ones. How are you going to interact with the team today to ensure that you are taking ownership for success rather than blaming others for the challenges you are facing?

PART TWO

Individuals

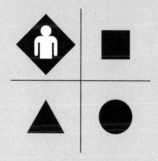

All change starts from within. As we build teams to solve the problems of our stakeholders, we start with ourselves, recognizing that we bring skills, attitudes, and tactical emotions to the table.

When we decide to join a team that produces commercial software, we must take responsibility for managing the commitments we make. How well we do this will impact our relationships and careers, for better or worse.

If this sounds reasonable, it stands to reason that we must ensure our contributions are the strongest and most comprehensive they can be. There are a number of ways we can do this, and we will explore them here.

CHAPTER THREE

The Right Stuff

We bring a variety of attitudes to everything we do, whether it is in software development or in everyday life. We need to understand how these affect our ability to participate in our activities and work to cultivate the most effective attitudes we can.

In this chapter, we explore some of the attitudes that make for highly effective team players and suggest that leadership matters regardless of role or title.

Cowboys and Unsung Heroes

On almost any project I've been on, there have been one or two people who really stood out from the crowd. They have gone beyond the call of duty to bring the project home—picture John Wayne riding off into the sunset. These are the legendary cowboys of software development fame, the "go to" people who can solve the tough problems, who seem to know all the critical information about the project, who are indispensable.

 Indispensable? Have you ever been involved in a project where the hero has disappeared? Suddenly nobody knows why those arcane design decisions were made, and you sure don't want to touch that indecipherable code that he wrote before riding off. Hmm. Life isn't quite as rosy, is it? Individual indispensability has become corporate liability. Tom DeMarco once noted, "Can-do attitudes escalate minor setbacks into true disasters."

There is another class of hero, however, that doesn't bring along such negative side effects. They're the ones who won't compromise on doing the right things as part of the job, the ones who do so much behind the scenes but never seem to see their share of the limelight or recognition. Although they may not be the source of miraculous solutions, they are rarely the source of major gaffes, either. They rarely break the software baseline. They won't overpromise on their commitments, and they will not let their estimates be negotiated down by aggressive managers (which often causes consternation with said managers).

They are less likely to put in large amounts of overtime, usually because they don't need to. Their methodical approach and lack of stress are often seen as plodding along with a lack of interest, giving the appearance of "not pulling their weight." When they leave, it's pretty easy to pick up where they left off. Their work is clear and understandable, with no hidden surprises. Although not often viewed this way, these are indications that these people were doing their jobs the way they should be done, not that they were just doing simple stuff. Their planning and attention to detail just made it look easy.

These are the unsung heroes of software development whom I've learned to appreciate. Although few of them bask in the glory that the cowboys receive, they can be just as recognizable and are far more valuable to the organization. Given my druthers, I'd rather have a team stacked with the unsung heroes and let the cowboys introduce uncertainty in the competition's camps.

Enthusiasm

While waiting for a taxi to whisk me off to the airport, I noticed a couple of people who were canvassing our block with pamphlets in hand and was a bit concerned that they would arrive at my door before the taxi did. They indeed did (had they picked up their pace?), and the elderly gentlemen struck up a friendly conversation. They were Jehovah's Witnesses out to spread the word; but instead of diving into an anticipated hard sell, we somehow got to talking about how he went about engaging people.

My original concern with the situation was that in principle, I don't subscribe to the one-size-fits-all approach. In software, I've seen more than enough new approaches that are supposed to save the world (and don't forget the latest must-have language or the obligatory architectural framework) and the corresponding poor fit for many shops.

I was pleasantly surprised in this case. The sell wasn't hard. It wasn't even perceptible. It turned out to be quite an interesting chat. His key point was that he believed in what he was doing so strongly that he couldn't foresee a time when his enthusiasm would wane. He just couldn't keep himself from talking about it with others. I was actually a bit disappointed when the taxi arrived on time.

I gained an appreciation for how we can be carried forward by our enthusiasm, and how carefully splashing this energy on those around us can serve us well.

I carried this thought into the training session we had that week, and it was by far the most positive engagement I've had to date with that very large organization. The majority of the group was still actively engaged in the afternoon of the second day. I even had to apologize to one of the participants for cutting short an energizing discussion after the session (because I had to rush to the airport to get home). All of us who had planned the session felt that it had exceeded expectations, with very positive feedback.

 Looking back, one of the key drivers for success at that session was the enthusiasm for the topic that the group's planners carried with them. They had devoted the last couple of years of their lives into the topic, and it showed. Even though they were relatively low-key instructors, they clearly believed in their message and knew its adoption would make a significant difference to the group.

Enthusiasm can be infectious in a group setting, whether the team is pumped up for building a cool new product, or making the big sale, or kicking the competition's butt. All it needs is a few people to get it started; the energy then flows to the others. Generally, when you grow beyond a core group, enthusiasm can be difficult to sustain. If you look under the hood of any large company with sustained enthusiasm, you will likely find a conscious effort being made to prevent it from being diluted.

Enthusiasm is not something you can mandate into the group; it requires a common motivation and is something that is best seeded through action rather than words. When you've got it, do what you can to feed it to keep it going.

Channel it. Never crush it. The output from an enthusiastic team can be absolutely phenomenal.

Being Reasonably Self-Critical

I've worked with a large number of different organizations, helping them become more effective at getting software out the door. Part of this involves the challenge of measuring the value of our improvement efforts.

Many argue it just can't be done. Most groups don't have the appropriate benchmarks, and many factors influence the overall results. It can be too easy to differ in the interpretations of which factors contributed the most or to conclude that the change is merely a function of noise.

Although there has been some success in quantifying value for some organizations, there has also been a nagging problem. Some companies that score well on the quantified results continue to struggle to get their product out the door. However, others that score relatively poorly show dramatic change and remarkable results with their efforts. The process data does not tell the whole story.

In retrospect, it appears that the component missing from the hard numbers is how well the organization can look inward and recognize that there is room for improvement. Call it openness for change, or an ability to be reasonably self-critical.

For some shops, improvement just won't happen. It's the equivalent of that unanswerable question "Do these pants make me look fat?" The messenger will be damned for telling the truth, but the company will make no progress with a lie. Others will gladly absorb any feedback they can get and act on it accordingly.

It is easy to take a list of clients and place them on the continuum between totally closed to criticism and totally open to an external perspective of their performance. This is a phenomenon that starts at the top, and as it trickles down the chain it manifests itself in various ways.

When having an open discussion about practices and the resulting performance, some teams will be open and engaged, whereas others can't wait until the meeting is over. Body language gives great insight, which is one reason why these sessions are most valuable face to face. The same managed session can be as short as 45 minutes with some groups, and more than 3 times as long with others. Perhaps there is a new metric to be gathered here.

In particular, senior management engagement speaks volumes. Some don't bother participating or even attending at all, and others will argue that the information discussed is irrelevant for their organization. On the other end of the spectrum are those who are interested in the results, actively involve themselves in the discussion, and solicit the input from the rest of the group in analyzing the information presented. Bravo!

An organization's ability to be self-critical is a key leading indicator of the success of any improvement engagement. It is one thing to change a few token practices for one team, but it is another thing entirely to internalize appropriate practices so that they don't fall back under pressure. To be able to look inward to identify potential changes that are within our own sphere of influence is essential. We all have room for improvement, all the time.

Simply admitting we have room to improve has value. We need to be open to external feedback without defensiveness. Although it may be one thing to maintain a public persona of strength that can border on puffery, it is another thing entirely to retain that boastful image internally, where it can often be interpreted as denial.

> We need to find a reasonable balance in the continuum of self-criticalness. Being able to recognize our ongoing potential for change, and to reasonably act upon it, is an extremely valuable strength.

Emotions

In the software development field, we get plenty of training in software languages, frameworks, operating systems, and databases. We get a bit of training in methodologies, and perhaps a little experience in the overall product life cycle that includes the maintenance phase of a product. We may get some more experience team dynamics through project work. Unfortunately, in the classroom environment, team projects often become an exercise in which one person carries the rest of the group along to get the assignment done on time. For many, this is probably the closest to real-world experience they will have at school.

All this assumes a software engineering or computer science track. I've got a physics degree from a university where I didn't have to touch a computer to graduate, and there are many others working in this industry with similar backgrounds. Relevant training often comes through work-based training courses, peer-based experience, or the school of hard knocks.

What about training in the area of emotions and their impact in the workplace? Many of us reluctantly sat through Psych 101 as a mandatory course in school. Although it might have been relatively easy and even interesting at times, few of us expected it to have any relevance in the workplace. Emotions aren't perceived to belong in the workplace, and they're certainly not to be exposed to your peers.

 With that perception, and the fact that we ignore emotions in the training curriculum, we generally work in environments in which exposed emotions can be shocking. We rarely expose our true feelings, repressing them until we hit our boiling point, then bang! When emotions are seen in the workplace, they are often exaggerated, because they are exposed at a time when we have the least control over them. Tempers flare, relationships are eroded or destroyed, and the team dynamics are crippled. It can take a long time for the team to recover from an inappropriate outburst.

Emotions are very real and cannot be ignored.

The degree to which we display our emotions on our sleeves seems to vary significantly worldwide. This is not stereotyping. These are simply differences that we need to deal with. It is clear to me that there is not one right approach for managing emotions in the workplace, but we must acknowledge that different approaches do exist.

In Asian cultures, emotion appears to be repressed from the workplace. Greetings are always cordial. There is a steady state of neutrality in the workplace. Those with a strong Asian background are very careful to preserve the respect for others and are emotionally steady.

In Eastern Europe, the opposite appears true. Peers can have a knockdown, drag 'em out brawl over a design review, and then break bread together over lunch and laughter afterward. Working with a number of Europeans on a large project years ago, it was striking to observe the strong emotional tides that occurred in the workplace. Indeed, the exposed emotions were so strong that there were others on the team who would go out of their way to avoid what felt like excessive confrontations.

Here in North America, we seem to fit somewhere in the middle. While surprised and sometimes shocked by the range of emotions exhibited by our European teammates, we can at the same time be frustrated by the inscrutability of our Asian counterparts.

The degree to which we expose our emotions appears to be driven by our upbringing, which in turn is heavily influenced by our culture. It is not an accident that the way we present our emotions aligns closely to the degree to which our cultures are "high or low context."[1] Asian cultures tend to be high context, taking a wide range of information into account as they make decisions. They tend to see things in terms of the "big picture." In low-context cultures, lives tend to be more compartmentalized, and decisions tend to be made with a narrower range of information.

As the diversity of our teams grows, we need to recognize that we will be exposed to a broader range of presented emotions in the workplace. We need to manage that diversity more consciously.

It is important to tune our actions so that they are appropriate for ourselves and for the people around us. We need to be sensitive to when emotions are being repressed, and we must provide an outlet where they can be safely expressed without eroding team relationships. We also need to be careful that our expression of emotions is not offensive to others.

 We are all humans after all, not automatons. There is certainly room for emotions in the workplace, to the degree that the team members are comfortable with exposing them and experiencing them from others. In a strong team, fear, elation, joy, sorrow, anger, and others all have a place in communication.

We all have a role in supporting and working through the appropriate emotions from others and ourselves, working to ensure that the entire team experience is as full as possible.

Stepping Up

On almost any project, there comes a time when we realize that some tasks that should be completed are being left undone. When that's the case, we need to consider whether it is appropriate for us to step up to the plate. Our considerations need to include the relative benefit to ourselves, the stakeholders of the product, and the business. These dropped balls can take many forms and have a variety of root causes:

- **Sloth.** There will always be, especially in larger companies, those who spend more effort in avoiding the work they are tasked with than it would take to do the task itself. Unfortunately, sometimes their avoidance will impact your ability to get your work done. Call this *known ignorance.*

- **Neglect.** Given an overwhelming list of things that are demanding our attention, along with an inadequate system for prioritizing our efforts, some important things will inevitably fall through the cracks. We're all human, after all. Here, we have *unknown ignorance.*

- **Skills shortage.** Whether we are moving into a new technology or a new position, there will be times when we know what needs to be done but don't know the most appropriate way to solve the problem. This is the *known unknown* stuff.
- **Lack of awareness.** Differing from neglect, these are the things we don't even know should be on our radar, the *unknown unknown*.

Root cause is one thing, but how we choose to deal with these dropped balls is more important. For the last three root causes, even if someone else drops the ball, it is generally a straightforward path to solving the problem. For lack of awareness, once the concern is discovered, we can simply act based on this information. Proactively, we can also learn from our past mistakes to ensure that we can tune our awareness for future projects. When we encounter a skills shortage, we can address this by importing the appropriate skills or by training existing resources. From the standpoint of neglect, we can work to continuously improve our prioritization schemes to ensure that we are focusing on the right elements.

It's when we encounter sloth that we can run into conflict. Team-based success is predicated on the assumption that all the participants have the intent of collaborating to achieve a common goal. When the goal is ill defined or when we don't manage the alignment of personal motivations to project goals, we open ourselves to the distinct possibility that these problems will arise.

It is easy to simply complain that others are not doing their job, and to use that as a reason for our not being able to achieve our goals, but this does nothing to solve our problem. There can be a strong reluctance to step up and deal with the task ourselves, because of our natural distaste for rewarding negative behavior.

There are political, interpersonal, and technical issues in these situations. As we progress from politics to technical issues, our sphere of influence increases. In these situations, we need to separate these three issues to help us determine how to respond.

In many shops, we have little control over the political environment in which the team operates; and in the larger shops that seem to harbor slothful behavior, it is well beyond our sphere of influence to change the politics at play. For most of us, our best bet is to recognize the situation for what it is and to consciously choose to participate or disengage. It can be very stressful to feel trapped in a political environment that doesn't fit our personal vision.

If we choose to stay engaged, we can look at our interpersonal options. It can be extremely difficult to empathize with someone who chooses to work at odds with the rest of the team, especially if we have not honed our communication skills. Empathy, however, does not equate to agreement, and truly understanding the underlying motivations of someone else can reveal either a deep-rooted conflict or a common motivation that can then be leveraged to resolve the situation. To merely continue to blame others for not doing their job is not a productive alternative.

 If the situation cannot be resolved interpersonally, there will come a time when we might need to just decide to take on the work ourselves to move the project ahead. Most people would not actually do this unless there was something in it for them—altruism only goes so far. We also need to reconcile that we may be consequently helping out the person who is causing the problem.

Often, we can find a reasonable set of benefits. Then, we can deal with a situation that is impacting us directly, which means we can get our job done more effectively. If this doesn't result in fewer hours of effort (because this is often a cultural or management-driven imperative), it will result in greater accomplishment and reduced chaos, which usually counts for something. We might have gained new skills in the bargain as well, which is rarely a bad thing. Politically, we might also raise our stature as someone who can do what it takes to get things done, despite the barriers.

In any case, as with all situations, our actions should be transparent, and open communication should be used to project our intent. Our actions should not be executed in a manner that goes against the accepted norms of team behavior.

We should work in a way that drives toward the team's overall goals, and at times, that will mean stepping up to handle whatever it takes to get the job done.

In these cases, be careful to ensure that you can find some sort of benefit to compensate for the effort expended.

We're All Leaders

Ken Blanchard unleashed *The One-Minute Manager* on the world quite a while ago.[2] One of the superb elements of the book was an extensive list of the characteristics of a good leader. More than a few bullet points or a "top-ten list," he provides close to 75 characteristics that capture the breadth of what it takes to lead, follow, and generally collaborate effectively.

Through our experience, we have all learned that being a boss is not the same thing as being a leader. There's nothing in the list about giving orders, belittling others for a sense of power and authority, commanding a high salary, or wearing an Armani suit. Indeed, the vast majority of the characteristics that Ken describes don't require you to be in any position of authority to practice them. Being objective, humble, and inspiring loyalty, along with many others in the list, are characteristics that could be attributed to any strong team member, regardless of rank.

We can distill a lot of these characteristics into the areas of strong communication, trust, and open collaboration. It is important for everyone on the team to possess these characteristics so that the team can function effectively.

There will be times on any project when we are given the task of leadership. Whether it is as fleeting as chairing a meeting or an ongoing role for which we are charged with ensuring that the group works together to achieve an overall goal, leadership is something we all engage in every day. Many times, we can be the most effective leaders when we stand back and allow others to take the spotlight.

 As with the notion of quality in collaborative projects, leadership isn't merely something that is the responsibility of others. Instead, it is something that guides all our activities, every day. We could easily perceive borrowing from this list of characteristics as good grooming for when we gain the official title of "leader," but it is more appropriate to embrace the elements of the list as part of our core beliefs today. Acting the part is a long way from living the role, and in the real world it is easy to discern the difference.

Don't wait to move into the corner office before living the characteristics of a good leader. Indeed, many of these traits are also the characteristics of a good team player.

If you wait until you are already in charge of people, it is already too late. There is a good chance that you didn't get there through a reasonable selection process.

Regardless of position or role, applying these characteristics in your interactions will inspire the same in others and will reveal you as an effective leader today.

Summary

Consciously or not, we bring a variety of attitudes and emotions to the table that will drastically impact our interactions with others and will significantly impact the overall outcome of our efforts.

There is great value in consciously understanding how we approach our interactions and working to manage these in an effort to improve our contributions over time.

How Is This Relevant?

Attitudes. As you approach a new assignment, are you filled with excitement or dread? Are you looking forward to working with the team or hesitant to deal with new people? Do you consciously consider these elements?

Heroism. Do you thrive on the rush associated with being recognized as the one who made the project a success? How has this affected others on the team? Did these heroic actions expose the project to a reasonable amount of risk?

Assertiveness. As you work on a team, do you actively ensure you are contributing the most you can? Or, do you passively await the next task assignment? Do you take it without considering the ramifications?

References

1. Mary O'Hara-Devereaux and Robert Johansen, *GlobalWork: Bridging Distance, Culture and Time* (Jossey-Bass, 1994).

2. Kenneth Blanchard and Spencer Johnson, *The One-Minute Manager* (Berkley Trade, 1983).

CHAPTER FOUR

A Quality Focus

Of all the attitudes that we carry into our activities on software development, the appreciation of our responsibility for quality is perhaps the most critical.

In this chapter, we explore some of the dimensions of quality, with the intent of reinforcing the notion that we have a vested interest in taking genuine ownership of the quality of our work.

A Quality Attitude

I was working with a company to see whether there was any way we could improve their approach to quality control. We looked at samples of their specs, followed through with their test plans, test cases, and results. What I saw was a great example of great attitude in action.

The team of three had taken it upon themselves to supplement the software spec with enough information to build a testable understanding of what was to be constructed and made that part of the baseline for the development team to use, too. They had a clear understanding of how well the product had fared with the huge number of test cases on a per-build basis, and they had the underpinnings for an excellent metrics program around the theme of product quality.

Several years earlier, when the code was simply thrown over the wall, they had started improving on the relationships with the development group and now enjoyed a healthy, dynamic environment. They had a good handle on the issues that were being tracked, and they served as the perfect customer representatives. As one of them noted, known bad software would only go out the door if it were "plucked from his cold dead hands." Even with all this, they were still eager to improve.

Going in with the expectation that it would be relatively easy to find significant problems, I was faced with the challenging task of working to find ways to streamline their current approach, which was exemplary for the industry. We talked about different approaches for automation, how to work with the development team to clearly specify product quality and ways to leverage their existing measures to identify trends to support project decisions and process refinement directions.

One of the highlights of the day was when the general manager dropped by in the afternoon to check on the proceedings. Rather than sit quietly in the back of the room and leave after a few minutes, he quickly became engaged, eagerly participating in the discussion about how to make an already strong approach to quality even stronger. We discussed comparisons with other groups I had worked with, and he was surprised that there was such a distinction with his shop. "You mean that there are companies that will knowingly ship inferior products?"

That's where the penny dropped for me. It was not just the quality control team's attitude about product quality. This attitude went all the way up to senior management. It was this attitude that separated this group from most of the crowd out there.

The company breathes the right attitude, and this is what allowed a group of three with little prior experience to set up a state-of-the-art quality-control program. Everyone takes personal responsibility for producing a good product, all the way to the top. As a result, they ship in a reasonable timeframe, their customer base is happy, they maintain an appropriate balance of project factors, and they want to get better.

> When the general manager asked my advice about how to scale up the team in the near future, my advice was simple: "Do everything you can to sustain the current quality attitude in the team as it grows, and everything will be just fine."

Quality Is Your Job

Many software development teams have a twisted perspective of what quality means. A QA group beats up on the product after it has been thrown over the wall by the development team. These testers poke at it from all sides and pass back their issues, whereupon the developers argue from the position of "well, we wrote the stuff, so we certainly should know how it is supposed to work!" This internal bickering continues until

- The project times out and they ship the product anyways, or
- The QA group stops looking for bugs, so with "no new bugs," the product can be shipped, or
- Someone in senior management repeatedly diverts the efforts in another direction, and few products ever get shipped.

I've seen all of these in action in the real world and usually it is not a pretty sight.

Generally in software, there is the notion that "quality is what other people are responsible for" on a project. We will put new hires into the QA/Test group so that they can familiarize themselves with the product in a place where they can't do much harm (or help, for that matter). The prima donnas get the cushy design and architecting gigs and all too often the relaxed standards of practice, too. Those who don't quite cut it end up elsewhere. We appoint a quality director that sits with the management team only when quality standards are forced upon us because we want to sell to Europe or to build medical devices or defense products. Then we'll do our best to work around these pesky people that are trying to stop us from shipping our product anyways. Our goal is to get the job done, right?

I don't think so.

The goal should be to get the job right, because just "getting it done" usually means we'll deal with it again later when someone else finds our defects. If we are lucky, it's those new internal testers saving our bacon. If we're not so lucky, it's a disgruntled customer.

The process of developing a product, software or otherwise, involves a chain of people each doing his or her part to contribute to the whole, and the notion of quality should be on every person's mind throughout that chain. As humans, we all make mistakes, but it is unfair, inefficient, and very risky to expect that the last person in the chain is responsible for all the mistakes injected throughout the process. To name these victims of our deeds, the quality-assurance group simply perpetuates the notion that it's their job to clean up the mess while you move on to other things, and hope they don't interrupt you with their seemingly trivial concerns.

 Quality needs to be on everyone's mind, at all times. We are all responsible for the quality of the components we contribute to the overall product, and we should all be explicitly aware of what quality really means for our contribution. Quality assurance isn't the people at the tail end, the people who are given little time to find our nasty problems. A quality assurance team is best thought of as part facilitator, mentor, support team, and objective auditor. Someone that is really doing quality assurance is working to ensure that everyone else has the skills, knowledge, and resources to do a quality job.

No matter where you are in your company's food chain, if you think that quality is simply someone else's responsibility, you have completely missed the point. It is your job, whatever your role, to ensure that your contribution does not degrade the overall system.
Quality is your responsibility.

Outsourcing Quality

When I was growing up in southern Ontario, everyone either worked in the automotive industry or had at least one relative or close friend who worked in the industry. There was always a strong sense of brotherhood, and the oil crisis in the 1970s was not an easy pill to swallow. If someone showed up driving a Nissan to work, there were times when that car could be flipped or torched just for being on the lot.

Even though there was a strong commitment to local brands, there was also an understanding about the product and the business. Nobody would buy a car that was built on Monday morning, and *partnership* wasn't a word you would use to describe the relationship between the unions and management.

Fast-forward to today and the landscape has changed. Although there can still be some animosity toward foreign car makers, there has been a growing acceptance of the foreign cars here. Not only have these foreign automakers opened plants on our soil, they have grown to a point where most of the cars they sell here are built here, with parts from here, and using North American workers.

I drive a Mazda that was built in Michigan. The engine block comes from a Ford foundry in Windsor, Canada. When I travel in a rental car, however, I am reminded that there is still a significant difference between the quality of a car from an American manufacturer and one from a Japanese one.

Before proceeding, I'd like to point out that there are winners from North America and duds from Japan, too. We had to replace the engine block in our Toyota minivan after only a couple of years. Not everyone who works in a North American factory is indifferent to the work they perform. There are widely fluctuating levels of quality across the industry, however, and it goes beyond the soil where the manufacturing plant was built or the ownership of the company lies. As we think about outsourcing our software products abroad, can we learn something now that the shoe is on the other foot?

As the Japanese outsource the production of their products to North America, they do so not because the labor or material rates are significantly lower than in Japan, but because of the "Built in America" demands of the consumers here. They have identified a business challenge to manage, and they have done so very successfully. Domestic brands continue to lose market share, while foreign brands continue to rank higher in terms of quality and customer satisfaction.

One of the things that the Japanese have done very well is to outsource their attitudes toward building their product. These are the same attitudes that made them initially successful in Japan. When plants initially open here, Japanese management runs them. The Japanese style is quite different from the typical North American style. Everyone contributes to quality. All employees are respected, and there is a strong sense of working together to build a strong product. Only when the attitudes are institutionalized and the quality approaches are ingrained are the reins turned over to local management, and only those who have been carefully groomed get the job.

 The big three automakers here would like to suggest that there is an unfair advantage. Domestic cars are hampered by the higher wages driven by unions and the huge pension obligations. The newcomers are too agile to catch. For these newcomers, although the workers get reasonable compensation and flexible pension plans, these arrangements were crafted as a partnership rather than out of being overpowered. Management has been able to succeed in building both a quality product and a sustainable business at the same time, and there is an ongoing conscious effort on both aspects.

Successful outsourcing involves the active management of values and attitudes during the transfer process.

If quality is on your radar, and if this is consciously transferred to your team, regardless of location, success will follow.

Software Hygiene

I spent some time in *the chair* a while ago for my semi-annual dental cleaning and checkup. As usual, due to the circumstances, I didn't get much of a chance to get a word in edgewise, and my hygienist carried the conversation. When the topic of flossing came up, however, I thought I would do some probing of my own, and a very interesting conversation ensued.

We talked about how people floss. By her off-the-cuff guess, maybe 5 percent floss regularly, and another 30 percent floss regularly enough to make a difference. At the other end of the spectrum are those who floss for a few days prior to their visit, and the results show when it is their turn in the chair. She noted that for those who do floss regularly, they are rewarded with a much shorter visit and a much lower likelihood of developing some serious problems down the road. These people also find that if they miss a day (and nobody's perfect), they *really* miss it, as most of us would miss a shower. For them, the practice of flossing is not a chore; it's just part of their daily routine.

And yes, I did ask the tough question. The response was no, my hygienist does not floss regularly. She did, however, make sure that I left the office with a new package of dental floss. No pressure, no shame, but a better appreciation for why we do, and don't do, the things we should.

In software, diligence in flossing can be equated to application of best practices in a number of ways. From my experience with a wide range of teams, regular use of estimation procedures, project retrospectives, and data-based project management (among many other practices) is very low (well below 10 percent). Most of us know that these are the "right things to do," but still don't do them regularly. Life gets in the way. In software, life can take the form of the latest fire du jour, ongoing pressure to deliver to schedules that have no basis in reality, or the fact that we just haven't yet been burned badly enough to be more diligent.

 Although most best practices actually take very little time when weighed against the cost or risk of not doing them, we still rationalize our way out of doing them, and we often face the consequences accordingly. For a parallel to those who only floss a few days before a dental checkup, ask someone in an ISO-certified or CMM-assessed shop what happens a few days before the auditor comes to town. Often, "best practices" become a disruption, and the hastily crafted façade is easily spotted during the audit.

Those developers and organizations that consistently apply the right practices are rewarded with predictable closure on their projects, with less plaque and fewer cavities for the client to find.

 To really work well, valuable practices should be introduced in small doses and applied regularly. For this to occur, the value needs to be appreciated, and the application needs to become routine practice. You need to get to a point where not applying them gives the team that I-forgot-to-brush feeling because "that's just the way we do software around here."

Best practices cannot simply be mandated, especially without the accompanying support they need to be applied effectively. The group will just get that sheepish feeling, try to apply them until life gets in the way, and then fall back into their zone of familiarity. Having not realized any of the benefit, they will then become jaundiced toward future attempts at improvement.

People, Process, Product—in That Order

 Few people in the software field would admit that quality is low priority for them. We lament the problems with applications and operating systems we use every day. We all promise high quality to our customers, but what does quality mean in the software industry? Are we really working to deliver on our promise of quality, or are we just paying lip service to the notion?

 Genuine quality needs to cover the three dimensions of people, process, and the product itself to deliver on the goals. Focus simply on the product quality, and you are likely to disappoint your client and yourself. Dependence on heroes might work for a while, but it's a high-risk path that is not sustainable. Neglect the process, however light it might be, and you may never finish your projects at all.

The quality of the people can be viewed in several ways: both individually and as a team. Strong individuals can internalize many of the elements of a high-quality process and compensate for gaps in explicit process focus. This can be effective, but only if the team is small, if they have worked together sufficiently, and if there is a shared understanding of the vision.

Individual strengths are rarely a scalable solution for process quality. The emphasis needs to be placed on the quality of the team: its consistency, attitudes, and internal dynamics. Individual and team quality can definitely be managed and improved, through training and experience in both the hard skills of software development and soft skills of team dynamics.

The process applied in building a product serves as a structure around which to work. Few organizations adequately emphasize the quality of their work structure or recognize that there is no single solution for a "good process." An approach that works well on one project might be disastrous on the next, even with the same team in the same organization. You should take time on every single project to determine what the right approach should be, within the context of a well-considered framework.

 Process quality is extremely context sensitive. It depends on the size and objectives of the project; the size, culture, and maturity of the team; and a host of other factors. On top of this, some elements of the process are far more critical for success than others. An agreed-upon vision and well-managed scope are critical precursors for success.

 Retrospectives leverage the past experience, good or bad, for the benefit of future projects. Focus on managing the process for each project, with an understanding that mid-course corrections may be necessary.

 Although product quality significantly depends on a strong process and team, these in no way guarantee great results. A clear and explicit definition of what quality means for each project is the only way you can ever achieve a high-quality solution. The definition needs to come early enough to allow you to build the appropriate quality into the product, and it has to be explicit enough to prevent you from artificially declaring completeness just because the target date is looming.

 Indeed, the ability to define what quality means and to execute on that definition for your products will only come after your people have gained expertise and experience and when your process has matured to a sufficient level.

If you truly want to deliver a quality product, focus first on the quality of the team that will do the work, and then on the quality of the process you are going to use to build the product.

Only after these have been established can you reasonably expect product quality to result. Anything less than this is simply lip service.

Summary

It can be frightening to see how an organization perceives the concept of quality. Respect for quality indeed starts at the top, but the attitudes and practices, for better or for worse, flow through everyone in the organization.

Strong attitudes toward quality need to be internalized. Respect for doing the best you can needs to be in your blood. Without the right attitudes toward quality in the team, the resulting product quality is not likely to be much better.

How Is This Relevant?

Internalization. Where does quality rank in your overall list of priorities? Are you personally focused on meeting deadlines or on meeting the true spirit of the task? How does your respect for quality manifest itself in your ability to control where you spend your time? Are you spending a great deal of time working on things you previously thought you had completed?

Ownership. If your organization works with third-party vendors, either for outsourcing system components or for separate activities, do you retain responsibility and control for the quality of the product?

How do you communicate the expected level of quality to your vendors, and how rigorously do you enforce it?

Priority for quality. Where are you in the product cycle when you start to think of quality? Do you build it in, or try to test it out? Does everyone focus on building quality into every aspect of the product, and is this done consciously? Do you have a quantified definition of what quality means?

CHAPTER FIVE

Facing Challenges

For all of us, there are times when things do not go according to plan. How we behave in the face of adversity speaks volumes about our ability to work successfully in a team environment.

In this chapter, we explore some of the issues around the behavioral patterns we often fall into when we experience challenges and some of the approaches we can take to deal with the difficult times in a more positive fashion.

Feeling the Pain

In the early stages of growth, few companies recognize the need for an explicit focus on quality assurance. Indeed, with the heady rush to develop your ideas into a product and get it out into the marketplace, most activities beyond coding and debugging are an afterthought for many organizations. Although this can sometimes be enough to carry a small group through their first release, at some point it will invariably result in a traumatic event, and extreme pain.

 This trauma is a self-inflicted pain that many in the industry believe is the inescapable norm, whether it takes the form of late deliveries, poor delivered quality, or total project failure. Software projects are seen to be hard, unpredictable beasts to tame, so your best plan of attack is apparently to attack rather than to plan. Teams feel the need to "hit the ground running" and don't really know what the end is, but are all driving as hard as they can toward it anyways.

Team would be more precisely described as a collection of individuals who are driving toward their personal perception of what the finish line is. Their views on the scope to be built, the level of quality of the product expected, the overall goals of the organization, and who is responsible for what within the group will vary widely. The consequence of this anarchy is assured pain. Without a common set of objectives, there must be disappointments, even if victory can somehow be declared.

Pain is there for a reason. Our bodies use pain to tell us that we have injured ourselves, that we are hungry, or otherwise need to pay attention to an area that is usually taken for granted. For an organization to benefit from the pain that individuals are feeling, that pain needs to be somehow transmitted to the top. Until it is clear that the pain exists, there will be no incentive for doing anything different on a project. Although people in the trenches might be experiencing a great deal of pain, there will be no organizational shift until those at the top experience the pain themselves. The brain is usually sympathetic to the nerve endings throughout our bodies, but senior executive are often distracted with their own unrelated challenges.

 For pain to be used as an effective precursor for improvements, it is not enough to simply express the pain experienced with the chaos at the project level. A translation needs to be made into a pain that can be related to at the top. Lack of predictability, poor delivered quality, and ultimately disappointing cash flow are pains that have stronger impact with those who can ensure that there is commitment for change.

 Only after the issues have been acknowledged and the organization recognizes that there may indeed be a better way to do things is it possible for a culture of quality to take hold. Those essential initial project elements such as a project vision, clear organizational goals, reasonable technical estimates, and defined and managed project scope will be respected for the value they bring to overall success. All of these elements need to be worked out and communicated in advance so that all participants can start working toward the same goal. Seek decent footing and a clear path before running off toward your destination.

To get to this point, it is imperative that you raise your hand when you are feeling pain. Ensure that when you are not getting the information you need from others that you tell them not only that it is insufficient, but also how it is insufficient and how this gap adversely impacts those around you.

Technical issues experienced at the working level translate to profit/loss issues at the executive level. When trying to communicate your position, be sure to use a language that can be appreciated by the recipient. If you are communicating to someone motivated financially, you must translate your issues into that form.

Unfortunately, exposure to pain is often the only way you will be able to motivate people toward an effective quality attitude.

Dealing with the Pain

There is likely a time in everyone's career when a catastrophic project failure hits—you have just been burned. The organization's credibility is shot, the pressure is on to make amends, and there is an expectation that strong action is required to remedy the situation. How the company and individuals react and recover from such a situation is a strong indicator of resilience and maturity.

Especially in software development, it is impossible to guarantee that catastrophic events will never happen. Even the simplest systems cannot be proven to be bug-free, and virtually any software warranty is filled with disclaimers intended to deflect responsibility. The challenge lies in the massive number of activities and tests that could be performed on any system to validate its functionality and performance and the constraints of time and resources imposed upon us by Mother Nature.

 Fool me once, shame on you; fool me twice, shame on me. You cannot predict and prepare for every eventuality, but being burned more than once with the same problem should not happen. When a problem arises, the intent should be to do the following:

- Fix the problem.
- Understand the root cause that allowed the problem to occur.
- Find and fix the class of problems that share a common cause.
- Put in place measures that prevent that class of issues from occurring in the future.

The result is not just a fix, but is a deeper understanding of the system and a stronger infrastructure that supports and guides the team in the future. Problems of this type are less likely to occur in the future, and that time saved can be used for other work.

 Take ownership rather than placing blame. Although there are times when an individual failed to meet explicitly stated demands despite having adequate resources, it is far more likely that the organization at all levels contributed to the failure. Is it the individual that has failed the system, or the system that has failed the individual? Too often, the situation is remedied by hanging someone out to dry. A reasonable infrastructure would have checks and balances in place that would have identified the problem before disaster struck. At all levels in the organization, it is insufficient to take someone's word that things are "done." The term *done* needs to be a validation of previously agreed-upon standards rather than an expression of a lack of time, boredom, or insufficient insight.

 Develop a credible rationale. "I'm done with this development task because it has been tested against the completion criteria. The issues have been remedied and objectively verified, and the system accurately reflects the changes at all levels." Note that the vast majority of this statement is not centered on the task or the individual but on the infrastructure that allows for a common understanding of what *done* means. Without this, there is a tendency to claim completeness at the first possible opportunity, and then lay blame afterward. The responsibility and accountability aren't at the same level as the authority in the system. It should be the same at the project level. "We're done with this project because we have confirmed that it adequately meets the end user's stated needs. It has been exercised against a reasonable set of specified conditions, and we all agree that it is reasonable to deploy with the known list of deficiencies." The story needs to hold water at all levels.

There is no practical way to be completely assured that you will never get burned, but you can take steps to reduce the risk of being burned, and you can follow approaches that can significantly reduce the risk of being burned twice in the same manner.

Plan your actions, validate completeness, and learn from your mistakes. These steps and approaches take time, effort, and diligence. There's nothing like getting burned to reinforce the need for a more supportive infrastructure.

To get burned and not grow from the experience is to lose twice.

Demonizing Mistakes

Recently, I had an interesting experience with the dealership where I had recently bought my new car. After my son came into the house to show me the interesting lug nut he had found, I investigated and found that there was only one left holding the wheel on. My wife had just arrived home from a trip on the highway, picking up the kids. Because the tires had been rotated a few days earlier, I had my suspicions as to how this had happened.

I dropped by to speak with the service department and was far from satisfied with the response.

The first word out of the mouth of the service manager was that the technician doing the work would be punished. When I noted that was not my intent for the visit, the story quickly changed to an explanation that the foreman wasn't working on Saturday. I informed him that the service was done on a Monday, whereupon he noted that the foreman was sick on the Monday, too.

> You get the picture of what was happening here.
>
> A few weeks later, after escalating this concern, he told me that the person who performed the service was no longer working at the shop. Clearly, he had spent far too much time formulating his next excuse, instead of listening to what I was asking for. What I wanted was some sort of assurance, not that this person would be punished for the mistake, but that there would be reasonable checks and balances to reduce the likelihood of this ever happening again.
>
> My problem was never with the person who rotated the tires. It was with the shop that failed to catch the problem before I drove off the lot.
>
> As you might expect, I get the car serviced elsewhere these days.

We all make mistakes, each and every one of us. To claim we don't is to not take full responsibility for our actions, and to lose the opportunity to learn, evolve, and improve over time. A prime reason for putting in place a system to support a team is to catch the mistakes that are made before they can do too much damage, and to provide an infrastructure within which the system can be continuously refined to prevent the same kind of mistake from happening again. Mistakes are the things that we improve upon.

As an opportunity to learn, mistakes provide a compelling starting point. We need to recognize that mistakes can take both an active form and a passive form: the things we do incorrectly and the things that we fail to do that result in challenges. Indeed, passive inaction can be the most insidious and dangerous alternative: not doing the expected, not following through, forgetting things, or not doing things because you did not know they needed to be done. This is where learning and infrastructure can really make a difference to teams, through sharing knowledge, setting appropriate expectations, and focusing change on the areas that have a real impact on progress.

Those in the organization that are stretching themselves the furthest are also the most likely to make mistakes. They are pushing the envelope, often because the envelope is inadequately defined or because they are working to go beyond the call of duty.

Demonizing mistakes is a sure way to sour participation, even if people are only bystanders to the incident in question. *Blame* is too harsh a word, and my preference would be to never blame under any circumstance. *Responsibility* is a more appropriate term, and responsibility for mistakes usually lies further up the corporate ladder than most situations may indicate. A mistake should result in appropriate action—shoring up team practices to reduce the likelihood that this kind of mistake will be repeated rather than penalizing the person who acted without adequate support.

On the other end of the spectrum, rewarding only the people who do not make mistakes will suck the life out of your organization. Nobody will take the initiative to take on more if there is a risk of making a mistake. You will end up with a consistently predictable passive organization, which might not be much better than a place that demonizes mistakes.

Embrace mistakes as your richest learning opportunity and leverage them to strengthen your team and the infrastructure within which they can do great things.

Denial

Our lives are a continuous cycle of absorbing information, and then formulating and executing a reaction to that information. We have little control over the information that comes streaming in through the news, interpersonal communication, and myriad other sources. The information comes to us whether we ask for it or not, and shutting down a source of information today usually means that it will still trickle to us in some other form later on. How we interpret all this information and, more important, how we act in the face of this information are the factors that determine our ability to survive.

In working with one client, this point was brought sharply into focus.

It Just Can't Be Us

We ran through the results of our Web-based performance diagnostic with a couple senior executives of a small company. They met with us in advance to discuss the nature and workflow of the engagement before proceeding, and they wanted to get a quick heads-up on the data before running the session with the entire team. Not the usual approach, but we had assurances that the advance session was for information purposes only, not for censorship. Up to this point, all was according to plan. The responses rolled in as usual, and there was no indication that anything was amiss. For the first 30 minutes of the debrief, all was relatively calm.

Then, the penny dropped as the president started to see some themes appearing in the data. The group didn't perform many industry best practices, and their consistent responses showed that this was the case. The group's own feedback indicated performance was below average compared to the overall benchmarks provided. In short, the data suggested that there were challenges within the organization.

Remember, what we walked through here was simply the team's responses to the questions they were asked. There was no distillation of information or drawing of conclusions. This was just raw data, rolled up to be statistically anonymous.

Suddenly, it became clear to the president that there were all sorts of flaws with the diagnostic instrument itself. Inappropriate terminology was used, we asked the wrong questions, and the information was simply invalid as presented. The questions needed to be reframed if there was to be any validity in the data, and all the existing benchmark information was apparently irrelevant to their group.

What we were all looking at were merely their group's responses to a set of questions. To my mind, we had uncovered a rich set of information that could be used as a basis for refining practices within the organization, specifically to improve overall performance. Experience shows that the numbers have a strong correlation to what is really happening in an organization. Other companies that had leveraged the diagnostic have validated this.

This person saw something entirely different. The president quickly built up a protective barrier from the data. He saw a broken tool, but only after looking at the responses to the questions. Whether or not the questions and approach were flawed, the answers were theirs, open to interpretation in a variety of ways.

What we have is imperfect real-world data, indicators rather than hard and fast metrics. The value in the tool is primarily in the discussion it generates within the team. It is often the first opportunity for everyone to get together to debate many of the issues that are exposed.

Unfortunately, this group will not have that opportunity.

Sometimes doctors tell patients something they don't want to hear, anything from "you should quit smoking" to "get your affairs in order quickly." Although there are clear stages in the absorption of information, people will progress through these stages at different rates. Some will never get past the stage of denial, whereas others will quickly take affirmative action on the information and have the greatest chances for survival and growth.

Neglect

I recall that the standard way to deal with assignments when at university was to complain bitterly when they were assigned, and then to hang out in the pub for three weeks until the night before the assignment was due. Then, it became a matter of getting the assignment done as expediently as possible, instead of learning the concepts and truly gaining from the experience. There was always time to try to learn the stuff before the final exam.

At least, that was the practice of the other students in the class....

The demands on our time are generally much greater today than they were back in school, and most of us are not much better at focusing on the tasks that are important before they become urgent simply due to the passage of time. We rarely make the distinction that Stephen Covey would recommend, pulling apart the urgent from the important. We are caught up in the "tyranny of the urgent," from our Pavlovian response to the notifications that we have new e-mail, to dropping whatever we are working on when someone wanders by the office, or racing to pick up the phone before it goes to voicemail. As suggested in *Peopleware,*[1] these behaviors prevent us from ever attaining our peak effectiveness.

Anything can serve to put off the current task. We are all guilty of procrastination at one time or another, whether it is because we loathe the job ahead or because we don't feel up to performing the task. E-mail and the Web are often excuses for procrastination instead of being the communication tools they were intended to be. Neglecting important tasks is frighteningly easy to do. We rarely intend to neglect issues, but we do little to guard them from being overcome by events.

Whether it is keeping tabs on the progress of the project, going through with the annual performance appraisals or adequately testing the module we just coded before we check it in, we all must deal with important tasks every day. Although putting them off or finding other things to do might not have an immediate impact, ignoring them can come back to bite us in a big way later. We constantly need to ensure we are spending enough time on these items, and let the lesser issues fill the cracks, rather than the other way around. To do this, we need to properly prioritize our work.

 The first step is to capture everything we need to do in a single list. Include the mundane chores, the repetitive tasks, the novel activities, and the large projects. Only when everything is on the table at the same time can we truly sort between them in terms of importance. Do away with the post-its on the side of your terminal, the lists you keep in your head, and all the other systems for remembering what to do. Capture everything in a single place. Take the massive tasks, the ones that are too daunting as a single item, and break them down until they are manageable bites that will allow for gradual progress rather than leaving them so large that they stay on a "back burner" forever.

We need to be honest with ourselves to deal with neglect. The big problems rarely go away on their own, and our list of tasks will not shrink without effort on our part. Although everything on the list will have a due date (whether it is a hard deadline or just intent), we separate the wheat from the chaff by clearly identifying the things that are critical to our success, differentiating them from the things that would not be noticed if they weren't done.

 Set reasonable expectations as to how long it should take to complete each task, and you gain a valuable tool to manage where you should allocate your time. Learn from your own experience where you typically have spent your time, and the tool improves dramatically. Ruthlessly defend your right to spend some focused time on important matters, and you are well on your way to overcoming neglect. Most important, ensure that everyone shares your expectations.

 With this approach, you will be equipped to spend more time on the things that are truly important to you, which in turn will improve your sense of accomplishment. You will have a clear understanding of your capabilities and a strong position against the unreasonable requests of others for you to just take on one more thing.

Neglect is not a strategy for dealing with your workload. Chances are that simply organizing where you spend your time can reap huge benefits in overall productivity and job satisfaction, and the best of all this is that you don't need permission or corporate initiatives to make it happen.

In Support of Perseverance

 Adversity comes in many forms. It is a rare organization in this industry that has not faced significant adversity at one time or another.

I often see companies just hunkering down in an attempt to weather a storm. They take the approach of cutting costs and hoping that some external mechanism will magically transform the economy, get things back on track, and re-create the positive business climate that they previously enjoyed. This is a dangerously passive strategy.

Tactically, every company experiences highs and lows at all levels, from the individual meeting that didn't go as planned, to the client engagement that didn't meet expectations, to the reporting period for which they failed to meet the numbers. There will always be numbers above and below the average. Although the highs are generally considered positive, how we perceive the lows will define us as an organization. Do we see the lows as problems for which we feel the need to lay blame, or do we perceive them as learning experiences from which we can determine the root cause of the results and work toward preventing similar situations in the future? Blame is bad in general, and blaming external circumstances is taking the easy way out. This is an attractive but misdirected tactic.

 The dictionary defines perseverance as the "steady persistence in adhering to a course of action, a belief, or a purpose; steadfastness." Whether it is tactical or strategic adversity, maintaining a solid vision of purpose, either personally or at a business level, is the key element required to support the perseverance required to allow you to get through difficult times. Often called the mission statement, this is the verbalization of a solid purpose on which a business is built. This purpose is not only the rallying call that can bring the organization together in difficult times, but it also the defining essence of the organization itself and can be used as the arbiter of strategic and tactical business decisions. Weak strategies and tactics that are not aligned with a strong purpose can be easily weeded out from the list of options.

At all times, and especially in tactically or strategically challenging times, nothing is more important in supporting perseverance than strongly holding on to a valid belief, a purpose, or a *raison d'être*.

Mental Models

To manage the ever-increasing volume and complexity of information that confronts us, one of the key coping mechanisms that prevents us from losing our minds is that of simplification. Just as meteorologists take massive amounts of data from all their sources, and then reduce and simplify it in models to the point where they can sometimes tell us whether it is going to rain later today, we cope through employing massive simplification and the construction of mental models.

These mental models are constructed from our wide range of experiences, and generally they serve us well. They allow us to make complex decisions in the blink of an eye; they allow us to focus our analysis on the difficult or novel portions of a larger issue. Indeed, we would be hard pressed to interact without mental models in today's world. They are necessary, but they can carry underlying evil.

 Throughout history, a generally accepted set of mental models has always governed our behavior. As we look back, it is easy to recount any number of invalid models that have held us back. The flat-Earth model most certainly slowed exploration to new lands. The belief that humans could never run a mile in under four minutes held most athletes back for some time. After it was broken for the first time, the floodgates opened, and 17 more runners broke that barrier in the 3 years that followed. All manner of mental models have been crushed over time: Man can't fly; we'll never escape earth's gravity; the list goes on.

Our mental models form the box within which we live and often overly constrain our ability to creatively resolve the issues we face. In software development, several mental models severely limit the capabilities of people or teams that lean on them:

- The *Software Is Intangible* model is an argument that is often made when a project is out of control. It is a rationalization for the lack of careful planning, analysis, and change management. Any complex task is difficult to perform and tough to grasp if there is insufficient effort to manage it appropriately. Software is no exception. Pick the right models to express different aspects of the problem, and software is just as easily communicated as the hardware it runs on. As Ellen Gottesdiener demonstrates in *Requirements by Collaboration*,[2] no single model is sufficient, and there are many, from both the structured and object-oriented world, which may be relevant for some aspect of your product.

- The *We Don't Have the Time to Plan* model is often used by those who haven't measured where their time goes and aren't astute enough to even compare their actual performance against their intent. Done practically, it is safe to say that the shorter the fuse on a project, the more critical the planning activities become.

- The *We Must Use This [development approach | language | platform]* model, although sometimes reflecting valid constraints on a project, often have more to do with religious fervor or gaps in our toolbox than true constraints. No project demands a specific development approach, much to the chagrin of process consultants everywhere. Business solutions are rarely language constrained. Except for embedded software, even platforms are becoming less relevant these days.

 We need to take stock of the mental models that we use to guide our actions and critically assess where these models lie in the continuum between being useful mechanisms to make sense of the complex world around us and constraining us from accomplishing great things. History is full of people who have said "that's impossible" only to be proven wrong, a trend that isn't going to change anytime soon.

> When you hear someone say "that's impossible," it can be valuable to see this as a challenge to overcome, a mental model in want of adjustment.

Summary

We all experience setbacks from time to time. It is important to understand the root causes of these challenges, acknowledge any part we have played in causing the problem, and strive to change the circumstances that allowed these root causes to occur in the first place.

Pain is the greatest opportunity for learning, both as an individual and as an organization. Don't brush these events under the table; instead, use them to grow and evolve. The strongest changes are the ones designed to ensure that something that burned you once will not occur again.

How Is This Relevant?

Feeling the pain. Consider some of the most challenging events in the workplace. Was the pain felt at your level adequately communicated to others in the organization? What translations had to take place? Was the pain leveraged as an opportunity for change?

Dealing with challenges appropriately. Have you been able to objectively identify your part in challenging situations? Have you managed to persevere through challenges and come out stronger for the next time around? What adjustments have you made?

Managing our models. What mental models are you clinging to that are holding you back? Have you adjusted your models in any way to achieve more than before?

References

1. Tom DeMarco and Timothy Lister, *Peopleware: Productive Projects and Teams, 2nd Edition* (Dorsett House Publishing, 1999).
2. Ellen Gottesdiener, *Requirements by Collaboration* (Addison-Wesley, 2002).

CHAPTER SIX

Proactive Effectiveness

Knowing our own skills and limitations, being reasonably organized, and following our tasks through to completion make us more effective. These are also all attributes that we can consciously improve with effort.

In this chapter, we look at the power of introspection to help us understand who we are and to help prioritize our improvement journey and explore some of these very learnable skills.

Know Thyself

There is an adage out there that is so pervasive it is difficult to find the source: *You cannot manage what you do not measure.*

In the software industry, where almost everything at the product level is new, a lot of uncertainty is associated with how long it will take to get things done. Because this uncertainty is rarely communicated, unrealistic expectations are set, and disappointment often results. We've all been there. Many of us wallow daily in this pool.

Although software development is generally a team sport, when you get right down to it the team is a collection of individuals, each with his or her own capabilities, weaknesses, and performance characteristics. A project gets into trouble one step at a time, many steps because of optimistic rather than realistic estimates that individuals make. To generate realistic estimates, you need measures of how long it took for you to do things in the past.

There is plenty of benchmark data about performance in other organizations; the problem is that it is likely irrelevant for your needs. There may be some information about your team's past performance, but chances are that this is not the case, and the relevance to your specific tasks is somewhat dubious. Another adage is that *if you want something done right, you've got to do it yourself.* Who better than yourself to monitor your performance? Until we in this field achieve the status of sports celebrities, we certainly won't be afforded the luxury of having a timekeeper or statistician track our activities for us.

 Assuming you are even in a position to set expectations about the tasks on your plate, effectiveness is all about self-awareness: knowing your own past performance with similar tasks. Armed with this knowledge rather than anecdotal recollection (which is notoriously optimistic), one can create estimates that are much more defendable. This approach eliminates the problems that come with playing the "fudge factor" game, where the resulting number has no relevance to the actual effort.

 Ted the developer thinks, "They always cut my estimates in half, so I'll double them."

Bill the manager says, "Ted's always padding his numbers, so I'll divide them by three."

 Knowing your own productivity and the variability in that productivity can be compelling in negotiating enough time to do the job right.

Asked how long your commute to work is, chances are you have a good data-based response at your fingertips. Why is it not the same for what we do while at work? Understanding your own productivity in developing software starts with you.

Be careful to avoid getting caught in the delusion that it's a huge job to collect reasonable measurements. Although the effort involved to leverage the Personal Software Process from the Software Engineering Institute (SEI) can be daunting, the results can be worth the effort, but there is no need to start with that extreme.

Start by picking the things that you do often and simply collect some measures of how long it takes to do them.

Additional information such as how often the task is
revisited can help, too.
Very soon you will have a deeper understanding of your
performance, giving you far more credibility.

Gamblers and Risk Takers

If there is one certainty in the software industry, it is that nothing else is
certain. We rush to develop products based on an unclear schedule, without knowing whether there is a real market or what the competition is up
to. Will we get finished before we run out of cash? Will market acceptance
really reflect our hockey-stick projections? Will somebody else beat us to
market with yet another Great Idea?

We need to live with uncertainty, because we clearly cannot remove it
all. How we live with uncertainty, however, separates us into two groups:
gamblers and risk takers.

Gamblers are the ones who will blindly rush forward without regard to the
magnitude of risks they face and are usually disappointed with their results.
Unfortunately, we have all heard the wild success stories. Just one more
quarter in the slot machine (which is carefully programmed to turn a profit
for the casino), just one more dotcom startup (with a technological solution
dangerously in need of a problem to solve), just one more target to push the
team (usually based on expectations set elsewhere rather than a realistic
understanding of effort required). Some gamblers do very well, but they are
clearly the minority. That allure of the big win, however, continues to bring
them back to the table for more abuse. "Little Bobby needs a new pair of
shoes…" as you roll the dice one more time is not an astute call to action.

Risk takers do what they can to understand and manage as much uncertainty as possible. By doing so, they tip the odds in their favor, because being
aware of the odds is already a vast improvement. Certainly all the internal
elements of risk are within your ability to understand, if not influence,
and over time they can be clearly quantified. Diligence with your market
and your competitive analysis will allow you to better understand your
odds and make reasonable choices based on the more realistic risk/return

that you can see. You will understand that some alternatives just don't make sense. For the risks that you cannot control, at least you will understand their magnitude and likelihood and be prepared to deal with them if they should arise.

The distinction is not about being pessimistic in comparison to the gambler's optimism. It is all about being realistic: pulling your head out of the sand rather than avoiding reality. There are gray areas between the two, of course. There are those who will sit back and study the slot machines, only approaching them when they believe their system is pointing them toward a winner, but this is still hit and miss.

I suggest that a strong correlation exists between where you and your organization are on the gambler to risk taker continuum and your ability to achieve your objectives.

Designing Our Environment

Look around. It is pretty easy to pick out a software product that has benefited from a conscious focus on design elements. There is clear consistency across different areas of the application. It works well to support the client's needs. Indeed, it can be a joy to use. Under the hood, the same focus has simplified the task of building the application and has reduced time and effort in the process.

Even with these clear distinctions, there remain a number of software teams that give the design of their products less respect than they should.

In a similar vein, as we look at distinctions from one work environment to the next, it becomes pretty easy to pick out the environment where there has been a conscious focus on the design of that environment. There are few overwhelming distractions. The required resources are close by. The space is conducive to getting work done: People don't have to "get away" from the office to be productive.

Few software teams reap the benefit of working in a well-designed environment. Given that most of the factors driving productivity are related to the teams, and that differences in work environment will significantly impact productivity, small changes here can reap significant rewards.

In many places, individuals are working in conditions that make it almost impossible to be effective. Note that the responsibility does not all lie with management.

 You don't need to wait for the organization to mandate a wholesale change to the environment. There are usually things that you can do on your own. Appendix A, "Core Tools," describes a number of elements to consider in refining our workspaces and work habits.

 We all exercise a great deal of control in our immediate workspaces, and we need to take responsibility for our half of each and every relationship we are involved in. With reasonable reflection and forethought, we can do a great deal to manage the design of our work environments. The leverage gained in doing so is tremendous. Personal productivity for many people can quickly improve by 25 percent or more as we take back much of the time that is lost and never quantified in timesheets.

Just as we recognize that conscious design of our software will result in more stable and organized products that have a higher likelihood of achieving our goals, the same holds true for the design of our workspace and activities at work.

Take the time to adjust your environment and work habits that will make you more effective overall on the job.

Not Nearly Juggling

 All too often, we hear that someone is "juggling too many balls" or that someone "has dropped a ball or two." Although they might be trying to do a lot of things at one time, when you really get down to it, what they are doing is significantly different from the "discipline" of juggling. Whether we are managing one or more projects or just acting as a team member with a lot of things to do, most of us could learn a thing or two from jugglers.

The act of keeping two or more objects in the air at one time by alternately tossing and catching them is not something that most people can do the first time they try. Initial playing around with two or three balls (it is actually easier to juggle three balls than two) results in a great deal of stops and starts as we chase balls around before anything that resembles more than chaos appears.

Jugglers endlessly practice their skills until they appear to be effortless. From those in world-famous circuses to those who work as street buskers, they break down the techniques and study them in detail until they can perform them without thinking. They focus on the steps separate from the context of their performance, adding complexity and pressure to the situation. How many of us as project managers regularly step back to truly understand and optimize our approach outside the context of a critical project?

Jugglers set things in motion with precision and accuracy. The ball is tossed in a specific direction, at just the right speed, with as little spin as possible; the pins are released with just enough spin so that they will fall back into the hand at the right moment. On software projects, we often rush headlong into coding as it is seen to yield tangible progress, instead of ensuring we have a strong start by establishing good understanding of the vision, scope, and resulting reasonable schedule.

Jugglers focus their attention where needed. They know better than to focus on one specific ball at the expense of the others. They appear to gaze at a point in space while actually they are surveying the entire scene. Through experience, they know what early signs of trouble look like and can adjust accordingly. They know when to compensate for a trajectory that is slightly off kilter, and they don't let one miscue cascade out of control. On projects, we need to have control mechanisms in place so that we can focus on the trouble spots, not the normal flow of expected activities. Most important, for those of us who have grown into management ranks through a technical stream, we can't allow ourselves to delve into the details and miss the big picture.

Jugglers are in control. They know precisely where their limits lie. When performing, they stay comfortably within these limits, while appearing to manage the impossible. More often than not, when they drop a couple of balls at the beginning of a performance it is just part of the ruse to make their show all the more fascinating. Early mistakes on a project shouldn't necessarily be planned in but should certainly be taken advantage of to focus the team. All in all, the team needs to be aware of their capabilities, provide credible technical estimates accordingly, and recognize that chances of success will diminish if the constraints on the project are too severe.

 Jugglers often work as part of a team. They won't toss a ball at someone unless they know it will be caught. They rehearse their dance and know their teammates' every move. They have the skill to leverage their partners' strengths and can compensate for their weaknesses. All of this is balanced to build the best performance possible. At any moment in time, they are aware of their role relative to the overall context, as well as their expected interactions with the rest of the team. How often have you or one of your teammates been caught off guard by interactions that could have been predicted or communicated?

Decisions

All our lives, we face decisions. As we gain experience, some decisions become more straightforward and others even become mundane. It would seem silly to angst over which socks to wear, which salad dressing to use, or what movie to watch. Time also brings more responsibilities. We continue to be presented with new situations, including some difficult-to-make decisions.

Tough decisions can take many forms. Which way to turn for a new career, whether to take a leap in a new uncharted direction, whether to hang on to something that appears to be better off left alone, whether to move or stay put. Tough decisions can often impact relationships, quality of life, and your personal sense of self-worth. They are high impact, and hence there can be significant resistance to making the decision.

Consequently, they can be frightfully easy to defer. At some point, these decisions will be made, either for you or by you. Given a choice of participating in the decision making or just letting nature take its course, chances are that actively driving the decision will provide you with more satisfying results. With that in mind, you can do some things to start moving down the path of actively making that decision.

 Recognize that there will be an emotional side and a logical side to be addressed for any decision. The heart may say one thing while the head says another, and each of us will tend to favor one of these perspectives over the other in most situations. Seek support and guidance where possible to help balance this dilemma. Respect that there is strength in collaboration. Different perspectives of a problem can provide a more complete understanding of the situation, and consequently a more comprehensive and better-fitting solution. Brainstorm, analyze, and consult in turn to converge toward the right decision that balances emotion and logic.

Understand the constraints of the problem. Be clear about what is known, what is unresolved, and what simply doesn't matter. Clarify the context of the problem and know your degrees of freedom. Does it need to be settled by a certain time? Who are the stakeholders impacted by the decision? Are there monetary constraints that need to be addressed? There is great value in capturing all this information, especially for those tough decisions that won't be settled in an hour. Even if you are the sole participant in the decision making, memories are imperfect and subject to change over time. Seeing that current perceptions are different from what was captured earlier can be a clear indicator that all is not as clear-cut as it once seemed.

 Break down the problem as much as possible. List and understand the different aspects of the problem. This categorization itself will often help you gain a clearer perspective. After some elements have been settled, iterate to identify further steps. Like chipping away at a sculpture, continue to attack and refine the problem where you can.

 Don't delay. The longer you wait to get started in the decision-making process, the less time you will have at your disposal and the fewer options you will have to choose from. Delay too long and the decision will be settled for you, whether you like it or not. As quickly as possible after you have clearly framed the problem, get a handle on the things that are not clear so that you can focus on reducing uncertainty and simplifying the problem. Recognize that we often delay because of our fear that the decision will be binding for all time. In reality, this is often not the case. Clarity, even if it will need to be revisited later, will usually be preferable to the uncertainty of an unsettled problem hanging over our heads.

When all is said and done, difficult decisions are like projects that you have been handed. They can be effectively attacked with project management practices.

As with more traditional projects, the degree to which you proactively manage the solution will have a strong bearing on the degree to which you are satisfied with the solution.

Start today to chip away at difficult decisions, and gradually the pieces will fall into place.

Follow-Through

Follow-through allows us to think beyond the immediate target and recognize the extended impact of our actions. As we do this, the range of possibilities of what *done* means quickly narrows. We drastically reduce the likelihood that there will be a difference in expectations and a corresponding disappointment with the results. We gain a deeper understanding of impact of our practices, a wider appreciation for the consequences of the influence and interdependence of our actions.

Follow-Through in Sports

In almost any sport, the first thing a pro will talk to you about when you take lessons is body position, focus, and the notion of strong and consistent follow-through. These are fundamental skills. Although you can still play the game without strong follow-through, you will never become world class. The pros and the better amateurs drill themselves on follow-through until it is second nature. In some sports, such as archery and golf, many pros believe they can leverage the follow-through to continue to influence the trajectory after the arrow has been released or contact has been made with the ball. The shot is complete only when the target has been hit.

In martial arts, we are taught to kick or punch through the target, not just to meet the target. From the perspective of physics, striving to simply meet the target drastically reduces the momentum and effectiveness of the punch. Without follow-through, we're more likely to bruise knuckles rather than break bricks. With proper focus

> beyond the immediate target, we pass right through that target as though it is not there.
>
> The first time you break a brick, it is surprisingly effective and painless.

Follow-through is like starting a fresh pot of coffee in the office when you've taken the last cup. It's about managing expectations beyond our own.

We're not really done with requirements when the document is saved. We're not done with the project when the product is installed at the client site. We don't go through an analysis phase just to produce a requirements specification. We are trying to capture the information needed for us to successfully complete the remainder of the project. We are developing the information that drives the schedule, the design and development effort, and the validation effort. We need to ensure that we have adequately addressed these goals. Having produced the document is merely making contact with the target. All too often, that target is only superficially impacted.

We don't produce code so that it compiles, we produce code so that it solves a problem. It's not about unit test, although that is a strong part of it. It's not even about integration test, although that's part of it, too. It's about ensuring that the end user's experience is complete and satisfying. It is the follow-through that we must focus on to ensure that we have accomplished our goal.

Don't swing just to make contact with the ball. Swing for the fence. Ensure your actions have the strongest impact possible. Follow through.

Explicit Completion Criteria

With two young children at home, it's interesting to see how we interpret the term *done*. Whether it is clutter in the playroom or the dinner on their plates, it's rare that we have a common understanding of *done* up front.

Throw something exciting in the mix, such as heading to a movie when we're done, and the interpretation usually appears to be something like this: *Do as little as you can get away with, because there's something much more fun around the corner.* And the grumbling when they have to go back to do the job right—oh my!

It's not enough just to say you're done, it is critical to agree in advance what *done* means.

Software organizations often play the same game with completion criteria. Always working to aggressive schedules, with pressure to get the system out the door and the excitement of looking forward to the next big thing, it is easy to get caught in the trap of saying "we're done" early. We've met our schedules; it's in the customer's hands, let's get going on something else.

Unfortunately, the real world can be even crueler than parents. The zeal to work on new and exciting things can be dampened as the customer finds the equivalent of dirty laundry under the bed or peas hidden behind the chicken bones. If you find that you are still working on things that you previously declared done, your interpretation probably needs some refinement.

 The term *done* can have many different meanings in software development. On one hand, often when not explicitly stated, it is anything from "we're tired of slogging through this" to "we've reached our target date" to "we've convinced our clients to take it." At the other end of the spectrum, it can be "we know we have a system that meets our reliability criteria," "our defect profiles have been ramped down to our expectations," or "we have little risk of problems if we release now." If what defines *done* is not stated clearly, it will certainly be loosely interpreted.

Done will be interpreted in a way that allows you to apparently meet your deadlines, but have they really been met? Realistically, all the effort spent cleaning up afterward is preventing you from working on the next big thing, and you weren't truly done after all. Instead, you need to set explicit completion criteria, for both the project and each individual task. Identify up front exactly how "doneness" will be determined. What test cases will be successfully run, and what test infrastructure is required to perform these tests? Is done having a system with 99.95 percent availability? Does done merely mean that the code correctly compiled? If so, state it—and downstream expectations will be managed accordingly.

When you have explicit completion criteria that all can agree on, you can actually agree to move on to other things.

Summary

We can do a number of things to make us more effective in the workplace.

We can strive to better understand our own capabilities and attitudes, preferably in a quantified form so that we can determine whether we are improving over time. Most of us have significant organizational challenges in today's workplace, and seemingly minor tweaks can dramatically reduce our wasted time.

If we more clearly identify what closure means and communicate it clearly, we can better manage expectations and eliminate a great deal of rework.

We need to continuously strive to refine our effectiveness through vigilance in these areas.

How Is This Relevant?

Risk. Do you clearly understand the risks you face, or do the same issues repeatedly surprise you? Is the direction you take based on achievable goals and management of risk or are you rolling the dice? Are you being realistic in your approaches to work?

Juggling. If you are trying to keep too many things going simultaneously, are you really juggling or is it perhaps something a bit less elegant? Is there anything you can learn from the discipline of juggling that you could apply to keeping all your tasks moving at once?

Follow-through. Spend the next day considering follow-through in everything you do. Are there situations in which you can complete the activity with simple tasks that will drastically affect the overall quality of the outcome? Can the simple act of saying "please," "thank you," and "you're welcome"—and meaning it—make a difference?

CHAPTER SEVEN

Sustainability

Most of us are in the software game for the long haul. Marathon runners don't try to maintain a sprinting pace. They recognize the importance of replenishing their resources along the way.

We explore approaches to maintaining our sanity as a critical component to sustaining our ongoing personal effectiveness.

Pressure

Both of my children went through the pressure of a piano recital recently. My daughter was familiar with the game, and my son was performing for the first time.

Although my daughter had been there before, the technical challenge in the pieces she was performing had been really ratcheted up this time around. Both kids independently expressed the feeling of pressure leading up to the event.

Both did very well, and both were visibly relieved afterward.

Around the same time, I had just finished an engagement in which I was running a day of customized training with a group of 50 astute, sophisticated engineers. I, too, felt the pressure beforehand and the corresponding relief and satisfaction of completion afterward. Generally, the feedback was positive, so I believe I achieved my goals for the event.

As my kids were heading into the recital, we talked about the pressure they were feeling as a very positive feeling. It showed that they both cared about the quality of their performance, they recognized the importance of being in the spotlight, and they knew they were going to be externally assessed. With that knowledge, their practices leading up to the event took on a different complexion. It was less of a struggle to get them to sit down at the piano bench, and they practiced with better focus. Keeping this positive perspective in mind, I also found it easy to prepare for my engagement.

We had all experienced a reasonable amount of pressure and learned to leverage it for better results.

 So it goes with pressure on project teams, too. It is important to ensure that team members feel an appropriate amount of pressure and that this pressure is reasonable with respect to the context of their roles as well as the overall objectives. Too much or too little and individual contributions as well as overall team effort will fall apart.

Too little pressure can come from several causes. If there is no clear completion date, work can very easily be placed on a back burner, possibly to languish there forever. I've had a number of these "on-hold" projects simmering for some time, and they only really get promoted in urgency when a potential is translated into an actual, by establishing a firm delivery date. Generally, this date becomes firm primarily through a commitment with an external stakeholder (a piano recital, a training engagement).

Insufficient motivation can also occur when the owner of the task doesn't see the real benefit of getting the work done. There may be an extremely relaxed deadline, such as "I'd like to get it done sometime this year," or it could be something that just isn't recognized as sufficiently important, the proverbial shuffling of deck chairs on the *Titanic*.

On the other hand, too much pressure can be just as de-motivating for people.

 I've heard stories about developers having to present their intermediate product results periodically to senior management, where the pressure is so great that some are physically ill leading up to the presentation. Being asked to perform beyond your capacity, either because the work is beyond your skill level or the performance expectations are clearly outside the realm of possibility, or the consequences of failure are beyond your sphere of influence, is debilitating.

We need to be careful to apply the appropriate level of pressure to our team, and to be vigilant to ensure that this pressure is tweaked to maintain optimum performance. Individuals react to pressure very differently, and we have to be careful to avoid painting the whole team with a broad brush. It can be useful to discuss the importance of appropriate pressure with the team directly; their feedback will be instrumental in helping you keep the team flowing effectively.

Whatever role you may have, it is useful to carefully monitor the pressure you are feeling about all the tasks on your plate. Is the pressure keeping you motivated to do a good job in the expected timeframes, or do you find yourself procrastinating and leaving it to later? Are you so worried sick about some things that it's tough to focus on getting the job done at all?

Is there a reasonable level of pressure from your peers? There can be a healthy level of pressure, driving you to do well so that you don't let your teammates down. Alternatively, there can be too much pressure, if you are the one carrying the team, or are trying to make up for not carrying your share in the past.

Stay tuned into the pressures you are feeling (and the pressure of those around you).

Consistent pressure at the right level is a strong motivator for people, and great things can be achieved with the right balance. Keep the pressure high enough to maintain motivation and performance, but no higher.

What's Important?

Each of us is motivated by different factors, both in our careers and personal lives.

In software development, it has been shown that the greatest variation in performance is driven not by technology but by the personnel side of the equation. Motivation and morale play a large part in determining the effectiveness of the individual, the team, and ultimately the organization.

Studies have shown that programmer-analysts rank personal life much higher than managers do. The inverse is true for responsibility. Achievement is very important to both groups, but salary and job security consistently fall well down on the list. If salary and job security fall so low on *everyone's* list, why is it that the world seems to revolve around keeping our jobs, and why is the size of our paycheck such a critical issue around review time? A lot of it has to do with Maslow's hierarchy of needs. The fact that we have not gained stability in these fundamental hygiene factors around the workplace (job stability, reasonable work environment, and so on) prevents us from critically dealing with the real factors that we are interested in. To heck with the important, we're sweating the urgent concerns. We're trying to stay afloat. We are being driven by our job. We are not driving our career.

 Where are the organizational activities that nurture achievement in most companies? Even for those companies that are providing a stable environment with job security and reasonable pay, little is still done to properly manage and sustain these critical factors. Quite often, we get busy in our careers, to a point where we lose track of the primary drivers that motivate us. The organization gets busy in getting the next project out the door or fighting the current fire, instead of taking the time to ensure that the tools that create value, the people, continue to be well tuned to run at peak performance.

Without constantly nurturing our primary motivators, they will wither to a point at which they are lost. Stress and inefficiency will insidiously creep in as motivation drops, and it can be difficult to see the problem before it is too late. Often, it is only after you have left a poisoned situation that you realize how bad off you really were. Auxiliary benefits of moving to a better environment can be powerful. You stop getting so many colds, those headaches go away, and people tell you how much more relaxed you look. It's no coincidence.

To truly flourish in your career, it is important to find an environment that supports your primary motivators. It's a two-phased approach. You need to understand what drives you (which can be a challenging rediscovery process in itself), and then you need to recognize whether your environment will support those factors. Be careful to look beyond the Dilbert-like stated policies to the actual practices in the organization, from senior management to the individuals you interact with. If there is poor alignment between stated intent and action, it is a safe bet that when push comes to shove, the stated intent will fall by the wayside.

Recharging the Batteries

We've all been in the situation where we have a problem to solve, we have a tight constraint in which to solve it, and the pressure is on. We continue to struggle, effectively pounding our head against a wall as we ineffectively deal with the issue. We're stuck in a rut. Creativity is stifled as we try to use the old tools to solve new problems, even if that tool didn't work in the first ten attempts. At these times, our best strategy is often to step back and take on something entirely different. We need to recharge our batteries.

This is an apt metaphor. It requires significant energy to continuously attack a problem, and we only carry a finite amount. Studies have shown that developer output drops precipitously as a function of schedule pressure and hours worked—not unlike a rechargeable battery—but many persist in slogging on, burning the midnight oil, with disappointing results.

Contrary to the way many organizations drive their staff in this industry, battery recharging can be an effective business strategy. There are valid reasons why pilots and air traffic controllers have strict quotas on the time they are on the job. Although loss of life is rarely a driver, those reasons hold true in software development, too. Sending people home after a reasonable workday rather than offering to spring for pizza on a regular basis will often lead to higher productivity, greater creativity, and of course, lower pizza costs.

Recharging the batteries can take a variety of forms. It may be as simple as stepping back and dealing with other things briefly, such as checking e-mail or getting a coffee. It might involve bouncing the problem off another set of eyes for a fresh perspective, which will often identify flawed assumptions or inspire the "aha" required to resolve things. It may mean getting a meal with a little more nutritional value than that obtained from a vending machine or a drive-through window. For the persistent challenges, it might require a more significant break from the action: heading home before midnight, or taking a few days off without looking at the problem.

Recognize that persisting against a stubborn problem is a losing battle. If you find yourself beating your head against the wall, don't continue to do so and hope that numbness will set in to ease the pain. Step back. Do something completely different, preferably something you enjoy. Recharging the batteries may be one of the most effective and most underutilized tools we have in our toolkit today.

Stepping Back to Smell the Roses

Note to self: Take advantage of the time off. Running hard all the time can take its toll.

A vacation is a great time for us to reflect. We can step back and look on the past, and recharge our batteries for the future. For many of us, it can be a time when we are reluctantly forced to step away from the computer and focus on things that we know are more important, things that might have taken a backseat to our work throughout the year.

There are all sorts of arguments against individuals running hard for an extended period of time. Elite world-class athletes will train for months for a single high-intensity burst of a few hours. There are longer endurance events, but there are participants who can sustain the energy levels to complete them. The events really take their toll, and careers are relatively short.

Research has repeatedly shown that working longer hours negatively impacts productivity. Benchmark data from my own work has shown that companies with a more reasonable workweek outperform those with higher average working hours. Despite the evidence, we still tend to burn the midnight oil, and many companies reward heroic efforts and ongoing insane work schedules.

In speaking with a neighbor recently, an interesting distinction between academia and industry came up. Educators will get several opportunities over the year to take a reasonable break. When they return, they start with a clean slate, a class full of fresh students to work with for the new term.

In industry, we often run into the situation where we take a week or two to relax, to get away, only to find that the backlog of issues has grown while we are gone, and we return to work having to run harder than before. The burst of advance preparation doesn't really help, and it only takes a couple of weeks to settle into our old familiar chaotic pace. We rarely ensure that our breaks are actually beneficial for us.

When we take a break, whether it be a plant shutdown where everyone is off, or a vacation during which the work moves on (and piles up) in your absence, we need to set up a structure so that we aren't further behind when we get back than when we started. Here are a few things to do to ensure your time away provides a net positive return:

- Set expectations with peers and clients well in advance. You are going to be gone, and reasonable adjustments can be made. Arrange for alternative contacts regarding critical information and schedule work to be done for the period that you are away.

- Coordinate with that alternative contact to be sure that they know what may be coming and are prepared to deal with issues appropriately. Provide background information as required. Walk through tasks to ensure they are understood.

- Identify all the things that would normally be done while you are gone and shuffle accordingly. Get them done early, pass them along to a peer, or put them on hold until your return. This can be a great opportunity to identify things you have been doing as a matter of routine that aren't even necessary at all.

- Leave contact information if you must, but warn people that this information is to be used only in extreme emergency. Threaten physical violence if that is what it takes.
- Give yourself a real break. Hanging out on the beach with your laptop or BlackBerry is really just extending your office space. Bring along a good book, one that's not work related. Take the time to connect with the people you are with and rediscover what's important in your life. Get away from the urgent.

Next time you have an opportunity to take some time off, do some preparation. Take the time to reflect and to recharge those batteries. Step back and really smell those roses.

Navel Gazing as Business Strategy

We all hear about rousing business success stories, but we also know in the back of our minds that few start-ups get to the point where they can proudly tell people how they survived. If venture capitalists only expect to hit a home run with one out of every ten companies that they back, and go through hundreds of pitches before finding one that is worthy of an investment, well…you do the math.

What happens to all those that fail? There are probably more reasons for business failure than there are businesses that fail. There just wasn't enough cash to get the product out the door, or the industry was just too volatile, or the customer base just didn't understand the message. It is easy to come up with reasons why the company wasn't part of the latest acquisition or IPO.

 The vast majority of all these reasons are just excuses. Blaming external circumstances while neglecting to look internally to see whether there is any way to pull the situation out of the water doesn't help at all. Nothing has been learned if you fail to look within to see whether there is anything within your control (or at least your influence) that you could do differently. My guess is that for most failed start-ups, there would have been plenty of remedies the team could have applied to address the challenges they faced.

Mature companies that measure their time usage average 40 percent to 50 percent of their time in rework.[1] The Hawthorne effect (when people know they are being observed in a study, their behavior or performance temporarily changes) may bring these numbers down from where they really are. Start-up companies that are running hard, working long hours, and being tossed around by a dynamic business environment can easily have much higher rework numbers. I measured close to 70 percent rework with one client. How many companies would have survived to be around today had they been twice as effective in spending their development budget? It is not how much you make, it is how much you save that makes you successful.

 Young companies striving to build the next big thing often find themselves immersed in a sea of evolving standards, unproven technology, and fierce competition. Even in the most volatile of business environments, what matters most is not how volatile the industry is but how you deal with these challenges.

There's always value in considering the ramifications of your actions instead of allowing yourself to be chaotically jerked around by every potential change that comes your way. Although some would say that he who hesitates is lost, I've never encountered a situation in which a brief look before you leap has had a negative effect. External change needs to be tracked and managed. Internal change must be controlled.

It takes considerable analysis and research up front to be sure that you are actually building the right product, and just as much effort afterward to sell that product. Despite the focus of many start-ups, most customers don't care in the least about the technology under the hood. They are concerned about whether the product solves a real problem for them. If the message does not appear to have been received, perhaps there was room for improvement in how the message was sent.

It can be easy and comforting to blame external circumstances for the challenges you face, but such an approach is a recipe for repeated failure.

Try looking inward to focus your energy on opportunities that are within your control.

Quality of Life

Some of us live to work, others work to live. Unfortunately, too many people are stuck in the former category, even though they might prefer to be in the latter.

There is always pressure to find those nasty bugs that we just can't seem to put enough band-aids on or to meet that looming deadline. There are individuals, and indeed entire sectors, that relish the thought of putting in the long hours to get a seemingly impossible project out the door on time. It can become a badge of honor, a cultural norm that makes those who are interested in a different balance in life appear to be misfits. From what I have seen and experienced, however, this is not a sustainable approach. Individuals will burn out, and organizations will face ongoing turnover challenges. Brute force doesn't appear to be the long-term answer to the quality question.

 In an early issue of *Fast Company*,[2] there was an article about the team at the NASA Software Engineering Lab. They're the ones who build the software for the space shuttle and have an almost flawless record with their product. When they find a bug (and they still do inject bugs, but they find more of them faster), they fix the bug, they address that class of problems in their systems, and they address the process flaw that allowed that class of bugs to enter into the system in the first place. They work normal hours, they all have lives outside of work, and they develop some of the best software in the world.

Every time I relate that story to a group, there's someone who asks, "What about those failed Mars missions from a few years back?" Those systems were actually built by NASA's Jet Propulsion Laboratory in an era when their mantra was "faster, better, cheaper." They pumped out projects at a fraction of the cost of previous systems, resulting in a significant increase in newsworthy failures.[3] Clearly, the emphasis of their mantra was "*faster,* better, *cheaper.*" Unfortunately, major disasters on the job tend to spill over into home life, and there are reports that much of the team's fun vanished along with the funding.

 To some degree, the NASA SEL is immune from the challenges that the JPL faced. They have no real competition and are not in a race to be first to market. With a clearly identified platform, less-novel innovation, and a manned spacecraft that requires a greater emphasis on quality, the SEL can be seen as having a rather cushy job. What they do is still rocket science, however, and it is pretty clear from the drastic performance dip at the JPL that an emphasis on quality will make a difference.

Fortunately for the Cassini spacecraft, the project was so large and Saturn is so far away that the mission largely predated the "faster, better, cheaper" initiative. Fortunately for Mars, the JPL appears to be learning from its mistakes.

Faster, better, and cheaper can indeed all happily coexist, but it depends on which of the three adjectives gets the emphasis. With better as the driver, faster and cheaper are often content to tag along for the ride.

The quality of the approach we take to developing software significantly impacts the quality of the products we build and, in far too many cases, the quality of our lives.

Summary

There will always be pressure to perform on the job. Often, this pressure takes the form of long hours and diversion from your other priorities. Although it is reasonable to expect some bursts of effort to get a project out the door, we cannot sustain a breakneck pace forever.

We need to be able to balance our lives and to take a break from a constant focus on the workplace. Without this balance, our productivity will suffer, and the side effects will spill over into our personal lives, too.

We must focus on the quality of our work environment, ensure that we are managing to preserve what is important to us, and recognize that we must pace ourselves for the long haul.

How Is This Relevant?

Priorities. What are the most important factors for you: Are you in an environment where these important factors are being properly tended?

Reasonable workloads. How many hours in a typical week are you focused on work? Are you sacrificing other areas of your life to do this? Is your efficiency on the job suffering because of the effort?

Time off. When did you last take a vacation or break without thinking about work? When you are out of contact with e-mail, do you get antsy? Do you protect any activities that help you distract your mind from the workplace?

References

1. Steve McConnell, *Rapid Development, Taming Wild Software Schedules* (Microsoft Press, 1996). This summarizes findings from Barry Boehm and Capers Jones, and higher measures have come from other studies.

2. Charles Fishman, "They Write the Right Stuff," *Fast Company*, December 1996.

3. A number of Web sites address the failed JPL mantra and the decision to return to the "standard" approach for space missions. One of the better sites is www.findarticles.com/p/articles/mi_qa3622/is_200007/ai_n8887228.

PART THREE

Groups

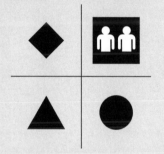

As we progress down the path of working as a team to solve problems, we quickly find that many problems are beyond the capacity of any one individual to solve. We must collaborate.

When we interact with others, even before we work together as a team, we are already dealing with the relationships within the group. One of the most challenging elements within relationships is the complexity of communication.

A deep, true common understanding is a difficult ideal to obtain, as each person brings his or her own perspectives, motivations, and expectations to the situation. We as participants within the group need to appreciate this diversity and learn to harness the value of these diverse contributions, while carefully managing the conflict that these differences will often unveil.

CHAPTER EIGHT

Communication

In team sports such as software development, the key to success is adequate communication. Peter Drucker once stated it is the recipient who communicates, and without the recipient, there cannot be any communication. If a tree falls in the forest to produce a specification that nobody reads, can a software system still be built?

In this chapter, we explore some of the critical mechanisms for successful communication, from being comfortable in your environment to active listening and feedback, as well as the need for trust across the group to facilitate the process of attaining common understanding.

Making Your Point

The notion that communication is in the hands of the receiver is merely the final part of the story. Although the correct receipt of the message is the acid test for success, the transmitter can do a great deal to ensure success.

It is important to understand the recipient from a variety of different perspectives. The recipient needs to be ready to hear the information, both in attitude and aptitude. Quite often, this will imply that you should carefully select your time for communicating and tune the content of your message to best fit the situation. The degree of detail, complexity of language, and tone of delivery can all be adjusted to help maximize the probability that the recipient is capable of receiving the information and that they actually want to receive it.

Recognizing the advantages and disadvantages of different media will allow you to select the best approach for communicating. Face-to-face communication is rich with visual cues that are lost in written communication, but it doesn't have the same persistence as something that has been captured on paper or disc. Phone conversations miss the visual nuances but still carry vocal intonations. E-mail and instant messaging lie somewhere in between and often seem to carry the worst aspects of written and oral communication. There are few cues beyond smilies, there is limited persistence, and we have to contend with spam and viruses.

In his famous 1971 study,[1] Albert Mehrabian came to the conclusion that three elements in face-to-face communication contribute very differently. Words account for 7 percent, tone of voice accounts for 38 percent, and body language accounts for 55 percent of the message. What medium are you using for the information you transmit?

It is always wise to refine the message before passing it along. Tactically, you can increase the impact of your message by proofreading or reviewing the content, and strategically you can add value by working to improve your ability to communicate in the chosen medium. Practice with groups such as Toastmasters can improve oral communication. Writing courses and templates or coding standards facilitate better-written communication. A well-polished message is much more likely to be received as intended. Typos or poor formatting in a résumé will quickly send it to the trash bin, and "ums," colloquialisms, and slang can significantly detract from the spoken message.

Feedback is critical for ensuring success. Just as any electronic communications protocol has feedback mechanisms to ensure that what was sent is identical to what was received, good human communication needs similar mechanisms. We need to be careful here, because differences in culture, position, or intent will introduce nuances to these feedback cues that can be disastrous. A nod can mean anything from "I heard what you said" to "I agree with what you said" to "You have just put me to sleep."

In written communication, reliance on a signing party to approve a specification or other important information can be just as misleading as a visual nod. A signature by itself can mean anything from "I've read the document" to "I agree with the contents" to "I managed to find the signoff page." The recipient needs to confirm that the message was received and interpreted as intended, and you need to ensure that the feedback mechanism means the same to all parties involved.

As someone who initiates communication, in any medium, you carry the responsibility for doing all that is possible to be sure the receiver is ready, willing, and able to hear the message. You are the facilitator.

The spoken word and documentation often fall short of our goal of a shared, common, consistent understanding. However, you can do plenty to increase the probability of successfully making your point.

Comfortable Communication

I'm sure you have run into situations in which your relative comfort level has impacted your ability to communicate. Consider, for instance, the following example.

Would You Like Crilladillas with That?

I've been to Spain a few times over the past few years. From the standpoint of communications, working at the client site is straight-forward, but all bets are off after business hours. I'm quite linguistically challenged (my family tells me they were still struggling to teach me English when I was 4), and Spanish is definitely not one of my strong points.

I managed to get by through a combination of multilingual menus, pictures, a lot of hand waving, and facial expressions. I have probably upset more people than I think, amused countless others as a foreign buffoon, but I survived. I have a few key phrases I relied on heavily. I slowly learned to push the envelope (although I fell back considerably between visits), and my comfort level is increasing.

That stated, I'm still at the point when I order meals where the need to finish the difficult and frustrating conversation overrides the need to get exactly what I want. I'll often get a surprise or two in my side dishes, and I sometimes even wonder whether the main dish is what I requested. Sometimes I try to clarify, sometimes I let it ride. I've never had any problem with allergies, and I've tried some very interesting dishes.

Some might say this is merely putting a positive spin on an otherwise challenged situation.

We see the same thing in the workplace. This shows up often with the globalization of software development, multicultural teams, and perhaps most important, different levels of comfort with the selected form of technical communication.

Agonizing Peer Reviews

In putting together my first object-oriented design, the combination of my uncertainty in an object-oriented world and a ruthless review team that easily picked apart my proposed design quickly made getting this review over with as soon as possible my primary objective.

Looking back, it was an extremely rich learning situation. Unfortunately, that's not what you see while immersed in the environment. Over the years, I have become more comfortable with object-orientation and can focus more confidently on the technical details.

About a month later, I was asked to present the refined design to an audience of perhaps 100 people, one of my first public-speaking forays. Like many people in this situation, I had little sleep the night before, plenty of nerves to deal with, and a couple of serious flaws in the presentation.

> Fortunately, most of the crowd was too far away to see the beads of sweat on my brow, and were already lulled to sleep by the previous presentations to catch my mistakes.
>
> Again, an investment in Toastmasters and a huge amount of practice has made it much easier to present material to a group.

As we communicate with our peers on software projects, we all have different comfort levels with our selected means of communication. We need to be sensitive to how this will impact the results. There may be a second-language challenge, a lack of experience with a tool or technique, or a lack of comfort with the others in the group. Regardless of the root cause, if not managed, the results will be diminished to some degree. Agreements can become a means to get past an awkward situation rather than a true meeting of the minds.

If there is discomfort, collaboration needs to be considered as an opportunity for learning and facilitated accordingly. Even for the most seasoned teams, these communications can still be regarded as a chance to clarify terms, agree on subtleties of notations or terminologies, or to ease tense situations for some of the participants.

> We all need to seek opportunities to make communication more comfortable among us, either through supporting others or through allowing ourselves to grow.

Full Disclosure

Walk up to anyone at a networking function and ask how business is and it is almost guaranteed that you'll get a superlative response about business being better than ever, being so busy that there's no time for a break, and so on. Apparently, only after that dance can you actually get down to discussing matters in more realistic terms.

Some people can remain cagey about what is really going on long after the opening salvo. They will keep the truth close to their chest as though they are in the final round of the World Series of Poker. The notion that retaining information provides some strategic advantage is a strong one, but we need to be careful about how broadly we use this approach. Just as in poker, we are participating in a situation in which someone will end up losing, and there will be times when everyone walks away from the table empty handed.

Full disclosure generally means disclosing all the known details of an issue. Whether it has to do with financial transactions, computer security, or interpersonal issues, the spirit of full disclosure is that all parties are working with a complete set of known information. This is more than mere honesty, which can be achieved to the letter if not the intent just by responding appropriately to the questions asked. Full disclosure also addresses the questions that are not asked, even the questions you didn't know you could ask. Everyone is on the same page, and there are no hidden pages to worry about. Full disclosure is about openness, about being genuine. It is a prerequisite for trust in a relationship.

Whereas intentional failure to disclose is a problem, we often fall into the trap of failing to disclose unintentionally, even when our actions are intended to improve clarity for everyone. We might be superficial in dealing with the current situation because we have other things on our minds. Or we might be passing along or capturing inaccurate information, given the subtle nuances of our language. Healthy disclosure requires feedback and attention from both sides to work.

We can use certain mechanisms to reduce the challenges associated with trying to get our full message across. The essence is to ensure that all participants agree that we have the same understanding of the "group memory." Whiteboards or flip charts excel in capturing information so that all can see and confirm that it makes sense. A digital camera can also quickly capture that information for the group. A data projector, if available, can be used to both capture and store information at the same time. If minutes are being taken at a meeting without flip charts, be sure to read and confirm the minutes before the meeting is over. You will save a great deal of grief downstream for each correction made while everyone is still together.

For those times when you run into an intentional failure to disclose, we need to work a little harder. Build some forensics into the conversation. Cross-reference with other sources and remember that a grain of salt can go a long way. Don't believe everything you hear, and don't assume anything about what you don't hear.

Many relationships, especially those based on strong trust, require full disclosure to be achievable. Being genuine in all interactions opens the door for all participants to win.

Trust

One of the core elements we keep coming back to when we discuss change in organizations is that a foundation of trust must exist among all participants. We need to be able to rely on others and ourselves for support. To do this, we need to have comfort in our own abilities (and in the abilities of those whom we are depending on). Without genuine trust, despite our best intentions, we will not make it to our shared destination.

On Belay!

Just after we were newly wed, my wife and I took a brief rock-climbing course at a local indoor climbing center. At one point, when one of us was up on the wall, we were supposed to test our trust in our partners by calling out that we were "on belay." We would then let go of the wall and let the rope and harness, which was attached to our partner, stop our fall. It certainly seemed better to try this in a controlled environment than to experience it for the first time out on the face of a mountain.

I was first. When I called out and jumped away from the wall, I dropped about a foot before the stretch in the rope disappeared. After that, I comfortably got back onto the wall and started to climb again.

When it was my wife's turn, she called out as expected. Then, despite pushing out from the wall with her legs, her fingers just wouldn't let go. She clung tightly to the wall. Even after having just seen the system in action, her lack of trust prevented her from placing her safety in the hands of others.

I would hope that if we were to try it again today, she would have built up the trust to let go.

Trust for each of us has its beginnings in our vast set of past experiences. Our perspectives of how we have fared in past relationships will go a long way toward coloring our approach to trust in new relationships. Whereas some of us will tend to assume the best in new relationships, others will enter into these same relationships with suspicion.

Over time, the amount of trust in a relationship evolves dramatically, based on the accumulation of all the interactions we have over time. If interactions go well, trust increases. If we have disappointment or failure, trust drops.

Think of this as part of our emotional bank account. When we succeed, we make deposits to the account, and sometimes we will make withdrawals. Each of us comes to the relationship with a different opening balance. Each of us has a different comfort level with where we think the balance should be. To belabor the metaphor, some of us borrow a bit too heavily on our line of credit, and we can have our credit taken away.

Trust is a function of the entire relationship. It is a cumulative outcome of experiences of those who share in the relationship, not of any individual. It is in the eye of the beholder to determine who is or is not trustworthy, a determination that can vary dramatically.

For our "trust accounts" to grow, we need to carefully manage the components of trust with each transaction in our relationships.

First, we need to ensure that we have a common understanding of what a reasonable destination looks like for our transaction. Do we share common expectations and do we both recognize how we plan to get to that end? For this to occur, we need to have completely open communications, as well as a reasonable structure for defining what our expectations should look like. A structure for managing dissent in a respectful manner is also very useful here.

Second, we need the knowledge and assurance that we have the appropriate capabilities to accomplish our goals. This applies to everyone participating in the transaction. Trust will initially come from credentials and other external references but becomes stronger over time as the team has more positive experiences together.

If either of these key components is missing, trust will erode, and the balance in our emotional bank account will drop. Next time around, it will be that much more difficult to work together successfully. Interestingly, when we have disappointing results, we tend to first place fault on others, but this is often an immature response. Especially if you are the one setting expectations, it is important to walk through both components of trust. Clearly define the completion expectations, but also discuss the capabilities of the group to determine whether they are reasonable. If they fall short, is the task one that can be used to stretch the group without significant risk? Or should other skills be applied to the situation?

> The responsibility for much of trust in relationships lies on our shoulders. The end product is influenced both by our personal biases and through the activities we undertake to foster trust in ongoing relationships.

Client Satisfaction

In one Dilbert comic, the pointy-haired boss realizes: "This job got a lot less stressful when I realized I hate my customers."

Having heard from someone in the real world that "If it wasn't for our customers, we'd get a lot of stuff done around here," it's clear that Scott Adams has his finger on the pulse of what ails businesses today, particularly where there is an ongoing dance between the client and the service provider.

Sadly, many software companies that see themselves as a shrink-wrap product company, with little ongoing client interaction, end up with more interaction than planned. Unanticipated and frustrating, but in the end they also fall into the "service provider" category, too.

Like *product quality,* the term *client satisfaction* is given plenty of lip service in industry. Unfortunately, there are few examples of companies that truly shine in managing relationships throughout the life cycle. As in personal relationships, the focus and attention that leads to that first kiss can be difficult to sustain over the long term.

Customer Disservice?

I tried to obtain a new cell phone after years as a faithful client with increasing usage. After many frustrating calls, I finally gave up and moved to another carrier.

As I notified them to terminate my account, they passed me on to their Customer Retention Department, whose first words were to offer me a new phone. Interesting approach. I had to move before they would take my requests seriously! This was like closing the barn door after the horse had bolted, and I was not about to back out of the new contract and give up my snazzy new phone at this point.

It is not the first time I have moved to a new cell provider. It appears the focus for most [insert your loathsome service provider here, be it a bank, utility, auto dealership, or so forth] is to try to win over new clients and hope that the overall pool is not diminishing, rather than to retain the clients they have.

It is important to note that the relationship needs to be viewed and managed from both directions to be truly successful, particularly in a service-oriented engagement. The interaction is a two-way street, and to attempt to improve the satisfaction of your counterpart at the expense of your own is clearly not sustainable. The imbalance will weigh heavily over time, and it is best to adjust the alignment or to disengage as soon as problems are seen.

As a service provider, I have explicitly chosen to disengage from a lucrative engagement when there was no way to bring alignment to the client. As many of the industry gurus would suggest, it was an entirely refreshing experience! I am dubious of claims of 100 percent client satisfaction on Web sites. There will always be cases where the cost of bending your values to build a working relationship does not adequately compensate for lack of satisfaction.

Remember also that client satisfaction is not found solely outside the organization. In almost any company, chains of dependency exist between groups, and all the same rules apply. Respect the needs of those you are providing a service for internally, eliminate the internal silos between departments, and the overall quality of your product or service will certainly go up.

In all situations, whether the relationship is internal or external, client satisfaction should be a major factor in how you measure your own success.

From my experience, both as a service provider and as a client, it is clear to me that the key to client satisfaction requires a healthy dose of active listening.

Clarity and Common Understanding

More of us than would like to admit tend to interact in conversations by "waiting to talk" rather than actively listening. We're busy formulating our next statement, pondering what we need to pick up on the way home, or focused on that errant eyebrow hair instead of trying to absorb and assimilate what the speaker is saying. We hear the words (or even read the words in a document), but the common understanding, gained through active listening, is missing.

Skipping Past the Deep Understanding

My favorite part of facilitating the two-day Requirements course we've run numerous times is a "bookends" exercise. We get groups to identify their greatest challenges in the realm of requirements at the beginning of the first day. Then, they rotate the challenges around so that different groups can identify how they would solve the problem at the end of the second day. In a very important way, the two-part exercise acts as a fine example of one of the greatest challenges we face in communication.

We don't really listen.

As the groups initially form to identify, list, and clarify the problems they face, there is rich discovery of major issues to discuss within the group. Come time to present the issues to the rest of the class, however, the first cracks in the communication ice start to appear. Despite warnings that one of the other groups will be asked to solve the problem being presented and that this is the best time to dig a little deeper to truly understand the issue, there is often little or no interaction across groups, even when prodded. Although part of this may be attributed to a couple of people steeling themselves for their turn at presenting, deeper forces are at work.

The presenting group has accomplished their goal of reciting what they have posted. The next group is ready to present. Everyone is ready to delve into the meat of the course. Just as with most real-life requirements exercises, the i's have been dotted and the t's have been crossed, and the document has been produced, but the intent to gain common understanding remains missing.

This becomes clear during the second part of the exercise. Many groups need to revisit with the original authors to gain clarity on the original problem statement or preface their solution by saying something like "We weren't quite sure what that other group meant, so we just assumed...."

In the continuum of communication from "I heard what you said" through "I parsed the words you spoke" to "I understand and agree with the intent of your message," how often do we get past stage one?

 The written word, which lacks the auditory feedback or the visual nuances of face-to-face communication, is the medium with the lowest fidelity in which to communicate, but we rely on it for most software specifications.

Instead of composing a document in a vacuum and passing it around for signature, use other forms of communication to obtain clarity and common understanding. Use the written form only to persist that common understanding.

We have two ears, two eyes, and one mouth for a very good reason. Actively listen and read. Use any mechanisms of feedback at your disposal to be sure that the intended message has been received.

The Dark Side of Communication

My spontaneous reaction to the word *spontaneity* is negative, but this needs to be taken in the context of the situation.

If we were to take a number of words we use every day and have each of us rate them from strongly negative to strongly positive, we would have a wide range of responses. For some of us, the responses to individual words would change dramatically with the context. Our differences in perceptions, in personal tastes, will strongly color our different views of the same situation.

For me, spontaneity is fine if appropriately balanced with a view of the strategic goals. By all means, it can be extremely rewarding to pick up and change plans on a dime, but it needs to be done in the context of getting the important things done. First understand what those important things are. Then make changes with some forethought—how each change will affect the whole—and our ability to achieve our strategic objectives increases dramatically. In the long run, the decisions for change still appear to be spontaneous, but less haphazard.

Although shared understanding is a difficult goal to achieve, requiring a great deal of thinking, empathy, and feedback, it is crucial to avoid the challenges that most teams struggle with.

At its most innocuous, a missed detail or incomplete context can change the entire perspective between the sender and recipient of the information. It is important to remember that all the information we process passes through our personal filters and that each person has an entirely different context from which they work.

Take a simple detail such as "Bob can't make it in to work today." If you know that Jane can adequately cover Bob's work without risk, this will have an entirely different meaning for you than if you know that Bob is on the critical path and is already behind schedule, with no one to cover for him. Avoid providing bullets of information out of context.

"Going dark" suggests a deeper issue. Hunkering down to solve a problem instead of raising the issue to the massed brain trust of the group is inefficient and risky. The person who should be receiving the information about the problem is left to assume the worst. As the mind wanders, usually based on past experience, the notion of what "the worst" is can quickly become very ugly. Ongoing communication of your lack of progress is better than going dark, because the recipient is at least aware of the real situation and can take action to help resolve the problem.

Misinformation is the worst-case communication breakdown scenario. Turning negative raw data around to put a positive spin on things is a major disservice to the organization, whether the intent was to simply maintain morale or to explicitly mislead. The best approach is to objectively identify in advance the information needed. This reduces the chance that statistics are skewed to defend a position rather than to provide guidance for informed decisions.

> As a team, we must sit down and come to a consensus about the deeper meaning behind the words we use. We need to explicitly discuss our different prejudices regarding our terminology and balance these differences to come to a satisfying agreement.
>
> Judicious use of paraphrasing to clarify meaning and an openness to learn and appreciate without having to agree are valuable tools to leverage.

Summary

Just as the root of most humor is someone's misfortune (try to think of a joke in which this is not the case—why *did* that chicken cross the road?), the root of most project problems is communication breakdown. Failure to adequately communicate comes in many forms, from simple slip-ups to overt misguidance.

Communication needs to be bidirectional. As a recipient, you should be striving to obtain the best information you can. Just as data streaming across the Internet is strewn with checksums, parity bits, acknowledgments, and the like, feedback is a necessity to ensure that the information that was sent is the information that was received.

Simply receiving data (such as status reports) is insufficient. You need to feed back what you have heard and probe deeper to ensure that you have the complete and correct interpretation.

How Is This Relevant?

Forms of communication. Are you using the most appropriate medium to get your points across? Would it be reasonable to make more of your communication face to face? How would this change interaction in your workplace? How has communication etiquette in the workplace changed over the years? Is this an improvement?

Trust. Consider how strong the trust is in all of your relationships. How consistently have you contributed to the trust account through managing expectations and following-through? Have you inappropriately withdrawn from the account by laying blame or disappointing someone? Could you have made deposits into the account by simply providing praise or credit when due?

Dysfunctional communication. Have you ever had challenges with missing information or misinformation in the workplace? How have you resolved the situation? Are some approaches to dealing with these issues more effective than others?

References

1. Albert Mehrabian, *Silent Messages* (Wadsworth, 1971).

CHAPTER NINE

Motives and Expectations

As we explore our relationships with others, we soon realize that many of our differences are not readily apparent. Without looking past the superficial and seeing these internal distinctions, we are often challenged to make sense of what we see.

In this chapter, we explore the nature of how our unique set of motives drives our behaviors. We also identify techniques to bring these unspoken motives to the surface. In exposing these elements, we may gain a better appreciation of how our expectations can color what each of us sees in the same situation, and how diversity can create a better, more robust solution.

Motives Drive Our Behaviors

The past few years have brought a slew of online collaboration tools intended to bridge the gaps between workers who are geographically separated, from across the campus to across the world. Although the best are excellent at communicating a shared understanding of activities, progress, and products, there are other challenges in working in distributed groups. Time zones and cultures are known issues that can be anticipated and managed. A software product, however, may never adequately address the issue of motives.

One could describe a motive as an emotion, a desire, or an impulse that acts as an incitement to action. It runs much deeper than the majority of vision and mission statements that I have seen.

Most of us are sensitive to the complexity of our own internal motives. When dealing with others, however, we have a tendency to build simplified models so that we can deal with the overwhelming information in an efficient manner. In turn, this tends to mask the complexity of the motives behind other people's actions.

Without this understanding, our first reaction is to assume that the motives of others are similar to ours, and therefore, we can't reconcile their actions. We become angry, frustrated, and prejudiced. We lump others into categories in our simplified model as a means of dealing with them.

At the personal level, a wide range of motives influences our every action. We can be motivated to burn the midnight oil for money, fear, personal satisfaction, or other reasons, both positive and negative. The positive drivers are more sustainable. The negative drivers drain us of energy and can quickly lead to burnout in a job situation. A "death march" takes a heavy toll on the team members. Recognizing our motives and the motives of others is critical for strong, clear communication and is an essential element for success in any team situation.

Marketing is motivated to get new features into their customer's hands, to facilitate higher sales. Developers are motivated by stimulating work and the desire to produce a high-quality product. Management just seems to want it done quickly and cheaply. Although motives don't have to be common, they must be acknowledged. We need to build stronger, more accurate models of what motivates our peers to be able to work with them as a team.

A project, too, can have strong motives that help sustain it to completion. It is best if these are explicitly defined for the participants and for the organization. More commonly viewed as project goals, these motives may include the desire to be technically superior, first to market, or disruptively innovative. Understanding these drivers up front can be a powerful force to coalesce the team into achieving them. It can also act as a sounding board for determining project priorities and whether potential changes downstream make sense. For all stakeholders, there should be a common understanding of why the project exists.

The mission statements of far too many organizations are filled with fluff, and it may take a bit of effort to identify the true underlying motives. Most appear to be driven primarily to increase revenue as high as possible, but for some, more powerful motives can align the team to achieve greatness. For those who are truly motivated to support and enrich the lives of their employees, the reward lies in strong commitment and reduced turnover. Some, organizations are truly committed to client satisfaction, and their ongoing sales are amplified with repeat business and strong referrals. These motives are independent of the organization's size and are simpler to institutionalize at the outset, instead of trying to retrofit them after a company has grown. Explicitly stating clear motives allows a company to recognize success in a variety of innovative ways.

> Recognizing, acknowledging, and managing the motives of individuals, teams, and organizations are critical components for successful interaction. This is unlikely to be automated in the near future.

Choice as a Motivator

It can be very interesting to compare the approaches used to drive software teams in extremely different markets: to see the similarities and distinctions, where the approaches work, and where they fall down. This perspective comes from reading a posting that was forwarded to me, the EA Spouse Blog.[1]

Although the assertions in the blog were corroborated by people I know in game companies, the thing that stood out for me was that this entry could well have been written by my wife—not because I've been in the game industry, but because I did my time working on an air traffic control system. A great learning experience, which simply confirms the adage that what doesn't kill you makes you stronger. The culture of extremely long hours (for a period, I was on call 24/7), heroic efforts, artificial schedule pressures, employee burnout, and feeble attempts to placate the spouses are in no way unique to game companies. These are almost identical situations, in sectors as different as they could get—from life critical to pure unadulterated entertainment.

The dedication of people I know in the game industry borders on obsession. The race to get their hands on the latest hardware can be huge. Almost everyone is an avid gamer themselves. Often after an extremely long day at the office, they unwind by picking up their game controller at home and playing more of their favorite title. Although those of us on the air traffic control project didn't have the opportunity of unwinding by directing air traffic at the end of the day, there was still a strong commitment to building a leading-edge product better than anyone else.

What appears to be a common element in both of the situations just described is the dysfunctional management oversight. With teams of extremely talented and highly dedicated people, success is often achieved despite the style used to drive the teams. In cases like this, any attempt to discuss concerns about the workload is often met with claims that you're not a team player and need to "get with the program." In high-profile projects, those who don't conform are seen as easily expendable, merely resources that are easily replaced by the lineup around the block of potential candidates who are eager for a shot at glory.

Often in these situations, there is no personal connection between senior management and the people building the system. Whether it is passive seclusion where management hides themselves in their offices or active animosity where the relationship has degraded to such a point that the team will clam up when a manager happens to be in the neighborhood, the impersonal distance makes it easy for management to perceive the people as mere resources, to be consumed as thoroughly as possible.

The stakes are high, and the result can be spectacular successes or dismal failures. Project costs such as rework and quality issues, along with human costs of morale, employee burnout and turnover, can take their toll. If success is only measured in dollars or delivery schedules, many of the real costs will never be exposed.

Equally positive results can be attained without incurring these costs and risks, but the prerequisite to this is the acknowledgment that the entire team is made up of humans, with needs and motivations. Heroic efforts can be drawn from the team in negative and positive ways. The strongest leaders motivate in ways that compel their team to give their best because they want to, not because they feel they have to. That ability to choose makes all the difference in whether this is a motivating factor. In consciously choosing to provide the heroic efforts, much of the human cost disappears. It is management's job to provide that true choice through understanding the team's motives, instead of posing ultimatums. This understanding can only be achieved by fostering a solid relationship with the team. It can't be done from an ivory tower.

EA has put out some amazing titles over the years, and the game industry is massive and growing. The air traffic control system we built is a technical success (note the qualifier), but in a different market. Unfortunately, as mentioned, the human cost can be very high, and thick hierarchical team structures make it easy for management to ignore that cost while driving toward their own goals. The pressure applied is by no means in the category of best practices, but in too many places, the end is used to justify the means.

Strong team relationships contribute more to success than any defined processes.

Exposing Our Motives

It becomes pretty clear for most of us sometime early in our youth that we are all motivated by different things. Despite that awareness, we often have a difficult time understanding and expressing what is driving our own actions, let alone figuring out what the hell could be driving the person across the table, especially when that person's actions seem to come from left field.

Our motives drive our behavior. If we are clear about our own motives, the link to our behaviors usually becomes self-evident. With others, unless we have some sort of looking glass, we can only evaluate them based on their externally visible behaviors. We have no insight into what drives them, so we have a tendency to assume the same motivations in others as we have in ourselves. Hence the perception that others seem to do things from left field at times.

To have reasonable insight into our behaviors, we need to find that looking glass. Difficult, yes, but essential to appreciating the motivations of all parties involved. Once we have that, we can start to bridge our gaps in motivation and work well together.

 In working with teams, I've used an instrument called the Strength Deployment Inventory (SDI) as a vehicle to help raise awareness of motivations within the group.[2] Although there are a large number of other instruments available (the Myers-Briggs Type Indicator is probably the most prominent), I've found the SDI to be very well received, and when properly deployed, it provides some incredible insights. There doesn't seem to be the same tendency to pigeonhole people as with other instruments (I'm an INTJ under Myers-Briggs, for what that's worth), and the approach has a very strong positive flavor about it.

The SDI is based on the work of Elias H. Porter, who derived four straightforward but powerful premises about our behavior:

- **We all do what we do because we want to feel good about ourselves.** With a bit of introspection, most of us would see this as reasonable; but on its own, this premise might not hold water for everyone. Even for those who appear to be self-destructive in their behaviors, down deep there is some need that they are trying to satisfy with their actions.

- **We tend to take different approaches to life when we feel things are going well and when we feel we are faced with opposition or conflict.** When things are going well, we tend to have a range of behaviors that help us maintain our comfort zone. In the face of conflict, however, we exhibit a predictable sequence of behaviors as the conflict worsens. We start out with a goal of solving the problem and addressing the needs of others (the classic "win-win"), but as the situation degrades, we will eventually get to the point where we don't care about others, and don't even care about the original problem—it becomes survival. Our behaviors will change, sometimes dramatically, along that continuum.

- **A personal weakness is no more and no less than the overdoing or misapplying of a personal strength.** Ah, here's a key premise for most people to recognize. Anything we can describe as a weakness in others can be translated into strength if we soften it up a bit. An aggressive behavior becomes assertive, someone who is wishy-washy becomes flexible, and so on. What's important here is that the behavior really could be overdone if we lean on our strengths too much, or simply perceived by others as overdone if it is not aligned with their values.

- **We naturally tend to perceive the actions of others through our own filters.** Tying back to the previous premise, this explains a lot of our miscommunication. If we are living within our own value system and use this as a means to judge the behavior we see in others, it is no surprise that we see others as over or under reacting to the same events we are exposed to.

Within each of our own motivational value systems, our behaviors appear consistent. Exposing and appreciating the differences in these value systems within a group can clarify many of the behaviors that have puzzled us in the past. The SDI provides deep food for thought as we explore all of this, both within ourselves and as part of a team.

For ourselves, knowing our own comfort zone of behaviors and our predictable sequence of behaviors in times of conflict helps us recognize and deal with many of the stressors we face in our lives. We can tune our activities so that they align more with our comfort zone, or we can consciously choose to borrow behavior that normally would not fit, to help ourselves get back to that happy place. Without this insight, we are often forced to use uncomfortable behaviors to mask this internal conflict instead of consciously choosing to borrow these behaviors, and our stress levels will rise accordingly.

As we interact with others using these new insights, we are more capable of working together successfully. Understanding what motivates others can help guide us toward more effective communication, by tuning the message toward the recipient's preferred value system. If someone is analytic, show him or her the numbers. If someone is assertive, be direct and to the point. Understanding the sequence of behaviors that others exhibit in crisis helps us recognize the problem much earlier and address the problem before it gets out of hand.

? There is far more depth to the SDI than can be reasonably covered in a quick overview, or even in a couple of days of intense training. I find I am discovering different nuances of insight from the instrument each time I deploy it with clients. As with other instruments, it has its relative strengths, and there are areas where it would not reasonably apply (such as part of a recruitment process, for example). It is best managed in the hands of someone who has been trained to deploy it.

Even if you don't have access to a trained professional, there remains value in acknowledging the premises that Porter identified. One of the most straightforward values is to recognize that we do bring different motivations to the table, especially when having difficult conversations.

Step back and consciously explore the motivations that each of you brings to the table. You might find that this appreciation will help you understand the different perspectives of others and to respect them to be just as valid as your own.

This insight can go a long way toward helping you resolve the situation so that everyone wins.

Rethinking the Achilles' Heel

The story of Achilles, like most Greek mythology, has relevance to what we all experience in our lives today. The complexity of our lives and relationships dictates that we can't possibly carry strengths across the board. How we deal with this reality, from tossing our hands in the air in despair to constantly working to manage our strengths and vulnerabilities, can significantly impact our overall performance.

On software projects, our vulnerabilities can manifest themselves in many ways. Project managers may be particularly susceptible to optimistic estimates. Developers can be repeatedly caught using brute-force approaches or gold-plating their work. Architects can tend to build impractical textbook-like designs. Testers can often be antagonistic toward the development staff. Finally, senior management can refuse to accept evidence that something might be awry.

Although these weaknesses are particularly evil for the roles described here, this is by no means an indication that these people are a bad fit for that role, or that others in different roles couldn't have similar weaknesses. Rather, these weaknesses can and often are shared by a large cross section of the population. It is the role that makes any particular weakness a nasty one. In another situation, the same weakness might not even be noticed or could be considered to be strength.

Elias H. Porter's work on Relationship Awareness suggests that we don't actually have weaknesses at all but rather these are just overdone strengths. The positive assertiveness of a tester can be seen as antagonistic by the development team. Those around him can see the "never-say-die" attitude of a senior manager as blind and unrealistic. Whether these strengths are actually overdone or merely perceived as overdone from behind the filters of the observers doesn't matter. In either case, there is a lack of alignment in the relationship. If the person feels compelled to act in this manner simply because of the belief that the role demands such an approach, rather than because it is a natural way to act, this can be a significant source of personal stress.

These weaknesses (or overdone strengths) can show up at any point in a project life cycle. They can be a symptom of a relationship challenge or they can be a function of the domain the person is working in. Wherever they arise, the exposure of these weaknesses gives us extremely valuable information. Until we are aware of our apparent weaknesses, it is impossible for us to adjust our behavior to remedy them.

There are opportunities throughout a project life cycle for us to expose and compensate for our blind spots. Initial team-building exercises or use of tools such as the SDI can provide insights into our motivations, comfort zones, and approaches to certain situations. This kind of information helps us to explicitly build a healthy team dynamic and cover for any blind spots the team may have.

At any point in a project where conflict arises, where mistakes are made, or where challenges need to be overcome, step back to see whether any weakness that may have led to the problem could be masked or removed so that the problem doesn't arise again.

Finally, during a project retrospective, focus at this level for lessons learned, rather than simply looking at the project, product, and process.

We cannot eliminate all the weaknesses we have, but in working as a team we can compensate for each other's deficiencies. The result becomes significantly stronger than the sum of the parts.

Think of all this as ongoing process improvement for the soul. If a problem arises on a project, fix the problem, fix the hole in the process that allowed the problem to appear, and fix the blind spot that prevented you from seeing the hole in the process in the first place.

We have no idea how many blind spots we might have, but we can choose to act appropriately when one is discovered.

Expectations

Expectations are powerful beasts. People experience elation when expectations are exceeded, but watch out if you fail to meet expectations!

Sadly, we can easily both fail to meet and exceed expectations of different people with precisely the same actions, at the same time. Although we cannot specify how people will react to events, we can often do quite a bit to manage their expectations, and in doing so their reactions, too.

What Are People Like in This Town?

I recall a *Reader's Digest* anecdote from my childhood:

A young couple moves to a new town and asks an old timer rocking on his front porch what the people are like in this town.

"*What were they like in your old town?*" he asks.

"*Well, they were all quite standoffish and cold,*" replies the couple.

"I expect you'll find them to be pretty well the same here," he says as he continues rocking.

Another couple moves into town the next week, and asks the same old man the same question.

To his same initial response, the couple noted that the people where they moved from were *"very warm and friendly, always willing to lend a hand."*

"I expect you'll find them to be pretty well the same here," he replied.

That old man was wise to recognize that these couples were merely changing their surroundings. Unfortunately, software development mimics life in that unless you explicitly change the way you do things internally, you can pretty well expect overall results to be similar to how they have been in the past.

Most in the industry are experiencing moderate to extreme pain in getting good software out the door on time. Yet we find that we're too busy to address the root causes of the problem. Despite the hope and desire that we'll somehow emerge from the swamp to an easier future, chances are that we will continue to slog along and business indeed will not get any easier. Quite often, it will just get worse.

Choose your metaphor. Whether you "don't have time to stop for gas," you're "up to your ears in alligators," or you are "continually fighting fires," if you don't explicitly change the way you do things, if you do not internalize change, change will not happen to you. If you can never predict when you will ship, or you are inundated with problems from the field (often problems that have already been "solved" at least once in the past), no superficial change in surroundings will make life rosy for you.

Change is not merely something that other people do.

Tangibility

I recently reviewed a book that was published while I was working on this chapter. In the book, the author wrote about Fred Brooks's

Mythical Man-Month and asserted that "programmers work with nearly pure thought stuff."[3]

He extended the notion later on, indicating that Microsoft produces nothing tangible, nothing that you can drop on your toes, as a justification for software development being difficult and software being less than perfect.

I then hunted down the original quote from the "No Silver Bullet" essay.[4] The issue being discussed there was that compared to other domains such as physical buildings, the high cost of change in software is not understood nearly as well.

Because of this, most software projects are more severely impacted by change, often because users like what they see and would like more, or because the software outlives its original intended useful life.

I think both authors are hinting at the same thing. A deeper issue is within our sphere of influence. This issue has been around since the *Mythical Man-Month* came out more than 30 years ago. We generally fail to appreciate the importance and value of making our software systems tangible as early and as thoroughly as we can.

Although originally expressed by Brooks as one of the reasons why we are subjected to so much change, it often sounds like an excuse for software being difficult, for the need to forge ahead into the code so that we can learn from our mistakes early.

Programmers work with "nearly pure thought stuff" not because it cannot be made more tangible but because as a group we are foolishly reluctant to understand and implement the approaches that are at our disposal to actually capture the structure of our systems long before we fire up our compilers.

We need to stop making excuses. Software development is hard primarily because we choose (consciously or not) to make it so. Software is only intangible because we don't respect the need to clearly specify what we intend to build (or clearly specify the question we are trying to answer if it can't be set in stone up front) and don't have the tools (read skills and allocated time) to do so on a regular basis.

For those who would like to suggest that innovative systems cannot be thoroughly expressed up front, this should be no excuse for failing to express your knowledge to that point and clarifying which areas require additional investigation.

Pure thought stuff indeed. Quantum physicists can't touch what they are studying or drop it on their toes (actually, it is the essence of what their toes are made of!), but they are careful to document their assumptions, hypotheses, and observations every step of the way. Their approach is disciplined and can be subject to rigorous peer review every step of the way. Their challenge is not that they are leaping to the final stage without careful consideration of the steps along the way, it is that by being careful they have been able to push the envelope and dramatically expand our understanding of the world around us.

We all place our code into safekeeping (check-out and check-in of code changes is the standard in many shops), but we still might have a partially completed copy of a specification on someone's desktop, or several versions kicking around (who knows which is the latest?). Worse yet, we might have nothing more than a marketing brochure or a back-of-the-envelope list of features we would like the system to have.

To imagine a group of carpenters gathering at the jobsite with all their tools and materials, hastily scrawling their intended structure down on a piece of paper and diving into the construction would be sheer madness, but there remains a large number of practitioners in the industry whose primary focus remains the code.

More people have indicated to me that the code is self-documenting than have said that the specification is the key description of what their product is or will be.

I worked on one project to extend a legacy air traffic control system. Expecting to head to the specs to see what needs to be resolved, I found myself having to pore over the code as the only reference for what is going on. That's right: an ATC system. Ponder that next time you settle into seat 13C.

Until we start to recognize that a clear description of all aspects of the system's functionality, characteristics, and constraints is absolutely critical to facilitate our actual building of the product, and that the techniques to do so are not rocket science for those who would simply take the time to investigate, software will continue to be intangible.

Every time I hear a purported thought leader in this industry suggest that software is intangible and that's just the way it is, I just shake my head. I'm sure that is not what Fred Brooks was asserting 30 years ago, but it appears to be interpreted that way more often than not.

We can certainly touch and feel a well-constructed speci-fication, which is the only embodiment of the final prod-uct in the early stages of development—that is, if we bother to take the time to construct it.

Managing Our Expectations

There are expectations in any relationship. We have expectations of every-one around us, as they have their own of us. We also have expectations of ourselves that we must deal with. Although it is important to set expecta-tions high, care must be taken to ensure that they are in alignment with precedents. Set too high and the likelihood of perceived failure is great. Set too low and we never realize our potential. Everyone involved has respon-sibility in building appropriate expectations. Failure to do so can result in hurt, resentment, and strained relationships.

When dealing with the expectations of others toward us, the perceived result ultimately matters—whether or not we met expectations. Set rea-sonable expectations with your peers up front, instead of leaving them to their own devices to set them as they see fit. Clearly specify what they can expect from the relationship and where the surprises may lie. Identify spe-cific things that they will see, and tell them what they won't see as a result of your interaction. Done well, clearly set expectations can turn even dis-appointing results into perceived success.

When setting your own expectations of others, be careful to be realistic and work to make sure that you start and remain on the same page. By letting the other person know exactly what you are looking for, you can eliminate many issues up front. Shared expectations are the basis of trust and effective teamwork.

The toughest situation to deal with can be your own expectations. We are at times our own harshest critics, whereas at other times we can be overly self-confident and brash. Those with the strongest sense of self-awareness are the ones who are most successful at setting reasonable expectations. Knowing their own capabilities, they will be able to set expectations just high enough to stretch themselves. Setting our self-expectations appropriately is an important part of managing personal growth.

Unfortunately, we often learn through the school of hard knocks how to tune expectations to avoid disappointment. Fortunately, we can all expect that we will improve with practice.

No News Is Actually Bad News

The old adage of "no news is good news" could not have possibly come from anyone with experience in software development. How many of us have been on projects that appeared to be going smoothly until late in the game when the whole house of cards suddenly fell apart? "No news" should set off alarms regarding the progress of a project.

Here's a case in point.

Fear of the Unknown

I was working with a project manager recently in an organization where there had been challenges with delivered software in the past. This project manager had the unenviable task of driving a high-profile project to completion, after the last project got into trouble just after shipping.

Overall, a lot of good things had been done to date. There was a strong team of stakeholders who had worked together to agree on the priorities, business objectives, and success criteria for the project. Given the iterative nature of the development life cycle, expectations were appropriately set. No promises were made for functionality planned for later stages; they hadn't even been specified yet. There were goals to try to achieve, but it was made clear that more defendable numbers were forthcoming.

There was even a well-coordinated effort with the stakeholders to prioritize and reasonably specify a great set of quality attributes for the project, something that few organizations even realize is important and feasible.

The project manager appeared to be doing all these things right, so what was the problem?

Apparently, it was the troubling news that had been recently received. Given the feedback on work to date, it appeared that intermediate milestones might be in jeopardy. Estimates to completion for work packages had been generally low (who hasn't seen that before?). The reasonable thing to do would be to compensate for this in the future tasks, expand the schedule accordingly, and make adjustments for a revised path to completion.

There was concern that the stakeholders wouldn't take the news well. My take on this was that getting this information a couple of months into a 14-month effort would be the best possible way to deliver this news under the circumstances.

Not only does the team now have insight into their true rate of productivity and a more reasonable schedule of downstream work, they have this knowledge early enough in the project to have greater flexibility to resolve the challenge. They didn't run into the brick wall as it appeared out of the fog in front of their racing vehicle. They have received an early alert that their path would have taken them to a wall in the future. They can now plan, rather than panic, and make a mature decision about what to do with the news.

With early news, they still have the option of adding resources to the project and having a positive effect. They can consider this information and choose to adjust priorities and scope to still meet a reasonable set of objectives rather than failing outright. They can choose to crash the project to meet some of their short-term objectives. They can work with stakeholders to accommodate different deployment approaches that still add value.

Instead of being handcuffed with bad news at the last minute, the information provides support for ongoing management of the project to completion. The project management system in place is doing exactly what it is supposed to do.

Consider the alternative: driving the project without a trackable schedule, only superficially validating the stuff that is built along the way. Many teams blindly rush headlong toward their target delivery date, and find out way too late that they will not be delivering as expected after all. For many projects, no news is actually the worst news of all.

Summary

The underlying motives and expectations that we all bring to the table in our relationships drive a great deal of the distinctions that we see across the team. Without understanding and managing these internal drivers, we are often driven to conflict and dysfunction.

Acknowledging and appreciating these differences is critical to successful relationships and forms the foundation of building a strong team.

If this foundation is not in place, no defined process or methodology will save us.

How Is This Relevant?

Your motives. Do you have a reasonable understanding of the motives that drive your own behaviors? Can you sense when you are transitioning into deeper levels of stress from your changes in behavior?

Motives of others. Have you ever been unable to reconcile the behavior of others in your group? What would be a reasonable distribution of motivational value systems across an effective team? How would you deal with any perceived deficiencies?

Tangibility. At what point do your products become tangible? Can this point be brought forward in the life cycle to help you more effectively manage change?

Expectations. Do your expectations get in the way of making objective decisions? Can you effectively manage the expectations of others to ensure that surprises are minimized?

References

1. http://ea-spouse.livejournal.com/274.html has the original blog; there are numerous updates posted throughout the Internet.

2. Elias H. Porter, *Relationship Awareness Theory: Manual of Administration and Interpretation* (Personal Strengths Publishing, 1996). Strength Deployment Inventory, SDI, and Relationship Awareness are registered trademarks of Personal Strengths Publishing, Inc.

3. David S. Platt, *Why Software Sucks...and What You Can Do About It* (Addison-Wesley Professional, 2006).

4. Fred Brooks, *The Mythical Man-Month: Essays on Software Engineering* (Addison-Wesley, 1995).

CHAPTER TEN

Playing Well Together

As we interact with others, we often face difficult situations along with the positive ones. Whereas many of these situations result from accidental misunderstandings, others stem from learned behaviors where individuals make choices that optimize their own interests over and above those of the group.

In this chapter, we explore some of the darker sides of relationships and look at ways to change our behaviors and attitudes to make the game more constructive.

Technical Ransom

We've all experienced projects where we rely on an individual to drag the team through to completion. It is tough to avoid on many projects. There may be a visionary with deep insight into innovative architecture or design to really differentiate the product. There may be a DBA or someone with other specific knowledge that is critical for the success of the project, or it might be someone who has the key relationships that will facilitate getting the product into the market. Great people to have on board, but there can be a dark side to these apparently wonderful assets.

In any team situation, heavy dependence on an individual may become a huge corporate risk. It is never safe to assume that this person will be with the project through to completion—ask any actuary about mortality rates. We all know how fierce the competition is between tech firms, especially for star performers. It is always important to work on distributing information across the team to mitigate your risks while improving communication. In fact, I can't think of a situation in which broader awareness of technical information becomes a liability. This is probably the practice where you will get the highest leverage for improving most projects.

Sometimes, however, the risk associated with a key individual becomes more than the usual actuarial concern. Sometimes, that key person abuses his or her role on a project, essentially holding the project for technical ransom.

Some project heroes truly believe that information hiding is a best practice for people and hold the project for technical ransom without even knowing it. Feeding the rest of the team small pellets of information that they believe are required to do the job, they eliminate any possibility of insight from the rest of the team that would improve the project's performance. At the same time, they lower morale for others who can't grasp the big picture and their contribution to the overall goals. In a sport with as much uncertainty as software development, a rigid-hierarchy model rarely works. The whole team needs to understand the broad goals so that they can proactively contribute to the solution space.

Others will deliberately hold the project for technical ransom for their own purposes. That ransom may take the form of more money or a greater share of the company, or control over areas of the project where it might not be appropriate. They may be the ones who consider themselves above the others when it comes to compliance of the agreed upon practices, such as change and configuration management, coding and design practices, or validation approaches. They place their own interests over those of the team's, and I have yet to see this behavior result in anything more than brief tactical gains for the individual. It always places the project at greater risk, and usually these risks are realized in some manner before the project finishes—that is, if the project ever does finish.

Teams need to take a hard stance against explicit ransom and work hard to educate the would-be "codenapper" about implicit ransom situations. Software development done well is a cooperative team sport, and those who would place their interests over and above the interest of the team should be viewed as a significant liability and dealt with accordingly. I'll take ten average performers who work well as a team over ten prima donnas anytime.

Don't give in to what are effectively ransom requests. Reward people based on their overall contribution to the team performance rather than for individual efforts.

Games People Play

As we interact with others, we're all playing a game, all the time, and the games that are played in the business world can have extreme outcomes.

Very few of the rules are explicit. The rules are often broken at surprising moments, and because of this it is rare that we are all playing to the same set of rules. At times, the rules to the games may be called cultural norms, at times they are seen as standard business interaction, and at times simply interpersonal relationships. If we step back and recognize that we are indeed always immersed in a game, if we consciously understand the rules and true motivations that govern our actions and those of our peers, we will have harnessed a very powerful tool.

A Fascinating Dance

I spent some time recently with a large group that, like many large groups in this industry, demonstrated the game being played in a wide variety of situations and responses. A diverse group always brings a number of different players to the table, and it can be fascinating to step back and watch the moves the players make. I'm sure this industry is no different from any other.

This particular group is dominated by what one could call a pack of alpha males. They are very bright and competent, to be sure, but also very adept at working the system to help them achieve their goals. They have advanced within this system through leveraging influence, exhibiting behaviors that demonstrate their superiority, and at times maneuvering craftily through the political landscape. Sometimes, they even leverage their deep technical knowledge, but this is not what differentiates them. They understand the game, play it well, and thrive in their environment. They play to win.

Others see the game for what it is and choose not to get caught up in the machinations. They have found their niche, their comfort zone where they can gain satisfaction from a job well done despite the game going on about them. They are not as deeply impacted by their environment and could perform well in a wide variety of different games. Although they might not come out on top as the winner, they are also less likely to suffer deep losses. Consciously or not, they behave in a manner that supports themselves and others, recognizing that working to win the game often means that most end up losing.

Finally, there are those who are frustrated by the games. They are often overwhelmed by the strong players, sometimes to the point of having to leave the game altogether through choice or because of exhaustion. It can be tough to realize that business is more than the reading, writing, and arithmetic that they fed us in school. Some never do realize it, or continue to hold on to the notion that business should be fair and have clear, transparent rules.

Although a few businesses avoid this negative environment, most play the games, and all of them have to work in a broader business environment where the games can be even tougher.

You have surely seen the games in progress at some point (perhaps a group of senior managers sitting in a meeting, all suggesting they can pull off miracles, not willing to be the first to blink). Maybe the executive can only show approval for an initiative by suggesting a change rather than shutting it down outright, essentially marking their territory. How about the team consciously setting fuzzy goals, making it easy to declare success whatever the outcome? All games. And there are plenty more examples that can be just as dysfunctional, just as damaging to the other players and to the organization as a whole.

If you are seeing this sort of thing, step back, recognize it is a game, and use it to your advantage. Give the players something to chew on, anticipate their moves, give them the opportunity to believe they have the upper hand if they need it, and think a few steps ahead of them—that is, if you, too, want to play the game.

Better yet, work with the team to understand a common set of objectives you can all work together to achieve. Give credit where credit is due. Take responsibility for your own shortcomings and mistakes. Demonstrate by example an approach where an inclusive attitude can serve to benefit everyone. By playing your cards right, not only can you achieve your goals, but you can also do it in a manner that makes others feel that they have won, too. Now that's taking the game to another level.

Negotiating or Grinding Down?

We recently had a company contact us with a tough challenge. They had someone who was scheduled to provide estimation training back out at the last minute. They were gathering their team together in one location from across the country, and they needed to fill the void.

They called us, because we were a known entity to them, with more than enough background experience to get the job done. We gave them a very reasonable quote for the work based on our need for some time to build up our lesson plans and provide the training, which was to take place in less than a week's time!

They said, "Great," but then we needed to talk about the price.

Ah, here we go again. The same scenario takes place thousands of times a day in software projects around the world. The estimate gets ground down, even if there is no defendable rationale for doing so.

Never mind the fact that it would have probably cost them more just to fly their original instructor into town and put him up in the area. Or that this person was quite probably someone who had inherited someone else's training material and may be less knowledgeable on the topic. What we provided was a fair, technical estimate of the cost of doing the work.

They really didn't have a lot of options at that point (because the people were committed to getting together, and they weren't talking to other resources that we knew of). It was like calling someone in on a Sunday afternoon to help fix a leaky faucet and then trying to steal their duct tape.

The result of the game? We gave in just a touch to preserve the relationship (as we expected we would have to), but not before we made it clear what we thought of the game, and exposed the irony that this game is one of the key drivers in dysfunctional software estimation, the very topic they asked us to train their team in.

They got the message.

This was the de facto practice of grinding down the price. The assumption that the first quote is merely an opening to the game of bartering, much like you would do (and is expected) when bartering for trinkets at a tourist trap somewhere.

 This game makes no sense in a business environment or a project environment. Economically, it is wastes effort and resources and leads to a weaker outcome. It assumes that the original quote was padded in the first place to compensate for the anticipated game ahead, and that those who pay the full price have been taken and those who are paid the full price have won. At some point, the whole point of a justifiable technical estimate of effort is lost in the negotiation game. The concept of fair value is overwhelmed in the win-lose jockeying for position.

 It is one thing to negotiate on the basis of fair value for both sides in business, and in software it makes sense to respect the technical estimate as well as the business constraints. Both perspectives are valid ones, and it is rarely good for the business or project to try to win the debate. In business and in software, if the costs need to arbitrarily drop, something has got to give. Preferably it is the explicit drop of scope, the (hopefully) careful degradation of quality, or something similar. Unfortunately in many situations, it is the collapse of the relationship and the unrealistic efforts to continue to provide 10 pounds of product in the remaining 5-pound bag.

If you look carefully enough, you can usually find a common ground that accommodates the needs of both sides. Although not perfect, it can get you to the endpoint without having to sacrifice the team to get there.

Be sure to investigate all your options, and be able to justify your rationale clearly based on what is best for the overall situation, not just for you.

Job Security

I've run into a number of people lately with interesting ways of looking at job security.

Some believe they have built up some job security by being the proprietors of critical knowledge for a product in their organization. Documentation just takes up time, not to worry—if there's ever a problem with that part of the system, you know who you can turn to, right?

There are all sorts of problems with this scenario:

- First is the general loss of productivity for this hero with all that information. There will always be questions and concerns about that area of the product, so our hero will spend quite a bit of time explaining the same thing to a number of different people, probably more than once in some cases. Maybe documentation doesn't take so much time in comparison after all.

- Second, being the sole proprietor of key information implies that others haven't had the opportunity to evaluate and contribute to the solution. Someone said once that there's no one here who is as smart as all of us put together. Anything done on a software project can benefit from additional eyes, and nothing should be considered done until it has been objectively validated as complete.

- Third, if this person were to disappear, either by choice (the grass is always greener) or by chance (the dreaded whacked-by-a-bus scenario or something less spectacular), the organization is left with a big hole to fill. What could have been a relatively simple retraining exercise with existing documentation and shared understanding now becomes a complete relearning exercise that may never be adequately accomplished.

Fortunately for these people, they are usually working for companies that don't recognize the massive risk in allowing this situation to persist. An astute organization would take measures, drastic if necessary, to ensure that the risk is mitigated as soon as possible.

It would be far better and wiser for everyone to build job security through the open sharing of information: Become indispensable because you are valued for your support of the organization, not for the jealous hoarding of information.

There are also people at the other extreme of the job security spectrum, giving selflessly to their job, their boss, and their co-workers to the point where they are taken for granted. It is sad to see the number of employers that take advantage of tough times and neglect to reasonably compensate their staff for years. Most companies are quick to scale back and ask everyone to tighten their belts in lean times; fewer are as quick to offer participation on the upside. "No, I don't think we can give out raises again this year…too bad there are no other jobs out there. By the way, how do you like my snazzy new car?"

Just as the hero above is shortsighted with the information-hoarding tactics, the employers that sell their staff short are in danger of having their tactics backfire, too. The job market will turn around, and people remember how they have been treated in lean times. When the market improves, a number of companies in the coming months will see more departures of critical resources than they would like. People eventually recognize that there is some job security that's not worth having.

> Job security can come in many forms. It is important to recognize that by definition, security has to be positive and strong for all parties. Consider the relationships you are involved in with your job. It's a two-way street out there, and if you are not taking care of everyone else you are working with and if they are not taking care of you, maybe it is time for a change.

Rumor and Innuendo

Elvis Lives! Aliens Abducted My Wife! Secret Lives of Talk-Show Hosts Revealed!

Got your attention, didn't I? Where would we be without the latest news about celebrities in decline, the latest solved crime that made headlines, or the latest prediction of our total demise? There's a vigorous market for juicy stuff like this in the tabloids, and the cover stories are interesting diversions in checkout lines, but most of us recognize the stories for what they are: entertaining fabrications designed primarily to make a buck.

Unfortunately, there are those who seem to believe that this relatively harmless approach to creating spectacular headlines is also a reasonable approach to ensuring that all appears to be well in software development projects. You may have worked with someone like that: The information they provide seems to be tailored for the current audience. The people at the top see things through rose-colored lenses, the people in the trenches are kept in the dark. Information becomes this pliable substance that is shaped in ways geared to benefit the provider. All the glory is gathered, and all the problems are deflected. Even if it stops short of what could be construed as lying, twisted information can be damaging in many ways.

Just as the tabloids seem to stop at nothing to get a headline that will sell, there are times that information on a project will be withheld or otherwise abused in the cause of generating personal power. Often, however, this personal power comes at the expense of the organization as a whole because there is no benefit to the team in hiding information at this level.

If this manipulation of information is done too often, damage can also be self-inflicted. Just as most of us are unlikely to put much weight on the headlines we read in the tabloids, we will also tend to discredit the source of misleading information if the outlandish stories occur too frequently.

Software development is a team sport, and teams need to work together to win. In a team-based project environment, if the information you are receiving doesn't appear to make sense in the context of everything else you know, question it. If the information you are providing doesn't appear to be arriving intact to its intended destination, ensure it gets there yourself. If it is third-party information, strive to seek out the source for clarification. It has been said that rumors are the ripples caused by insufficient information, and like tsunamis, ripples have a way of growing in impact.

Avoid the trap of relying on rumor and innuendo as a guide. Be critical of your sources of information. As Joe Friday used to say on Dragnet, "Just the facts, ma'am."

Minimizing Disruption

It's been said that surprises are bad for software projects, that an easy, predictable path to completion is easy on the soul.

I'm not sure about you, but having some sort of surprise isn't all that bad. After all, there's really nothing in the term "surprise" that is intrinsically bad. Surprise can bring astonishment and wonder, and it can easily be as refreshingly positive as it can be negative. Surprise can indeed be good.

The same can be said of change. Naive software teams are caught off guard by change, and then will staunchly reject any change (with equally dismal results). Change, like surprise, is a double-headed coin. It can bring opportunity, or it can be a threat, but it definitely should not be avoided. Change can be managed. Surprise brings variety and the potential for innovative solutions.

It is really disruption that we need to be careful of and what we want to minimize in our projects.

Everything about disruption is negative. By definition, disruption implies confusion and disorder, impeding progress, and breaking things. These are all terms we aren't too keen to associate with our projects. Although some would argue that a little directed disruption is valuable to triggering change, this is not something that makes any sense in the context of a project, something we are working to successfully bring to closure in a reasonable timeframe.

Our goal as project managers, or indeed as any participant in a team, is to do everything in our power to minimize disruption on our projects: to ourselves, to our teammates, and to the project itself. This requires a proactive, constant vigilance for the signs and symptoms of disruption, which may appear in several forms.

 We're all familiar with project disruption. This is often disguised as the more generic element of change. Internally or externally driven disruptions to scope and schedule probably derail the majority of projects. However, if we drill down a level, most of these disruptions can at least be anticipated, if not eliminated.

Internally, this often takes the form of finding out that an intended approach just won't work or will take far longer than originally planned. This is something that can be well managed through prototyping and peer review. Identifying issues and potential solutions early, and recognizing the risk or uncertainty in the time required to tackle the unknown on a project, allows you to accommodate for this in the schedule. Failure to factor these variables in may still allow you to squeeze a schedule into your targets, but it will also almost guarantee an unhealthy dose of disruption downstream, near the target dates when it is least convenient to manage.

Externally, we see project disruption when significant changes are proposed to the scope, often close to the intended delivery date. All we are left to do is throw up our hands in dismay. Engaging the external stakeholders as true team participants (rather than those pesky clients that just seem to get in our way) and leveraging the same approaches previously discussed can go a long way to managing these issues.

Process-related disruption is less commonly identified. Generally, most of us don't explicitly consider the approach we take in developing software until it is seen as a problem. This often takes the form of too-little intentional effort applied to ensure that step A is really completed before step B can reasonably begin. It can also come from the other direction, when the mandated activity adds little overall value but continually disrupts the healthy flow of creativity and progress.

In the former case, we need to be careful to agree on what *done* means to avoid unanticipated rework downstream. In the latter, whatever we do should effectively contribute to help us get our jobs done. In either case, most of us need to step back and consider the approach we use on our projects, at the highest level as well as for each specific task we tackle.

Finally, personnel disruption can come in the form of individuals (or groups) departing from the scene and leaving the rest of the crew to clean up the mess. A more insidious form of dysfunction occurs when issues between various members of the team remain unresolved and continue to eat away at relationships within the team.

We must recognize that we are all living, breathing individuals with distinct sets of motivations, perspectives, and circumstances that we bring to our relationships, instead of simplifying our perception of the universe by assuming that those around us work from a framework or context that is identical to ours. Acknowledging these distinctions helps us appreciate the actions of others in a different light and allows for much more spontaneity, creativity, and appreciation in our teams. This in turn will drive positive surprises, healthy change, and much more effective collaboration.

Chances are that whenever you recall something that put your project out of kilter, you can categorize it into project, process, or personnel disruption. Consider these sources of disruption. Look for the signs that may be readily apparent. Work to minimize the disruption around you.

Quality Circle Genealogy

It has been variously argued that the notion of quality circles has been around for perhaps half a century, and that Kaoru Ishikawa, of the fishbone or cause and effect diagram fame, is credited as the "father of the quality circle movement." Common in manufacturing environments and ISO-based quality initiatives, quality circles bring a small group of people together voluntarily to solve their work-related problems or to improve their work environment. Handled appropriately, the shared participation fosters teamwork, cooperation, and more broadly, effective solutions.

All good stuff, to be sure, but it is safe to say that solutions through peer collaboration are more than 50 years old.

Aboriginal Sentencing Circles

For hundreds of years, North American aboriginals have been managing affairs using circles of various kinds. Healing circles are used for supportive improvement and recovery. Sentencing circles are used to develop consensus on fair and reasonable consequences to crimes. Research shows that these long-standing practices have a number of strengths that would make adoption valuable as a means of managing change in software organizations.

One of the key elements of these circles is that everyone is involved in the decision, and the party to be changed (either healed or sentenced in the circles above) requests to participate in the circle process. It is not something that is mandated from the top down.

When participating within the circle, a safe environment is provided where people are free to speak their mind without recrimination. The focus is on solutions rather than punishment. Openness and honesty are critical for success. All participants are empowered in the process; they all have a voice and a shared responsibility in finding constructive resolutions for change.

Beyond the strengths of circles to address immediate problems, the shared decision-making process helps build a sense of community and capacity for resolving conflict, and it promotes these as community values.

Indeed, it appears that sentencing circles include healing circles for the victim and offender, as well as follow-up circles to monitor the progress of the offender. This approach provides a more

> comprehensive solution than the systems we are accustomed to and can be effective at addressing the underlying causes of criminal behavior, instead of just punishing that behavior or simply dealing with the symptoms.

Software development would benefit from a similar holistic approach. On a micro level, broad participation is critical to ensure that impact is appropriately analyzed and disseminated as we address changes through change review boards. Significant changes can then be effectively communicated through to the rest of the team. Maintaining an environment where any change can be voluntarily brought to the board in a proactive basis will tend to reduce the need for the more severe form of "sentencing and recrimination" that would be used to address situations where the build is broken and needs repair.

Broad participation will promote buy-in across the team and dramatically improve the quality of the ideas that contribute to the change process. Collaboration and shared awareness improve the sense of community, which can only serve to improve or sustain team dynamics over time.

Whether you follow the lead of the quality movement or acknowledge that the principles of collaborative problem solving have much deeper roots, there is great value in leveraging the practices and philosophies of circles within your teams.

Make Yourself at Home

Generally, we tend to look at work as a place we need to drag ourselves to in the morning, and home as that place that we look forward to returning to after a long day at the office. When we think of them as physical locations, the four-letter-word *work* conjures up more negative emotions, while *home* has a far more attractive ring.

For a growing number of us, myself included, home and workplace are often physically co-located, mixing things up a bit. For me, however, this blending helps me recognize that home is more than the place where I have a mortgage and put out the trash. It is more than the place where I sleep at night. I've learned that home can be wherever I am, with whomever I'm with, doing whatever I'm doing. Home is a state of mind rather than a place on the map.

One of the key factors for individual effectiveness is the notion of being comfortable with your environment. This includes being comfortable with your skills in the context of what is being asked of you, comfortable with your co-workers and your relationship with them, comfortable with your physical surroundings. This blends nicely into team effectiveness. If we scale up appropriately and the whole group interacts well together, if we are comfortable, if we are not wanting for any of our essential needs, only then do we have an opportunity to be effective.

It is important to ensure that this environment is optimized for all of us to thrive, whether we are in the environment where we are producing software or in the environment where we are reading bedtime stories to our kids. We need an environment where we do not feel threatened, where we are free to do what we want to do. Our actions need to be aligned with the overall needs and goals of the group.

The only way we can achieve this is to openly discuss our needs and goals, and to find a collective set of these for the group that is congruent with our own. In that context, we can then select activities that work well for ourselves, do not conflict with the needs of others, and support progress toward the overall goals. Without open collaboration, without free expression, we cannot understand whether there is congruence. Therefore, we can't act appropriately.

To complain that your needs are not being met without having clearly expressed them is pure folly. To exist in a team environment of any kind without regard to the needs of others is neglectful.

Physical location is irrelevant. Home is the state of mind where you have the freedom and confidence to exercise appropriate choice in what you do. It fits in quite nicely with the building of an effective workplace. Make yourself and others at home in the workplace.

Summary

We often face individual behaviors that are detrimental to the group as a whole.

If we learn to recognize these behaviors in others and ourselves, we can work to minimize their negative impacts.

There will be times when this means we need to step up and actively take control of our surroundings. At other times, we might not be able to immediately change things, so we need to tolerate the situation, at least for a while.

How Is This Relevant?

Managing group dynamics. How consciously do you manage the dynamics of the groups you are involved with? Do you step back to consider the different perceptions and behaviors of the group? Do you adjust the norms of engagement to keep the relationships flowing smoothly?

Our role in groups. When was the last time you were positively surprised in a group environment by the actions of others? When have you done something that pleasantly surprised others? How could you do this today, and who would benefit the most from this?

Defining *home*. When was the last time that you had an open discussion of wants and needs in the context of the workplace? Are you in an environment where you can truly thrive, where you do not feel threatened? Do you have the freedom, within reasonably structured boundaries, to act in accordance with your needs and the needs of the group? Do you feel at home?

PART FOUR

Teams

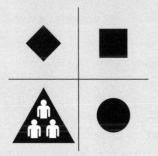

When groups decide to get together to solve a problem, there is a strong need to go beyond ad hoc random discussions. We need to understand how to behave in a manner that will bring us toward a common goal.

To do this, we need to first have an understanding of what this common goal is. We need to be aligned. Then we need mechanisms that will allow us to share information that we have and a common understanding of the relative importance of this information, including how it will evolve over time. Finally, we need to ensure that this agreed upon goal and approach is carefully fostered over time, because there are strong forces at work to break down this agreement.

Successful team interactions require established systems and mechanisms that support a shared understanding of the current and intended state of progress, but these need to be maintained. Although some might argue that this is the role of the project manager, the responsibility for contributing to this system in an ongoing fashion lies with every one of us.

CHAPTER ELEVEN

Alignment

For a team to be effective, we have to start by arranging all team members in such a manner that they are in their appropriate places and know where we are headed. We have to bring the team into alignment.

In this chapter, we explore the different dimensions of alignment, the reasons for maintaining a focus on this alignment throughout our efforts, and how team size affects our approaches.

Unifying a Great Team

In organizations of any size, the unifying presence of a consistent vision of where the team is headed is great for keeping the team pointed in the right direction. The challenges then lie in sustaining that vision and retaining a team that sees it through to completion.

Sometimes, however, a broad team of talented and passionate individuals comes together with what they perceive to be a common goal. As discussion starts among the team, however, they find that each one has a somewhat different perspective of that common goal. As in the parable of the blind men each coming upon a different part of an elephant, it is critical to coalesce the different perspectives together to arrive at that common vision for the team, making the whole greater than the sum of the parts. The somewhat oxymoronic notion of a steering committee is not sufficient to sustain the team; a clear unifying vision is critical in a group such as this.

A well-crafted and managed vision for a project will provide several key benefits beyond unifying the team's broad perspectives. In clearly describing the "what" of a project, it will allow the team to ensure that the "how" of the project is properly aligned with its business objectives. It can provide a reference point for decision making as suggestions for scope change arrive, identifying whether this proposed change will help you achieve your objectives. It serves as a great prioritization vehicle for action and provides a clear sounding board for continuously validating the business case for the project. Finally, and possibly most importantly for passionate teams, it serves as the basis for people to decide whether they want to remain involved with the project at all.

 For any substantial project, it is impossible to avoid the different perspectives that will emerge within a strong team. If channeled appropriately, these perspectives can significantly strengthen the overall result. A clear vision can unify a team of lemmings or cats toward a common goal. With all the additional challenges surrounding the management of a strong team (personalities, agendas, and so on), it is imperative to get a handle on the definition of why the team is together in the first place.

If the team does not have a single unifying vision, the team does not have a future.

Growing the Team

From the business perspective, one of the most important stages for a technology company involves scaling up the team. Whether it is done to meet current demand or in anticipation of future demand, whether it is handled through cash flow or done through some sort of investment in the future, the risk associated with expansion is massive. Few companies truly respect these risks. Consequently, the results range from loss of control, dilution of the passion that drove the initial team, to much worse.

From the perspective of the individual, joining a team can be equally risky, particularly at the stage when a company is experiencing growth. It is dangerous to assume that the business side is carefully managing the transition and important to recognize the responsibility you have in ensuring that this new relationship will be a successful one.

Far too much of this dance is left to chance in most cases. Hiring people is not the core business of most tech companies, and individuals are too often focused on the allure of a job rather than the advancement of their careers. In both cases, much more emphasis needs to be placed on determining whether there is a mutual respect for how the work is done.

The majority of software companies, despite any suggestions to the contrary, have a culture for getting things done in their organizations that overrides any set of standard procedures that may be on the shelves. In some places, this culture works better than others. In any organization, the approach that may be formally established is heavily laced with individual attitudes, team relationships, and organizational politics. Few businesses recognize this culture as an essential part of the workplace, and fewer actively manage this culture as a differentiator for success.

 When growing the team, although there is value in weeding through the mass of résumés to determine whether the appropriate skills are in place (although to my mind, many of the attributes sought in interviews, especially at the junior/intermediate stages, are easily trainable skills), it is important to acknowledge the existing culture and determine what the candidate's impact on that culture will be. Is there evidence (beyond the well-rehearsed answers in an interview) that the candidate will respect the existing approach to getting work done and can work in a cooperative environment? How many of the person's responses are framed in terms of "I achieved this…" versus "We achieved that…"?

Noting that they had a stake in previous relationships, what is their perspective of what happened in the past? It can be a warning flag if all previous positions turned sour because of what the "other guys" did. Hire for attitude, train for skills.

 When joining a team, delve deeper than what is shown on the corporate Web site, and recognize that this is much more than "getting a job" at any level. It is your responsibility to determine whether the environment is going to be compatible with your needs.

As an employer, my fondest memories of interviews are those where the candidate left me feeling wrung out afterward. The deep, probing questions were coming my way in the interview. They did their best to understand how things were done and whether there was a fit, instead of passively answering questions with responses that they thought would advance them through the gates. Alas, there have only been a couple of these in my experience.

Sitting down with a prospective employer is your golden opportunity to understand the cultural fit. In time, the allure of the paycheck will pale in importance to other concerns. It is these other concerns that are critical to investigate. Although the company's products might be part of the original attraction, remember that you will spend much more time in the process of building the products rather than in the glory of having shipped them.

Indeed, in some companies the time building the products can approach 100 percent, as they never manage to ship.

Just as employers will check references and other sources as part of their due diligence, you need to do the same to get past the rehearsed answers that are often a part of the interview ritual.

There is great value in candidly asking to chat with a relatively new or junior member of the crew to get their perspective of how things are done; and clients or past employees can provide rich insights, too.

Walking the Team Walk

We have all grown a couple decades before entering the workforce, and the habits and attitudes that are ingrained in us by that time are hard to change. Throw on top of that any time in an organization, and it becomes clear that attempts to indoctrinate, to sway, to encourage all to conform to one approach represent an uphill battle. We all have our comfort zone, the mode of action in which we believe we are at our best.

Somewhere along the way, the approaches that we have embraced for getting things done start to fail, and it usually happens when we start interacting with others—we become a team member. We get thrown into teams without advance warning that the skills and approaches that got us this far just don't scale up. Our approaches aren't exactly like the others, and quite often, they don't mesh at all. Carrying all our information internally doesn't work so well when others need that information to move forward. There are trade-offs and compromises to be negotiated and tactics needed to reach the team's end goal.

 There is great value in coordinating effort, but there is usually great resistance, too. We all feel the resulting pains when a team isn't in sync, and we'll quickly complain as we experience the results, but what do we do about it? Doing nothing is probably the worst thing you can do. Passive resistance is the most dangerous form of resistance to change. Active resistance, kicking and screaming about what to do, is easily observed and dealt with, but what happens when thing just don't get done?

Tracking time is a classic example of resistance that I've seen in software development teams. Everyone will complain about the failures to meet target dates and the overwhelming effort, but attempts to get a handle on where the time goes by tracking it and making informed decisions will usually fail. First, there are active resistance tactics, such as "tracking my time will take too much time." (How do you know that, by the way?)

Then along come the dangerous passive tactics. Especially after initial tracking exposes huge inefficiencies, you will often find that people suddenly become too busy to continue tracking, or that huge amounts of time get thrown into large catchall categories that don't provide much insight. The initiative fades in usefulness, and then eventually stops altogether. The perception is that this improvement stuff has again failed us.

 Two problems here: First, our intent for measurement is wrong. We often measure to report, rather than to learn. We translate the data into negative information, rather than into an opportunity for growth. Second, something for which we all need to take ownership is that we have killed the initiative ourselves through lack of participation. We have failed to walk the walk. We all mean well, but our priorities clearly show up in our actions. If something doesn't get done, it wasn't a priority for us, regardless of what was stated up front. Genuine buy-in is tough to achieve, but critical for success.

Any initiative will take a little time to implement (much less than the time saved overall if wisely chosen), and early returns will likely reveal some embarrassing or depressing news. It's easier to hide your head in the sand and get back to your old comfort zone; it is tougher to forge ahead and actually reap the potential gains that the bad news represents. Ignorance is bliss, but not progress. These pains will not go away on their own. Scream for what you believe is right, but are you ready to do something about it?

It is a lot tougher for a team to succeed than for an individual because of the increased coordination required.

When a team clicks well, the results can be spectacular. We all need to walk the walk to be truly effective team members and contribute to the success of the greater organization.

Our actions define us, not our statements.

Making the Rules

One of Carly Fiorina's achievements during her tenure at the helm of Hewlett-Packard was a corporate makeover that included a collection of ten statements called the "Rules of the Garage," to serve as a rallying cry for a company that had become an extremely diverse set of geographically distributed groups.[1] In my visits to no less than six Hewlett-Packard sites in three countries over the past year, this manifesto has been the most consistently displayed common element at all these sites.

Packaged up as an attractive poster and ad campaign (no doubt courtesy of their Imaging and Printing Group), the rules are superimposed on a picture of the garage where the founders apparently started up the business in 1937. The intent is to bring back the essence of what made the start-up successful so long ago, to return to the company's roots. It is interesting to note that there is nothing in the ten statements that talks about profit or following procedures, elements that would seem critical to huge, dispersed public company.

HP's Rules of the Garage transcend the tactical issues that people face as they work to get product out the door on a daily basis, while at the same time they serve as a set of principles to use as a sounding board for specific day-to-day practices. They are all about teamwork, flexibility, and making a difference, elements that don't normally describe an organization the size of Hewlett-Packard. There is nothing about specific products and technologies (HP's original product considerations included automated urinal flushers and bowling alley sensors, among others) and nothing in the rules that would even tie them to any specific industry.

Jim Collins and Jerry I. Porras identified Hewlett-Packard as one of the truly visionary companies in their book *Built to Last*.[2] Their criteria included having survived through multiple generations of chief executives and product cycles, and making an indelible imprint on the world in which we live, both of which HP has clearly achieved. Although even the most visionary companies will have their ups and downs, the likelihood of weathering the inevitable storms seems to increase considerably if the business is held together with some of this principles-based glue.

HP's Rules of the Garage were put together as an ad campaign relatively recently, but their genesis stems from 2 friends deciding to build a company that would make a difference almost 70 years ago. Their value system has survived changes that were unimaginable to the founders, and has served as a basis for creating a company that is as relevant today as it has ever been.

Most companies today hold profit or share value above all else, and entrepreneurs are focused on leveraging investments to a point where they can IPO or be acquired as an exit strategy. These elements don't appear high on the list of rules for companies with an interest in building a lasting presence or making a real difference. Just as speed and cost are often valued higher than quality at the product level, profit and market share are often valued over business-level excellence, and I think both perspectives are woefully shortsighted—probably because both product quality and business excellence are rarely well defined.

It can be an interesting exercise to work through these rules in your organization.

> If your company is large enough, try to figure out what these rules might be, and whether they are aligned with the rules you might set, given the chance.

The Conscious Team Contract

Some of the most compelling lessons that we gain out of training sessions are those where the results are not intuitively expected but are consistently arrived at by all participants. For an instructor, this phenomenon is intensified as it occurs each time the course is run, indicating global applicability, akin to a physical law.

I have worked with a number of groups specifically on teamwork. One of the exercises I've used to kick off the session is to get groups to brainstorm about their past experience: what the characteristics or attributes of their most successful projects were. The results will vary slightly based on the experience and terminology that the participants bring to the table, but at some level it is almost as if I could just post up the answers in advance.

It is rare that a team indicates that access to appropriate tools or technology is a driver for successful projects. Although some might note that this is just a given characteristic, I suggest that it is mostly irrelevant.

Successful projects are generally characterized as having highly motivated participants, appropriate skills, and challenging goals. Straightforward to this point. The people involved are interested in the tasks and have the capacity and motivation to move forward. A great deal of this has to do with the content of the product we are endeavoring to build.

Beyond this, a number of common characteristics stand out. All groups will also arrive at the conclusion that successful projects and teams share respect, integrity, trust, and strong communication, and have fun doing it. This collection of terms is an intensely interwoven mix of issues. Although critical for team success, these have nothing to do with the relationship between the product or application domain and the participants. They have everything to do with how the team members work with each other.

In all my years in industry, the primary emphasis in building up a team has consistently been in collecting the right set of skills and unleashing this pool of talent to get the project done. Sometimes there is a little emphasis on "team-building" activities such as going out for lunch, but mostly not. Sometimes there is a conscious effort to ensure that the goals are challenging but still reasonable to achieve, but often not. For the most part, dealing with team-dynamics issues has been an awkward reactive activity on the part of the project manager or HR.

As a participant, I have never been on a team for which there was any focus on managing how the team would work with each other. In my experience working with teams as a consultant, it is an extremely rare occurrence in the field. I have seen it consciously done in only one team when I hadn't introduced it into the group through training.

We all seem to acknowledge that successful projects rely on strong team dynamics. What can we do about it?

I think any team that is interested in success needs to consciously address this issue and should take the time to build a team contract.

Think of this as the rules of engagement, or the norms within which we choose to relate to one another. As noted previously, each group will bring different experiences and terminology to the table, so there is no universal team contract that can simply be purchased or downloaded and posted on the wall to mitigate these key issues. Each contract, to be effective, needs to be drafted as a group, respected and agreed upon by the group, and actively managed and reflected upon by the group. (A precursor to this, of course, is that all participants are interested in engaging in the success of the team.) The contract will probably have a number of key statements, each supporting some resonant aspect of relationships within the team.

Over the years, I've learned that these rules need to carry a few key elements to be the most effective:

- The rules need to carry positive, sustaining characteristics and include the negative aspects we want to avoid. It is just as important to identify mechanisms for fun, trust, and mutual respect as it is to address the issues of blame and defensiveness.

- There needs to be complete consensus and agreement for each of the rules and a mechanism for adjusting the rules as the environment changes. Anyone should be able to step up and say we need to rethink our team contract, and the entire team needs to respect the value of the time spent in doing so. This is an ongoing investment that is critical.

- Partially tied to this is the notion that the contract has to have a built-in safety valve, a nonjudgmental mechanism to identify that someone is in violation of one of the agreed upon norms that has been set out. (My personal favorite is to wave your arms like a chicken when someone is going against the contract.)

- At times, you might need to escalate that safety valve; and the group needs to agree that if things get too hot, it is okay to disengage. Indeed, this is imperative. It has been shown that in situations of extreme conflict, we have physiological mechanisms that actually shut down rational thought. We need to be able to safely step back and cool down before addressing the issues.

 Each team will have a very different contract, even if common themes exist in most. Just as with a specification of a product, however, it is critical to go beyond the drafting of the team contract. It has to be consciously put in use. Post it prominently. Take the time to reflect on it periodically. Use it as a mechanism to ensure that the team remains effective. Change the contract when necessary. Don't let it stagnate.

 One of the valuable uses of a strong team charter is that it provides a mechanism for introducing new members to the team, along with the normal "here is our development approach, here is our product and spec." Being able to point to the contract and say "here is how we have agreed to work together" can keep the team in sync, can drive the discussion of adjustment of the contract for new members, and can reveal to prospects early that they just might not fit in.

 It is imperative for team success (especially if you consider team longevity to be a success factor) that you consciously consider how to manage your team dynamics. Drafting and using a team contract can be an effective way of addressing relationships within the team and building mechanisms for dealing with conflict before they occur. Without this, you will end up with a collection of individuals rather than a team as the pressure rises. When that occurs, a shared common vision of success and achieving that common goal are significantly more difficult.

It Takes All Kinds

It is often said that having a single strong leader to drive a team in the right direction is critical.

 That can certainly work if the direction chosen by that strong leader is the right direction to begin with, and everyone on the team agrees that this is indeed the case. Problem is that if the leader possesses those attributes that enable her to drive the team, the notion of consensus building can be relatively dormant in her tool kit. The team may never have the opportunity to voice their perspective as to whether they feel they are headed in the right direction. The "right direction" becomes a single point of failure, and those who have not voiced their opinion will certainly do so when things go awry.

I have seen organizations try to remedy this situation in a couple of ways.

Some organizations try to make all decisions through consensus among the team members. This might be great in theory, but there are problems with consensus. The decisions that get made are the "easy ones." The watered-down results can work in situations when the status quo is fine, but when there are problems it becomes tough to drive the difficult decisions through the group. Also, even when times are good, this approach will only scale up so far. It can be impossible to get consensus on any decision when there are too many cooks. The soup will never be just right for everyone.

Other organizations approach this apparent conflict by trying to build the team in a manner that minimizes the variability of the perspectives. The hiring process gets distilled down to one where a specific mold is cast, and the effort becomes one of finding candidates who most appropriately fit the mold. Standard tests and questions are asked, results are collated, and the process becomes statistical. Personality-assessment instruments are often used, even those that are not designed to accommodate the hiring process. Even though the cookie-cutter team will accommodate the intent of the fearless leader and the risk of conflict is minimized, something is seriously missing. The absence of conflict can become apathy rather than harmony, and an organization bereft of balancing perspectives risks being blindsided.

In all of these cases, the capability for innovation is severely crippled.

There is a great deal of value in different perspectives (and in the appropriate channeling of these perspectives in a healthy environment of collaboration). It indeed takes all kinds of people to make a strong organization, with a balance of complementary strengths to leverage.

We need to respect the perspectives of others on the team, and we need to appreciate the differences among us as potential strengths to provide us with a more rounded and potentially much more unique solution. Instead of looking to replicate our current strengths as we grow the team, we need to understand where our blind sides are (both technically and emotionally) and work to fill them with new talent. We need to be open to the discovery of new ways to look at things, and we need to ensure that everyone has a voice, in the context of effectively getting things done.

Although it is critical to have a single vision to allow the team to collaborate effectively toward a common solution, it is best achieved by using that vision as a sounding board, a consolidating theme to balance the wide perspectives of a diverse and balanced team.

Manage broad diversity in your teams.

Near Early Warning

Back in the days of the Cold War (the younger folk out there can check with their elders), the Distant Early Warning (DEW) Line in the Canadian Arctic was a critical part of NORAD's (the North American Aerospace Defense Command) defense. This was intended to provide a warning system for nasty missiles headed over the pole to wreak havoc on us (although it dawns on me that, being in Canada where the line is located, *distant* can be a relative term).

Although it is not clear to me what we were supposed to do with this warning other than to counter the attack, the theory was that this system provided us some comfort in being able to predict our impending doom well in advance.

Fortunately, we've never put the system through its paces.

Most software teams have no DEW Line in place. When trouble comes, it usually arrives without warning. We're suddenly late not by a little bit, but by months. We throw an equally ludicrous revised target out there and continue to work like crazy. We start to validate things for the first time in a project by putting everything together when we are 90 percent into the project and are surprised that it is not a smooth integration. That pretty Gantt chart we painstakingly built initially doesn't reflect what people are doing in the least, and our expected completion date is a function of what we promised and how frustrated our testers are. Scope creep looks more like a scope rampage. We don't need an external evil empire to guard ourselves against. As the cartoon character Pogo noted years ago, "We have met the enemy, and he is us."

How to construct an early warning system for software projects isn't rocket science, even when building rocket systems. The reason it's rarely in place is that it requires time that you can actually put a finger on, and when weighed against the optimistic expectations of perfect code first time, we all know who wins. We don't have time for that early stuff; let's rev our code engines and start building. We fail to learn from our mistakes, and we relive them, project after project.

What it takes is a little discipline in the way of project planning and quality assurance. Understanding what success means for all stakeholders is a start. From there, recognize that there is value in putting together your best understanding of scope to be used as a basis for all work. After that, acknowledge that you weren't perfect and that you will spend a lot of time managing change (or even more time reacting to change, if you prefer). Clear common expectations for everyone are required, as is diligence and oversight throughout.

We're still not talking about a perfect development team here; issues will continue to be injected throughout the project. You'll identify and correct more issues in-phase, you'll have more flexibility in how to remain on track, and you will have more credible predictions to completion.

 Call it a "near early warning system." The checks and balances that ensure what you claim is done rarely comes back to haunt you. With these, less will fall through the cracks, and you have the flexibility to adapt to change throughout the project. Get the real enemy under control, and you will gain an assurance that feels a lot better than mutual assured destruction.

Scaling Up and Scaling Down

 As we move through our careers across projects, teams, companies, and industries, we usually find that each new situation differs appreciably in a number of different dimensions. Project magnitude, team size and culture, corporate governance, and business criticality are a few of the factors that drastically alter what is important to success in our new environment. For the most part, these factors will either increase or decrease in significance as the project changes in size. To avoid failure, you must correspondingly scale up or down in response.

When scaling up, the approaches that sustained success in the past are usually inadequate to deal with the present, and the change is definitely nonlinear. Increased lines of communication will force more rigorous documentation approaches. The higher cost of failure increases the importance for reasonable checks and balances along the way. Politics can become an overwhelming force to contend with, and the lifespan of the project can challenge the attention span of the best of us. For people graduating into the workplace for the first time, all of these factors can hit with an overwhelming culture shock. Significantly more focus on governance is critical to sustain success in the new environment. Although failure can occasionally be attributed to excess oversight, insufficient oversight often brings down these big ones.

To scale down can be a joy. Working on a smaller project, a smaller team, or less-critical application can be a welcome relief after a large project experience. There are sometimes fewer political issues to deal with, and success that is more visible sooner brings quicker rewards. Unfortunately, there are just as many risks in scaling down. It is all too easy to let down your defenses when moving to a smaller project or team to a point where there is insufficient respect for the controls warranted. At the other extreme, however, it is important to recognize that what worked in the large will often cripple smaller endeavors. Documentation can easily become needless overhead, and issues that demanded pomp and circumstance elsewhere can often be sufficiently supported with less formality. Without proper consideration, application of significant oversight can easily cause stagnation on a smaller project.

An awareness at all levels of where you have come from and where you are headed, along with those around you, will go a long way to helping you understand where you need to focus for success on your new venture. What worked in the past cannot be trusted to work in the future. Appropriate reflection and proactive observation of potential changes can prepare you for your new situation.

Summary

A well-aligned team is much more effective than one with diverse impressions of what the destination looks like. We need to focus on the arrangement of the resources that make up the team and ensure that everyone is clear about where we are headed.

For smaller teams, this can be relatively trivial (because we each take on several roles in parallel), but as the team grows, we need to ensure that our alignment remains intact.

How Is This Relevant?

Getting things done. Do you have a reasonable approach to getting things done? To what degree is it formalized, adhered to, and managed in an ongoing fashion? To what degree does culture, individual attitudes, and relationships play in how things get done? How does this change when the going gets rough, and how often does this going actually get rough? How much influence will you have in this environment?

Core job elements. Consider your current role (or past roles if you are currently job hunting), and ask yourself what aspects of this position are consuming your day. For many, it is not the skills you bring or the products the company ships, but the team practices, relationships, and culture that determine your satisfaction and ultimately the company's success. These are the elements that are of critical importance as you grow a team (or become part of that team).

Rules of engagement. Does your company have the equivalent of HP's Rules of the Garage? What principles does your company adhere to that make it unique and visionary? Is the primary emphasis to make a difference for your clients or to make a profit for yourselves?

References

1. George Anders, *The Carly Chronicles: An Inside Look at Her Campaign to Reinvent HP* (Fast Company, January 2003).

2. Jim Collins and Jerry I. Porras, *Built to Last: Successful Habit of Visionary Companies* (Harper Business Essentials, 1994).

CHAPTER TWELVE

Organization

After we have assembled the people into the appropriate positions and gained a common understanding of our goals, we need to build in mechanisms that will allow the team to complete their tasks in an efficient and orderly fashion.

In this chapter, we discuss some of the neglected aspects of building a process and some of the critical areas to consider as we try to gain consistency and efficiency without burdening the team with bureaucracy.

Everything in Its Place

 How do you deal with organization on your projects?

A Sailor's Mentality

Have you ever tried to find something around the house, spending much more time looking for it than it was really worth, or even forgetting what it was that you were looking for as something else distracts you?

If you are like me, you have at least one place in the house that is a catchall for the odds and ends—a kitchen drawer with the loose cords, can openers, scotch tape, elastic bands, and used twist ties. Maybe you have a drawer like this in most rooms of the house, or perhaps this is how you could categorize your entire garage or house.

Some have a sailor's mentality of putting things back in their proper place as soon as they are done with it. They never know when a rogue wave might hit. From experience, they know they would have enough on their hands without all sorts of stuff flying about inside the cabin.

At the other extreme are those who take things out and use them, and then leave them lying around with everything else in random piles. Some will happily let this go on indefinitely; others will hit a critical point where they have had enough, kicking off a frenzy of getting things reorganized again—the equivalent of finding out that the auditor is coming to town.

Not that a software auditor should be perceived as the equivalent of a rogue wave, of course.

We often treat our software development projects with similar approaches. There are the fastidious types who have a system where everything has its place, and everyone knows where to find things when they are needed. The system is well organized; and when something is not in its place, this omission stands out just as strongly as all the information that is in its proper place.

 Others, quite possibly the majority of projects with smaller teams, fall closer to the other end of the fastidiousness spectrum. There might be a few documents that have been produced and placed somewhere on a server (or worse, someone's desktop), but certainly not where everyone knows about them, and rarely put there in a controlled fashion. It's not clear whether there is sufficient information in the documents that do exist, and what usually happens is that when something is needed, there is a flurry of questions to locate the required information. "Where is the latest spec?" becomes the equivalent of "Where's the stapler?"

Often, when the item being sought cannot be found, some sort of substitute is identified. A new and different assumption for something that has been previously resolved becomes the equivalent of a paper clip replacement for a staple. Although each might serve the tactical need, the strategic implications can be more far reaching.

If you need to locate things easily, or understand whether something is missing, you need a system that has a place for everything, and everything in its place. For any reasonably complex endeavor—from running a household to running a software project—this system needs to be more than a single junk drawer or file folder.

 In software projects, there will be distinctions by phase, by domain or area of the system, and by perspective of the system (the "who, what, why, when, where, and how" distinctions). Layer on top of this an audit trail of the evolution of all of this information over time, and you can start to see the complexity emerge. It is useful to define the system and the expectations of the content for each specific project in advance, so that the holes in the information will be just as prominent as the information itself.

The system needs to be commonly understood. This prevents the proprietor of the system from getting bogged down. Although I know that everything in our kitchen has a place, for example, I don't always know where that place is. I sure know who to ask, however, much to her chagrin….

> Organization brings clarity, and clarity brings efficiency to project teams.
>
> Scrambling to clean up a software project, either when someone can't find the information needed or when an auditor is on the way, is rarely adequate for addressing the problem and does nothing to prevent the same scramble next time around.
>
> For any project, clarity on what information will be required and how it will be managed is a critical first step that should never be neglected.

Defined Approach or Work of Fantasy?

It has gotten to the point where I rarely bother to ask to look at the defined process in most organizations I work with.

 In most cases, it doesn't really exist, and in the shops where they have something captured, it is more often something they purchased or the figment of the author's imagination than something that reflects what happens on a day-to-day basis. Shouldn't a defined approach be used to bring new people up to speed, help in creating more credible estimates, support problem remediation, and help educate clients to the approach used by the group? Most attempts at capturing a defined approach are more "if-only" than "how-to" manuals.

Many process descriptions are written to describe what is believed to be a better approach to developing software than is being practiced now. Few companies ever make it to that higher ground. The problems that motivated the effort may have apparently gone away after a brief period, or that higher ground was just a bit too far out of reach to begin with. Far better to start by capturing what is happening now in an organization, so that you have a place from which to build. Chances are you will not be able to develop a complete picture that everyone agrees with, and the gaps themselves are valuable insights to leverage.

 Be pragmatic; start with the status quo.

A necessary accompaniment to a defined approach is the willpower to stay with that approach, or modify it if it is found to be wanting. This willpower unfortunately has to take the shape of a stick at times.

 If you are going to go to the trouble of defining an approach, it should be mandatory for everyone involved. If there are optional elements, there should be explicit descriptions of these options, as well as the steps needed to shore things up after the fact. A "suggested approach" is a waste of time for most groups. When push comes to shove, most people will not fall back on a defined approach unless they are appropriately incented to do so.

Remember, those who participate in defining the approach are more likely to follow it afterward.

Be firm; ensure that the organization is along for the ride.

The approach needs to hit the sweet spot of quality-based activities, and that will vary dramatically from project to project. For most organizations, that sweet spot is probably more than you are currently doing, but less than you would like to define. Beyond this point, there are actually diminishing returns for the project. It is not always true that if a little quality effort is good, then a lot of quality effort is better.

Although there is a clear cost of nonquality in the rework and uncertainty that scuttles so many projects, there is also a cost of quality, the effort required to perform the up-front activities, reviews, and tests that help avoid that rework. Too much quality and you may actually be paying more in the long run than you have to for projects that are not mission critical.

Certainly if we are developing a life-critical system, that sweet spot moves way over to a point with greater weight of process, as the cost of leaving issues in the system increases dramatically, but we aren't all in that boat. Be reasonable. Do only what is appropriate.

Make activities optional and they won't get done. The process becomes another work of fiction sitting on the shelves. Write it in a vacuum and few will buy into the approach. Make the process too heavy and with the resistance will be delays due to the effort spent applying the process. In any of these cases, the defined approach may as well have been written as though it were to take place on some distant planet. It is a work of fantasy.

Process Architecture

When building any large software system (and most smaller ones, too), it is generally accepted that there is value in the development of an architecture: identification of the major building blocks of the system and the mechanisms that need to be in place for the system to work as an efficient, cohesive unit.

There have been significant advances in the understanding of what works and what does not and in the construction of architectural patterns for reuse. Out of the study of software architecture has evolved a growing set of established mechanisms and protocols that can make the development of larger systems much more cost effective.

Generally, a software system expands along with the organization that builds it. The team may grow in size, the project may grow in duration and complexity, and the number of external relationships may grow. Although the software architecture can be developed to manage the growing application complexity, that notion is rarely extended to the approach used support the team that is building the system.

Just as elegant software architecture can make development of features on the project appear simple, a well-architected development process will tend to remain in the background to facilitate the effective interaction of the team.

Developers, designers, and testers are not handcuffed by the process, forced down paths of interaction that appear to be at odds with getting the job done (and that would invariably be undermined with shortcuts). Software architectures are built for the unique properties of each new software system being developed (built on a reasonable framework for efficiency), and the same should be said of process architectures.

A good process is developed with the combined intent of streamlining the work, addressing the challenges encountered in the past, ensuring that there is a reasonable audit trail, and supporting the development of a product that will meet the needs of the end user within the project constraints given. These different and conflicting views need to be balanced and combined together to solve the problem. No single perspective of what is important is sufficient for a comprehensive solution. Faced with particular development challenges, most organizations have a tendency to fix the point problem with their process, instead of stepping back and generalizing a more global, reusable solution.

 As with software systems, mechanisms that have shown to work well in the field are evolving for software processes, too. Although most organizations that are faced with communication challenges still tend to lean on documentation as a remedy, there are many reasons to suggest that this is one of the weaker solutions. Whiteboards facilitate open, immediate communication, but are less persistent. Databases are better at managing complex collaboration issues and lend themselves better to the management of information, but can be expensive to implement and are hardly immediate. Wikis are evolving to be an attractive alternative. There is not yet a global answer here, but we are clearly evolving beyond the stodgy document.

Who does the job of architecting a process in your organization? Generally, people with a broad range of experience in software development will take on the task of fixing things, much as we will fix our own plumbing leaks around the house. Unfortunately, the statistics show that many organizations aren't simply dealing with a leaky faucet. If the average project expends close to 40 percent of its time in rework and on-time delivery records and product quality are suffering, we have a situation more akin to a major flood, a task that few of us would attempt to repair without proper training. With limited training available in the area of process definition and management, real-world experience becomes critical.

Just as software architecture has evolved to a point where it would be ludicrous to develop a large system from scratch, both significant and minor process development activities can benefit from an understanding of the mechanisms and common elements that have evolved in the science of process development.

There is certainly no need to reinvent the wheel in this critical area of software development.

Reading the Fine Print for Packaged Methodologies

Quite often, as we decide it is time to get our developmental ducks in a row, we find a need to coordinate a collection of material that will form the basis of documentation. This is true both for our declared process and for the products that this process is intended to produce. A quick search will generate a huge number of candidate packages to use as a basis: standards-based packages from industry associations such as the Institute of Electrical and Electronics Engineers (IEEE), loose smatterings of random offerings provided from community-based Web sites, individual elements from locations hither and yon throughout the Internet, and comprehensive packages from many vendors.

There are pros and cons with each of these approaches to building a quality library. Here are some of the questions that should be swirling around in your head as you imagine what the fine print should look like for any of these approaches.

Who's behind this stuff? Although some of the brightest minds in the field are contributing to the knowledge base overall, there is no minimum standard for self-promotion of templates. Individual templates or checklists may offer some unique insights, but take nothing as guaranteed and use good judgment as you apply any information you find. Just because it comes from a book or the Internet, even from a well-revered Web site, that is no guarantee it is appropriate information for your needs.

Will this fit our culture? Just as with any tool, such as bug-tracking systems or project management software, packaged methodologies come as part (or all) of an assumed process, which may be agile and efficient or large and cumbersome. It should be relatively close to what you are doing now and for the most part support your current good practices. (Yes, every organization I've seen has at least some good practices that are worth focusing on and sustaining.) Most established organizations don't take kindly to major changes, and most new groups will likely have plenty of opinions about what the right approach should be. An external solution can serve to objectively mediate these different opinions, but in most cultures there will still be challenges to overcome.

What's the real motive? Is the source of this packaged methodology really trying to improve your effectiveness while collecting a reasonable remuneration, or are they trying to lock you into their approach, their tools, or their consulting. Is the methodology technology-centric (whether focused on a particular tool suite or not), quality-centric (focused on the definition and production of a well understood product), or team-centric (focused on maximizing the collaborative effectiveness of the group)? Do these motives align with yours?

How do the pieces fit together? In many approaches, the overall methodology has been defined and evolved over time to work well as a complete system, where the pieces complement and reinforce each other. Most comprehensive packages will eventually be tuned to fit together as a system, although there may be gaps and overlaps in version 1.0. If you mix and match from different sources, this should be one of your greatest concerns.

 How easy is the fit? The broad, all-encompassing methodologies usually started from what worked on a large project, and then grew over time to be more generally applicable across the industry, to a point where they cover all the bases but need to be dramatically tailored down to be reasonably useful for even large projects. Is there any guidance on how to make it practical for your needs, and how much will that guidance cost? Remember that for the best fit, the methodology needs to be tailored down for the organization and then tuned specifically for each project's needs. The more comprehensive the starting point, the more tailoring will be required.

What are the life cycle costs? If you are buying a product, how are the licenses structured, are there maintenance fees, and what will it cost to have someone come in and explain or help tailor this beast? On the other end of the spectrum, will you even be able to find the source of information for clarification if necessary?

Can we do it ourselves? There are plenty of reasons for tackling the challenges of creating your own defined methodology, with only light reliance on a packaged methodology:

- First and foremost, the team will embrace a methodology defined as a team for the needs of the team. Participation drives ownership and acceptance, and you can't buy that in a box anywhere.

- It is best to start small. Any wholesale change in approach will cause far greater culture shock than benefit for the group. The combined learning curves of many individual practices that comprise an overall methodology will be a major setback, one that some companies that I have worked with never did manage to recover from. Evolution as a gradual process has shown to work over millions of years.

- Grow organically. Methodology components (such as coding or design standards or review checklists) are best grown based on the internal findings of the group. Find a problem once, fix it. Find it twice, identify how it should be remedied in a standard fashion, and broadcast the news in a standard or checklist. They will become personal expressions of your best practices, rather than a generic set that will rarely apply to your situation.

- Play the field. Instead of locking into one source, learn from all that are available. Nobody has cornered the market on appropriate approaches for all software projects, and no one ever will. Take what works from wherever you can, and don't be afraid to mix and match if you have considered the ramifications. (Remember the notion of a cohesive system, discussed previously.) Remember the bottom line is improved predictability and effectiveness for your projects, not adherence to someone else's assumed approach. Best practices are only situationally applicable.

For all of these reasons, my leaning would be to take an internal approach to building up a defined methodology, at most using a broader overall methodology as a basis of defining the direction you are taking.

Don't take the sales pitch at face value; as with anything, you need to understand what you are getting yourself into. Consider what the fine print would look like if it were available.

Is This a Process Project?

There are always more things to get done in a business than there are hours in a day: weed through the spam to deal with the real e-mail, answer the phones, handle the daily backup and the monthly finances and the billing and receivables and status reports. Somewhere in there is the task of getting your product out the door.

Visit most mid-sized companies, and there will often be Gantt charts on a wall describing the planned approach for getting that product out the door (some, surprisingly, are even up-to-date). Almost every company recognizes the value in reduced risk, better coordination, and efficiency that project management brings to development of a product that you can see, touch, or execute, but many fewer extend this notion as far as they should.

A project isn't just Gantt charts and status reports and documentation, although larger, critical projects can benefit from these and other tools. A project is a managed approach to making a change to the world around us. The result of a project, the product, can often be something that is less tangible than an automobile or a new fence or a software application, but it is still something new that exists as a result of the activities performed to create it.

In the genesis of any organization, and in the renaissance of many companies, a very important product created is the process used for producing the traditional projects of that organization.

Whether it is required because the team is being ramped up for the first time or because the existing approach is clearly not functioning in the current environment, the importance of getting a reasonable process in place is enormous. Process improvement needs to be more than picking a few pet things to do differently, and less than taking an encyclopedic industry methodology and calling it your own.

For a development approach to be effective, it needs to be defined, disseminated, used, managed, measured, and evolved over time. It needs to fit the culture of the organization, address the shortcomings and leverage the strengths, and become institutionalized. When people say, "That's the way we do things around here," they should be talking about the intended approach rather than the shortcuts around it. The likelihood of getting this right with an informal approach is slim.

The process of creating or refining a development process is not new. Reasonable implementations and common pitfalls are well known. Taking on too much change, tackling items with little leverage, mandating change to a group that has not participated in the refinements and failing to build in measurements to validate progress can often lead to disappointment.

Next time you find yourself about to do "a bunch of stuff," especially in the area of defining how you are going to go about your core business, step back and determine whether that stuff is worthy of packaging into a project, with its clearer vision and expectations, planned approach, and better controls, particularly if it is a project to define a reasonable approach for your software projects.

You may be glad you did.

Optimizing for Speed

In the software development world, schedule constraints are the norm, whether valid or artificially generated. It makes absolute business sense to strive to get your tax software out in time for the tax season, or your game software out for the holiday buying rush.

 Throwing artificial time constraints at the team because someone arbitrarily agreed to a date without understanding the ramifications, however, is dangerous business practice. Compressing the schedule simply as a means to get the team to work faster is inexcusable.

Artificial Speed

Valid or not, schedule pressures generally drive the team to push for speed. Many teams seek speed by trying to eliminate all of those perceived "overhead" activities, such as analysis, design, and test. If you are not producing code, you are not building the product, right? You might have seen the cartoon where the manager tells his team, "You guys keep coding, I'll go and find out what the customer wants."

Quickly diving into the construction of a project without adequate planning may give the illusion that progress is being made, but the result is usually a great deal of rework to satisfy the client's real need, or worse yet, a disgruntled client that simply walks away.

Optimizing for speed is not rushing headlong into coding. It is planning enough to be sure that your efforts are pointed in the right direction.

Project managers focus on the planning and tracking of the project, but the planning often consists of constructing a Gantt chart that has all the known activities on it, squeezed in such a way that it fits within the schedule constraints handed to the team. The targets win out over the technical estimates. The original schedule either falls woefully out of relevance early in the project or the tasks are claimed to be complete, only to reveal their true state when the team tries to integrate what they have. This is usually so late in the schedule that there are few options for remediation available to them.

Optimizing for speed is not trying to cram all your work into the time you have been allotted. It is recognizing how long your activities can be expected to take, including the uncertainty in these estimates, and reasonably reconciling this information against the constraints. Deferring scope, adding time or resources, or explicitly relaxing the quality are all options for getting done on time.

Simply hoping you will make it is not.

True speed will only come with clarity. All the stakeholders need to have a common understanding of what needs to be accomplished, and why. The best way to be fast is to spend the time up front to gain that common understanding, reducing the downstream rework that is caused because expectations have not been met somewhere along the way. To have that common understanding, the unknowns need to be identified early in the project and attacked ruthlessly. Don't plunge headlong into coding unless it is recognized as a prototyping exercise focused on resolving a specific question.

One of the original Darwin Award winners was a fellow who met his demise after strapping a jet engine to the roof of his car. For a fleeting moment, he attained a great deal of speed, but he failed to plan out his actions well enough to recognize the threat of that mountainside in the distance. Just as in many software projects, I'm sure he had an exhilarating ride while it lasted, although few would suggest that his project was successful.

> Useful speed in software projects is gained through a methodical refinement of the information available, not through foolhardy sprints into the unknown.

Making Training Work

It is an unfortunate truism in the software industry that best practices represent tangible effort that needs to be taken into account and scheduled, typically at the early stages of a project. When these additional "overhead activities" are weighed against blind optimism and lack of awareness of the true costs of ineffectiveness, most companies tend to repeatedly fall back to code-and-fix software development. Even if the new practices are scheduled in, they are quickly dropped at the first sign of trouble.

A Good Mix for Training

In all the public training sessions I have provided (and in the majority of the onsite courses, too), I think that there has been less value provided at the end of the day than there could have been. Although feedback indicated that the material and instruction was up to snuff, my concern stems from the wrong mix of people attending the sessions.

Invariably, the courses are filled with people who can benefit from awareness and application of best practices. They contribute and participate freely and usually leave the session filled with enthusiasm to head back to their workplace and really make a positive difference. Unfortunately, the attendees are not the ones who need to appreciate the value of the application of best practices for the organization. Senior management needs to be involved, too.

Sometimes, particularly in onsite offerings, all the right people are in attendance: both the people who will be doing the things recommended in the training and the people who need to understand the additional value so that they can allow it to happen.

What often happens, however, is that management just can't seem to find the time to commit to the entire training session. They are too busy, focusing on the urgent rather than the important. With too much on their plates, they haven't got time to learn the value of best practices. They have fires to fight, and often excuse themselves from the session very early.

My view is that this is really a chicken-and-egg situation. They are fighting fires *because* of their lack of appreciation of the value of these practices. Most managers would benefit in improving their grasp of the fundamentals.

When the attendees emerge from training, full of vim and vigor and ready to change the world, they'll all too often hit a wall of existing work. Without communicating the value in change, there will be insurmountable barriers that prevent the introduction beneficial activities.

Most training sessions are doomed from the outset without the proper people in attendance. At best, the training will provide a deeper understanding of what is destined to be theory, a nice certificate, and another binder for the bookshelf. At worst, training without commitment can foster resentment driven by the deeper understanding of the gap between theory and practice.

For training to really impact your organization, make sure that there is the right mix of attendees: both those who will be doing things differently and those who need to appreciate the value in change so that they can allow it to even occur.

When Things Go Wrong

Despite everyone's best efforts, no matter how much diligence has been applied to the planning process, no matter how consistently you track against the plan and stay on course, things will sometimes go wrong on your projects.

The problem might be a new technology that doesn't live up to expectations, an external resource that fails to deliver on time, an internal problem of some kind, or something else entirely. Whatever the cause, be careful to avoid the usual knee-jerk approach of slapping a bandage on the problem and forging ahead.

The first thing to do, of course, is to recognize that actually knowing about the problem is indeed a good thing. Although you could probably plod along for quite a while ignorant of the problems that exist, acting like an ostrich will just get you deeper in trouble in the long run.

Make sure that the team knows you want to hear the bad news as soon as possible, and try to build your reporting system so that the deviations and problems stand out for attention. Avoid the same old status reports that clutter your inbox and that don't really say anything important. If you are in a situation in which you could copy last week's status report into this week's status report and nobody would notice, you know what I mean.

Usually, when a problem arises on a project, the first symptom that appears is just that: only the first symptom. It is important to dig deeper to collect enough information to act appropriately. Seek out the root causes to understand the true nature of the problem and its ramifications. Be sure that awareness of the problem is spread to all those stakeholders who need to know. Only then can the team use their collective experience and knowledge to solve the problem appropriately.

A problem is not really solved until you can clearly explain what caused it to occur, what you have done to correct it, and prevent it from happening again. A problem that has mysteriously gone away is actually still around. Chances are that it will reappear later, probably at a very inopportune time. Problems don't just go away on their own.

 Finally, at the end of the project when you run your retrospective (you do run retrospectives, don't you?), look back on all the problems that you have had to overcome on your project. There is a strong chance that you will see some trends that have developed, which are likely to point to some systemic challenges that you can't see from a single problem. It might be a specific area of the system that is particularly troublesome, too many design problems that don't manifest themselves until much later, or a developer who tends to cut too many corners a little too often (or a project manager who tends to accept too many "bandages"). If you take steps to find and correct the systemic issues at this point, you won't be forced to live them again in your next project cycle.

It is not how the team performs when all is going according to plan, but rather how the team pulls together to manage the crises that will inevitably arise that will make or break a project.

Analysis of our mistakes provides the best insights into how we should evolve our development process.

But We Aren't That Big!

At what point does it make sense to sit down and capture the approach you take for doing things around the office?

A frightening number of companies have at best a superficial description of their approach to developing software, often not even exposed to the entire team, and rarely reflecting what is actually done when push comes to shove to get software out the door. This description is usually put together after a project catastrophe, loosely based on some published best practices that might have worked elsewhere. Even if they are followed for a few weeks, there is rarely any focus on keeping them current or mandating their usage.

 A number of drivers indicate that it is never too early to start capturing the intended approach for developing software, or for that matter, any activity that is done repetitively around the office.

Even for an individual, making this information persistent can be critical. Motivations for actions will change over time, and it is easy to fall into the situation where you wonder, "what the heck was I thinking back then?"

How many times have you gone back to something that you started six months ago to discover you just couldn't figure out where you left off or why you had done what you did? A single person, over time, can exhibit many of the same communication dysfunctions as a larger team.

A good way to treat this information is as journal entries that are explicitly focused on how you do your work, as opposed to what work you are doing. Reflecting on this over time is a critical component for improvement. Not all of it will be relevant, but you can be sure that some of it will be a valuable reference, more than worth the time spent to produce it. The act of producing the material itself can be valuable, because it forces you to think through your actions before you start.

As the team grows from one to more than one, we encounter the first step-function in the importance of a defined approach. Without a shared understanding of how software is to be done, or even what *done* really means, expectations are sure to be missed.

Although a team of two can often get along with reasonable communication and little captured knowledge, it can also be a recipe for disaster. The differences in perspective that usually required time to manifest themselves for individuals can now occur instantaneously with two people, and often does. For events that impact more than one person and which will be done repeatedly, settle on the approach explicitly, up front, now.

One of the key challenges of growth is the cost of scalability for the team. With the knowledge that a common approach is critical, if it is not clearly defined, it is at best left to existing team members to train up the new team members, and at worst left to the new team members to learn from their mistakes. These mistakes will cost you twice: once when the mistake is made; and again as even more time from the group is consumed to shore up the communications, often at a point where the time required comes at a significant premium.

If initial steps were not taken to begin capturing the intent for development when the team was very small (even a team of one), there is a good chance that when you realize the need for fixing things, the task of capturing the intent is overwhelming. With deadlines looming and already crazy hours, nobody believes they can afford the time to stop what they are doing to define some processes. There is more inertia with a larger team, which prevents capturing the approach at all.

One of the reasons it appears to be a daunting task is the perception that the entire approach needs to be captured in a single monolithic event. If you prioritize the effort to focus on repetitive events that have the broadest impact, you will simplify the effort and reap huge returns.

In software development, think of change control and release management as two prime candidates.

It is never too early to settle on an appropriate approach for how you do things, especially if you are doing these things repeatedly.

Structured Debate

In the halls and offices of many organizations, a great deal of misdirected debate is taking place.

This project has to be agile. That requirements tool trumps this one. Sometimes passionate discussions, but misdirected just the same.

All the time spent debating which approach to use, which methodology to follow, which tool to purchase, is time away from focusing on the real task: completing the project that meets the client's needs.

There is an appropriate time to discuss these issues, but too many shops continue this discussion for far too long. We're too often deciding whether to use a hammer or a chisel. Choosing between Makita and DeWalt power tools, we're not getting our project done.

Heated methodology debates are a sure sign that the participants have gained just enough knowledge to be dangerous. There is an awareness of the value in the tools, but still insufficient consciousness of the cost of the ongoing methodology debate itself. We need to be careful to recognize that with methodologies, as in most other areas, perfection is the enemy of sufficiency.

The healthiest debate we can have on a project, and the debate that should consume the lion's share of the time, is debate that allows us to provide the best possible solution for the client. Debating scope, architecture, and implementation alternatives will lead to a refined product, and that is what we are here for. Debating the approach for too long is akin to the "angels on the head of a pin" discussion. We ourselves become pinheads.

Don't get me wrong. Methodologies and tools are important. They are so important that there should be time devoted to the beginning of every project where they are selected in a manner that allows us to focus on the appropriate debates for the majority of the project.

Indeed, this is the major benefit from the selection of the appropriate approach. Strong selection provides structure around our efforts so that our tasks are pointed in the right direction. Our approach should be put in place, then silently, invisibly do its job. If there is a conscious ongoing effort to determine the appropriate approach, or to remember how to use a tool, there remains a need to further standardize, familiarize, and institutionalize these elements.

Selected appropriately at the onset of a project and refined as required throughout, a reasonable methodology will serve to help the team ensure they understand the breadth of issues to consider, provide appropriate insight into progress, and facilitate the creation and cross-referencing of reasonable project artifacts along the way.

Just as it is safe to say that there is rarely one right tool for a specific woodworking job, and no tool works for all woodworking jobs, the same holds true for approaches to software projects. We need to look at the project we are dealing with today, and select the appropriate tools for the job. Remember that this is something you will likely never hear from a tool or methodology vendor.

Some tools have shown to be consistently valuable and will be used on almost any project. We need to become effortlessly fluid with these standard approaches, and the best way to do so is to continuously use them. Determining the vision and specifying scope should not require remedial clarification of the approach on any project. The suggestion that you can get by without doing these things should be closely scrutinized.

Some tools are useful for unique situations that occur rarely. These are essentially the custom jigs. We need to be flexible enough to recognize when they are needed and be capable of adapting accordingly. Scripting languages and esoteric modeling approaches can serve to get us out of the occasional jam.

We need to continuously hone our skills with the tools we know and use regularly, and we need to continuously seek to learn new techniques that could serve us well in the future, but we cannot let this effort get in the way of our prime objective: to best address our client's needs.

Done right, this effort facilitates our completing the job, by putting appropriate structure around our debates.

Summary

Regardless of the team's size, there is value in stepping back and figuring out the approach you will use to get the job done. For critical projects or highly repetitive activities, the value of clarifying and optimizing the defined approach becomes much higher.

In doing this, you will channel your time to focus more appropriately on providing the most effective solution for your customer.

How Is This Relevant?

Focus on the solution. Is there a lot of debate in your organization about the process that should be followed? Are there times when mistakes have been made because of an inconsistent or incomplete approach? Is this consuming time that would be better spent on providing a good solution to the customer?

A well-defined approach. Does your team follow a commonly understood approach? Is it practical? Has it been structured to accommodate each specific project? Can it be easily introduced to new members of the team?

CHAPTER THIRTEEN

Coordination

Even if we were to construct the perfectly defined process, coordinating the day-to-day activities of the entire team involves a great deal of effort. No predefined process can accommodate the nuances of discovery and change on a project, and we need to be careful to respect the need for ensuring that the team is working smoothly and efficiently.

In this chapter, we explore some of the mechanisms that we can apply to coordinate our teams, dealing with detailed issues while keeping an eye on the overall objectives.

Clearing Roadblocks, or Blocking Clear Roads?

Project managers (and their executive above them) come in all shapes and sizes, work in many different ways, and vary significantly in their success rates. I've come to understand that one of the best paths to take as a leader is to work tirelessly for your staff, no matter what level you're at. You need to be clearing roadblocks for your team to be effective.

 The best leaders I have worked with are those who embrace the role of facilitator rather than director. They get the team together to make sure that everyone is on the same page from the beginning, and generally listen more than they talk (you know...two ears, one mouth). They work throughout the project to maintain this common understanding, and remove all roadblocks as soon as possible—so that the team can continue to make progress expediently.

Although few project managers consciously try to undermine their staff, the blocks often seem to get thrown up just the same.

 Many leaders feel it is important to focus on the details. Indeed, if the leader has risen through the technical ranks, the details are usually where he is more comfortable. It is unlikely, however, that the leader was originally scheduled to deal with those details. While diving back down during a crisis, there is nobody minding the helm. In being displaced, the original owner of those details has lost confidence and credibility.

Project managers can unintentionally disrupt the team by injecting seemingly random change. Although actions often have good intentions, they can be catastrophic to team morale, and credibility. Whether it is an apparently simple promise to a client without checking in with the team, or new features thrown into the fray as they come up, changes will dislodge people from their anticipated path forward. Instead of clearing the way, roadblocks are often raised by managers as quickly as the team can get around them.

The only good promise to a client is "I'll get back to you with the team's decision."

If you are not doing everything in your power to prevent disruption and allow your team to get their planned tasks done by clearing roadblocks, you probably have room for improvement as a leader.

Managing with an Open Book

There are a myriad ways to categorize project managers and the approaches they use. Whether they use recent innovations such as critical chain or agile approaches or tend toward more established management approaches, whether they live and die by the Gantt chart or carry their information in a spreadsheet or the back of the envelope, whether they drill down and manage by the numbers or are more touchy-feely about their projects, you will find successful and not-so-successful project managers of all flavors.

Based on what I have seen, there does appear to be one differentiator that effectively distinguishes between those who are likely to bring a project home successfully and those who are more likely to struggle. Project managers who hold their cards close to their chest tend to be the ones who live in crisis mode, because key information becomes available to team members only after problems start. Those who drive their projects with an open book tend to fare much better.

This assumes that success is clearly defined, of course. It is much easier to artificially declare success after the fact if expectations have not been clearly set.

Communication is the primary key for success, and the project manager is the gatekeeper of information for the project. Information is collected here to form a current snapshot of project status. It is then massaged into a form that is presented further up the chain to the project stakeholders, internal and external. On large teams, there needs to be some sorting, culling, and simplification of the information to avoid a combinatorial explosion, and the project manager is a natural point to do so.

How communication is handled determines the path a project will take. This point could become a bottleneck where information is closely guarded (or worse, obfuscated), or it could become an efficient hub of current and relevant information for all participants. The project manager can act as the strong central hub for clearly disseminating information, or can act as the weak link that can virtually guarantee disappointing results.

 With an open-book approach, the opportunity for surprises to pop up and derail the expected path to completion diminishes significantly. Some managers would believe that it's best to keep people on the team aware only of the information required for their small contribution to the project. Additional information would cloud their focus, distract them from their task.

This couldn't be further from the truth, unless of course your project team is a collection of gerbils being fed food pellets and trained to run on a treadmill. In projects with human participants, we all share a hunger to know what is going on. Awareness is much more valuable and important to us than the prison of withheld information.

A wise old man once told me, "We all have our own book." Our collection of experiences and knowledge, combined with current information, blends to form our own perspectives and drive our actions. Although we cannot control many of the experiences of the team (indeed the variety of past experience can be a huge advantaged if harnessed), we can grow the team's knowledge base.

> As a project manager, providing an open book of current information available is the best thing we can do to allow the entire team to attack the project.
>
> As we all bring our own books to bear on the issues presented in the project, we create a formidable library of resources for success.

A Coordinated Effort

I recently had the pleasure to participate in an incredible example of teamwork and project success, with a group that had just met, many with no experience in the domain.

This was something I had wanted to do for some time. I finally took the plunge (literally) and signed up for a week-long ocean-kayaking excursion with Outward Bound. (Yes, this is an endorsement.)

There were 12 students from a wide range of backgrounds, from across North America. With two guides, we set out from Tofino with the gear and food we would need for five days on the ocean. For those in the group who had never been in a kayak before, this step was indeed a big one.

The guides provided some initial support, but only enough to ensure that we were reasonably safe and adequately prepared. A practice wet exit demonstrated what we were up against with the Pacific Ocean. We gained enough confidence to help us understand we could get out of the kayak when we had to (and enough cold to convince us that we would be more comfortable staying upright during the trip).

What the guides did from that point was wonderful. Instead of directing us during the week, they just suggested final destination for the trip that the group could agree to. From that point on, they merely acted as technical resources for the group as required. Weather reports from their radio and spot training on different techniques when desired were their major contributions.

All decisions—where to head toward for the day, what to eat, and where to stop for meals and bio-breaks—were group decisions, based on all the information available. We considered our progress against our overall objective, the current and forecast state of the water and the weather that day, the obstacles in our path, and the condition of each individual in the group. We consciously worked to ensure that all had a voice in these decisions. We were all free to offer up suggestions for debate at all times. There were times of disagreement, but we always resolved these differences so that we could forge ahead as a cohesive group.

For each stage of the journey, we identified a lead who would make tactical decisions such as when to rest, when to cross open water, and what formation we should take. More often than not, even these decisions were made on a consensual basis. At all times, we had agreement on the day's objective, as well as a couple of contingency plans should something come up. To a person, if the situation arose where it did not make sense to continue to work toward our goal, we adjusted our overall plan accordingly.

After a decision had been made, the group worked together to efficiently get the job done. People fell naturally into roles in which they could contribute, based on strengths, comfort levels, or interest in trying something new.

We had setbacks along the way. After making it to a certain point toward our destination with time to spare (finishing off the day's ride in significant swells), the weather forecast indicated gale-force winds for the next day. With one of our overall guiding principles being group safety, we decided to backtrack the next day and take a leeward route that would add another 12 nautical miles to our journey, while retaining our overall objective. Even with this backtrack, we had a couple of spills that we had to deal with before we got to calmer waters.

By that time, after a few days of cold water and damp conditions, our overall destination at Hot Springs Cove (on Vancouver Island) was something we definitely did not want to miss. We forged ahead, and as it turns out, the campsite that we otherwise would have missed became one of the highlights of the trip.

Overall, 14 people with a wide range of experience accomplished more than most of us expected, and any setbacks we had were really blessings in disguise. There were no Gantt charts, no dogmatic status reports, no decisions handed down to the group, no targets that were clearly not achievable. We were all clear on the goal. We made tactical and strategic decisions in a collaborative fashion based on a wealth of current information. We pulled together when we had to, and still let individuals stretch themselves when the opportunity arose. We worked hard and enjoyed ourselves immensely, and were all fully engaged participants. Although we didn't completely gel as a mature team in that brief period, we did have instances of storming that we managed well.

It's safe to say that we all grew during the trip. With the initial part of the week filled with trepidation, by the end I wanted to stay out there, and my confidence on the water had increased tremendously.

Despite everyone in the group coming away with very different experiences, we pulled together and all made it to the hot springs as a team, making the water that much more satisfying to bask in.

Merely an Employee?

I subscribe to a number of daily snippets from a variety of sources, and something recently caught my eye. In a Fast Company article,[1] a head-hunter made this comment: "Candidates who think of themselves as employees immediately tip the scales of power."

This statement resonated with me, but upon reading the article, I was disappointed to see that it had taken a direction I hadn't anticipated. The tipping of the scales of power suggested was that during the hiring process, if you already consider yourself to be more than merely a candidate, you can manage the hiring process differently. You can be more proactive in the interplay, you can demonstrate your ability to participate in solving the company's problems, instead of just answering the interviewer's questions as you believe they should be.

Although I agree with this approach in the hiring process (as a starting point), I wish the article had gone much further, to discuss the scales of power after you are actually part of the organization. At this point, the scales of power flip back in the other direction. Instead of thinking of yourself as "already an employee" during the hiring process, you need to think of yourself as "not merely an employee" after you are in the door.

 Thinking of yourself as merely an employee does indeed tip the scales of power, but in the wrong direction—away from you. Regardless of the compensation model you are working under, regardless of whether your title starts with a capital *C*, there is value in thinking of yourself as having a strong stake in the success of the business.

If you behave as merely an employee, there is at least an implicit, and often an explicit, relinquishing of control and influence in how the company behaves. The rules that have been established prior to your arrival, documented or not, are handed to you as gospel. You are placed in your appropriate spot in the hierarchy, and are rarely involved in the process of strategic decision making. The roles of "employee" and "leader" don't have a great deal of overlap in most people's minds.

As an employee, you aren't hassled with many difficult decisions, but you are also stuck with the consequences of the decisions of others. Yuk.

 You can gain some distinct advantages, however, by thinking more as an active participant in the organization. Even if your company doesn't offer employee share options, there is still a great deal of value to you to help make the company's success a reality.

 At the very least, your involvement will provide you with some insight that will clarify the rationale behind some of the business decisions. By exerting influence in the business's behavior, you have the opportunity to leverage your viewpoint through the group and drastically magnify its impact. Your efforts will be recognized, a necessity if you have anything that resembles career aspirations within the team.

Some suggest that you have a choice of either working to live or living to work. By becoming a more active participant and not merely an employee, you gain the opportunity to structure your work environment to be much more pleasant and productive.

Investing in the "living to work" side of the equation will spill over and dramatically improve your ability to live well outside of work. When you leave the decision making to others and make no effort to invest in your future, you have no reason to complain about the results.

Checking Out, Checking In

Minimizing the element of surprise on software projects is always a good thing. At all levels of the organization, surprise and redirection are pains that can have devastating results.

For the individual, having your priorities constantly shuffled by management can be demoralizing. There's nothing more frustrating than setting yourself up to work on the latest build of software only to find that it is in worse shape than what you migrated from. For the project, a constantly changing target will be difficult to meet, and an environment in which the team is busy with unanticipated rework becomes a ball and chain, making it even more challenging to reach your goals. For the organization, constant unanticipated change makes it difficult to plan delivery and meet expectations. Future projects are undermined, as individuals don't become available as originally expected.

Two primary touch points in software projects allow you to minimize these surprises: control of what you are going to do, and control of what you have done. These are the key pillars in a solid configuration and change management approach. From the perspective of developing code, the points correspond to the checking out and checking in of a source file, but the concepts can and should be extended to include anything that is done or produced on a project.

Checking out, or understanding what you are going to do, not only implies that there is an initial understanding of the intent, the scope, and the schedule, but that changes to this understanding are being managed throughout the project. All potential changes to this understanding should be managed in a common pool, whether it is change due to new feature requests, defects that have been uncovered, or just differences between what was scheduled and the actual time required to complete a task. Weigh all possible changes against the risk associated with taking them on, and be sure to set expectations as to what *completion* means for each activity.

At the other end of the pendulum is *checking in.* This is confirming that what was intended to be done was actually completed. Without this check, you are quite likely to run into the 90 percent done syndrome, as the avalanche of artificial completions comes crashing when you try to get the product to actually hold together around integration time. Try to maintain a culture in which everyone strives to keep a clean, functional development environment. As disruptive changes are added to the system, schedule and coordinate their incorporation so as to minimize the pain. Remember, too, that anything produced on a project can be subject to confirmation that it has been done correctly. A specification can be tested as rigorously as a piece of functional code, although in a different manner.

 As with everything software development related, communication is critical. Having the controls in place at both ends is a good start, but often you can run into perceived problems because the rationales are not clear for the decisions that have been made. If there is a known reason for changing someone's planned activities, that person is much more likely to accept the change, even embrace the change as being valuable for the project. If no reasonable rationale can be given for a change, this in itself becomes a form of communication.

Building in the proper checks at both ends of any change is critical to reduce surprises. Communication of the change and its rationale to all affected further reduces any remaining pain that may be lingering.

Attitudes Around Documentation

It never ceases to amaze me that people in software development have an almost religious aversion to documentation—anything from "we don't have time for that stuff" to "we got our documentation over with, now we can get on with the project" and everything in between.

 If the primary driver for success in the collaborative game of software development is communication, why do we all loathe documentation?

A number of dysfunctional attitudes around documentation contribute to its bad reputation. At the highest level, documentation is often identified as a separate overhead on the project. I have seen Gantt charts with "Documentation" tasks split out from other activities on projects, sometimes near the beginning of the project where it would have a chance of adding value, but often at the end of the project. The product is complete, now we need to get the documentation out of the way because it is a contractual obligation.

Where is the value-added activity in this?

In well-run meetings, the minutes capture the agreement of decisions that have been made and what action items will carry over from the meeting. Similarly, documentation on well-run projects capture the information that needs to be around for the long term so that it is available to everyone, and used by everyone.

 Documentation should simply be the minutes of the collaborations that took place throughout the project. A requirements specification should not be written by an individual and then given to the group. It should capture the common understanding, gained through discussions, research, and consensus of what the product needs to do. A project schedule should be the most reasonable agreed upon path to completion, rather than a network constructed by someone with a copy of Microsoft Project, and fleshed out with estimates that suggest all tasks will be completed before the target date. If constructed by an individual or small group without overall investment of effort from all stakeholders, any document is doomed to be ignored and fall out of date as soon as it is published. There's no shared ownership and commitment.

The author needs to become the coordinator and editor.

Similarly, if you do get to a point where you have created a massive document of some sort, be careful to make sure that people can agree to the content at the detailed level. There is nothing like the false sense of security you get in having a signoff party so that a dozen people can sign a 500-page document that they could not possibly have absorbed. Although you might have formally achieved an important milestone on your project, there is little assurance that you have a common understanding moving forward. Documentation needs to be more than empty promise.

People often push back on documentation because of the concern that the effort of building it will not pay back. This is often based on the narrow perception of the utility of the documentation and the assumed high degree of formality required. Capturing the intent for an individual to do something such as the migration of a database schema, for example, may take as long as the migration itself. However, this documentation also facilitates reasonable planning, independent early validation of the intent, and verification of the results, coordinating the overall effort and saving time overall.

If information is needed over the entire life of the project, documentation that is more formal may be warranted. Be careful to not force the same formality in all cases. The results of a whiteboard-based design review can be captured with a digital camera, literal back-of-the-envelope calculations can be scanned in, and e-mail threads can be dragged into a project folder. It doesn't have to be pretty, just retrievable and managed.

 If it is retrievable, it also needs to be used as a basis for future decisions. In many places, the culture is such that even if documents exist, there is little rigor in their use. They are treated more as recommendations or suggestions rather than binding information. People at all levels need to understand the importance of the documentation, not just that the documentation is available. Changes to that common understanding need to be managed well so that the information doesn't fall out of date.

Documentation is not evil. It is a necessity that for most software projects is managed poorly. It can be thought of as the practical persisting of a common understanding that has been achieved through collaboration, used to facilitate future work toward our common goals.

If you are not following this approach, stop wasting your time with documentation. You will probably need the time later to clean up the mess you have on your hands.

Lost in Translation

I was recently driving an online training session, with more than my fair share of challenges.

For those of you who have never run online training, from the instructor's perspective it is a little like being the Wizard of Oz. Remember the scene where Dorothy and the others finally manage to get in to see the Wizard, and Toto pulls back the curtain to reveal someone frantically pushing buttons, swinging levers? "Never mind that man behind the curtain," the Wizard cries out. To make the experience engaging for the students, the instructor has to monitor a range of different indicators, advance slides and use pointers or reveals to show where we are, watch for people with their hands up, respond to private chats, and talk through the presentation. This is a simplification of the challenge, but you can probably see where I am coming from.

In this particular course, we had already made it past some hiccups regarding the start time and the version of the online environment we should be using, and were only into the first session. I needed to know how many people were dialed into the phone bridge so that I could arrange breakouts for an upcoming exercise. I had a private chat window open with the support person for the training; I asked him, "Any way of determining how many people are on the phone line?"

The response: "Yes, you can do that."

Great! Here I am juggling more than a handful of students in the middle of the session, flipping levers and pushing buttons, and I am told that what I want to do is possible. Give me the phone sequence to press, or do it yourself and give me the answer, but don't just tell me that it is possible! Looking back, the response was reasonable given a literal parsing of my question, but it certainly did not meet my expectations.

The support for this company's online training had recently been outsourced, and there were still some kinks to be worked out of the transition.

We made it through the session, but I decided to minimize my expectations on the technology and support and focus on delivering a reasonable experience to the group primarily through discussion. Fewer bells and whistles than the Great and Mighty Oz might conjure, but the important points were delivered.

We Can't Easily Outsource Everything

In the book *The World is Flat,*[2] the author suggests that the convergence of technologies in the past decade have brought us to the point where anything can be done anywhere in the world. The lowering of trade and political barriers and the "digital revolution" has given everyone the opportunity to be as connected as they want. He highlights the influence of China and India on the global supply chain, and this is something that we are all seeing in the software domain. The author weaves a very compelling story, but I believe this oversimplification for the masses is hurting us.

Apparently, most of those who take their taxes to an outside company to be done actually have their taxes done in India. Often when we call for customer support, we expect someone to ask us questions from a script and walk through a flowchart based on our responses. More often than not, we can detect an accent, and there is a good chance that it is the wee hours of the morning where that person lives. For these well-structured interactions, either carefully scripted like first-level phone support or financially precise given the business rules of tax law, it only makes sense to do the work where it is most cost-effective.

For the challenges associated with real-time event logistics, or even worse, the novel innovation and creation of a software product, the world is not so flat as we would be led to believe. Basic fluency in the English language is a long way from a shared understanding of where the project needs to go, and we need to go well beyond Berlitz to ensure that we are all on the same page. Cultural differences are very real and very significant.

 In software development, most organizations are very weak in building a reasonable requirements spec for internal use. Confusion, misinterpretation, and disagreements are the order of the day. How can we expect to take this same weak basis for a product and send it halfway around the world and expect success while paying perhaps 40 percent the going rate for resources? There have been too many instances of higher costs, lower quality, and overall client dissatisfaction to turn a blind eye to the challenges.

 I don't know of a company that has succeeded in the offshore outsourcing model without a significant investment in management oversight, acclimatization to culture differences, and sensitivity to linguistic nuances. It is not simply a matter of passing the work out to the lowest bidder. The cost-savings argument has weakened, and we need to recognize other areas of value if we are to reap the benefits of outsourcing. Arguments could be more reasonably made for leveraging external expertise or managing demand fluctuations for our resources.

 The world is flattening, to be sure, but we have to be careful to manage the speed bumps we encounter along the way.

Balance with a Human Touch

In early 1992, Robert Kaplan and David Norton introduced the Balanced Scorecard as a means of identifying important corporate performance measures for an organization.[3] Since that time, the Balanced Scorecard has gained great support across many industries, an indication that the approach indeed provides improved insight.

In a nutshell, the Balanced Scorecard takes a sound approach to building a metrics program one step further, by ensuring that you cover the broad areas of financial, customer, internal business, and innovation and learning perspectives as you identify your goals, measures, and initiatives—an essential improvement over most narrowly focused approaches, where the tendency is to weigh heavily on the financial side for measures. One key element to note is that all areas are inexorably linked together, and analysis of the correlation between the areas helps you gain that sense of balance that is intended. In a Balanced Scorecard, a healthy bottom line is insufficient for success.

I have found in implementing this approach that there can be a tendency to give short shrift to the internal, employee side of the balancing act. Of the published implementations that I have seen, even the internal business and innovation and learning elements explicitly focus on measures and initiatives that are geared directly toward corporate performance, instead of addressing the human condition within the organization.

Software development is an intensely human endeavor, as I expect it will be for some time in the future. In most environments, it cannot be reduced and measured in the same manner as a production line or manufacturing facility. Motivation is a huge driver for productivity, which in turn ties to business performance. To neglect this factor is to severely cripple your ability to succeed strategically. Low morale will result in decreased performance and high turnover, and driving a team hard for tactical gains is not a strong strategic approach.

We've all seen organizations that treat their employees as expendable resources. Although they might reach a local peak in performance that is rarely sustainable, they will never attain industry-wide excellence.

 With this in mind, I would add an explicit fifth element to more reasonably balance my scorecard: internal employees.

Explicitly focusing on factors such as reasonable compensation and benefits, adequate working conditions, and appropriate autonomy and visibility will help to set the bar high for the management team. This will also balance against the traditional measures of success for the organization. It will demonstrate to the employees that there is a reasonable focus in their well-being as part of the overall vision, which will improve overall organizational effectiveness. It can also temper the employee's zeal to turn the organization into a country-club environment (there is no shortage of organizations that had elaborate lounges with leather sofas, beer fridges, and game consoles that do not exist today) by adequately balancing their needs against the overall needs of the organization.

Manage with a balanced business focus that includes reasonable respect for the human side of the equation.

Retaining the Context

 Many organizations I have worked with generally seem to have satisfied (or at least tolerant) customers, while there remains a lot of bickering and infighting internally between teams. Some people in these companies would say, however, that if the customer is happy, isn't that all that really matters?

I think not.

There are a number of dimensions to look at to determine whether a company is successful. A post hoc justification that things are fine because you have a reasonable share of the market and customers are not running away is extremely shortsighted. Recall that the Balanced Scorecard measures organizational performance in four separate categories: financial, customer, internal business, and innovation and learning. Although the customer may be happy, you can easily be suffering miserably in all the other three.

When there are problems in these other categories, we have internal challenges. Poor management from the internal business perspective and a weak focus on innovation and learning are often maladies in organizations that somehow manage to get the product out the door: In these cases, the financial side appears to be the dependent variable in the overall equation, and the overall financial picture is often bleak.

We need strong coordination: ensuring that the team knows what they need to do to achieve the overall goals, and ensuring the team knows how to do those things.

Knowing what to do is a function of breaking the overall job into individual tasks, and making sure these tasks work well together to achieve the common good. Usually, an internal chain of products is passed along inside an organization to produce an overall useful product. Something produced at any link of the chain that isn't adequate for those downstream will cause problems. Quite often, these problems can be fixed or masked by those downstream groups, but not without extra effort, which equates to time, cost, and often degraded trust. Compartmentalizing is a necessity for any large system to be produced, but the components need to work in harmony. Without clean interfaces, silos are built up, and inefficiency and waste grows across departmental interfaces. Are the immediate users of what you produce happy with the results?

Knowing how to do your job allows you to get your job done correctly and helps you find ways to do it more efficiently. Anecdotal learning of "how things are done around here" is often the approach taken in software organizations. Weak practices get propagated and institutionalized without a strong focus on reasonable training. This will cause inefficiency and waste within the group, and will often lead to products that are inadequate for those downstream. The costs mount. The bottom line suffers. It takes more money to get the same product out the door. How do you know that the widget you are producing is a good product, and whether you are producing it efficiently?

Having one team feel successful while the others need to perform heroic feats so that the customer can be satisfied is far from an optimal approach. Teams need to specialize in their respective capabilities, but all work toward the same goals within an organization. Coordination means that all the widgets that are being produced fit together properly for an overall smooth-running machine.

If you are of the opinion that things are good enough where you are because the customer seems satisfied, perhaps you should look at some of the other dimensions discussed here.

If the customer has been consulted, the team is aligned internally and trained to do their job right, my guess is that your company will have a healthy bottom line.

If you are struggling to make a profit or please your shareholders, some work may need to be done to coordinate the troops.

Summary

Recognizing that we are humans working together to creatively build a product, the defined approach we believe will foster the project along is clearly insufficient. We need to continuously emphasize the coordination of everyone involved.

This is an interpersonal activity, not an engineering activity. We all need to work to ensure that we remain effective in accomplishing our common goals. This requires active participation from all involved, all the time.

How Is This Relevant?

Information availability. Does everyone have access to the information needed to make decisions, or do people keep data close to their chest? Is information managed carefully, and do people know where to go to find the latest relevant information?

Retaining the big picture. Are decisions made in the context of the overall plans? Do the overall objectives encompass a broad range of perspectives, as a Balanced Scorecard would? Is everyone aligned with this big picture, and is it relevant?

Working together. Is collaboration effective in your organization? Can the team accommodate changes with appropriate mid-course corrections if necessary? Is everyone engaged?

References

1. Bill Breen, "Interview with a Headhunter," Fast Company (December 1998).

2. Thomas L. Friedman, *The World is Flat: A Brief History of the Twenty-first Century* (Farrar, Straus, and Giroux, 2005).

3. Robert S. Kaplan and David P. Norton, *The Balanced Scorecard: Translating Strategy into Action* (Harvard Business School Press, 1996).

CHAPTER FOURTEEN

Guidance

The problem of ensuring that a team works well together is a tough one. There are both strategic and tactical issues to deal with: deciding on a specific approach to take and coordinating the team effort from day to day. This information is important and labor intensive, but it still fails to provide a reasonable level of higher-level guidance to the team.

In this chapter, we look at some practical guidance in how to effectively keep a team running smoothly. We consider some of the attributes of reasonable process deployment and team behaviors essential for success.

Carrots and Sticks

Whether you are raising a child or trying to ensure that the right things are being done on a software project, one of your primary responsibilities will be that of providing the appropriate level of guidance. Those of us who have been in either role understand that there are approaches to the problem that are effective and others that are not, and success or failure is usually strongly correlated to whether the experience was an enjoyable one for the recipient.

We can provide guidance with carrots, or we can use sticks.

Unfortunately, for a variety of reasons, sticks often appear to be the weapon of choice. When people are given the task of defining a process for the software team, they often head off on their own for a period of time, perform some degree of research, identify and possibly purchase resources, come up with a solution, and then unleash it on the organization. "This is what you have to do on projects from now on." Although they have done what they were asked to do, it becomes an entirely different task to ensure that the defined approach is both reasonable and reasonably applied.

Just as you can go crazy continuing to tell a child to shut off the lights or clean his room, even if backed with consequences such as no TV, it can be difficult to get a software team to consistently "do as they are told."

Nobody enjoys being told what to do. Unpleasant directives drastically reduce the willingness of the team to heed the mandates given. One problem is that in software projects, when push comes to shove, there is a strong tendency for those who make the rules to not comply with the very rules that they mandated themselves. Consequently, this significantly eats away at any credibility there may have been.

 In all situations, we want people to understand the reasons for doing things, so that they understand the value in taking the right steps. When people know the underlying rationale, there is less likelihood that they will look for shortcuts and merely obey the letter of the rules rather than the intent. With kids, it can be hiding all the dirty laundry under the bed. With software teams, it can be the superficial validation of a document or incomplete testing of some code before passing it along. In either case, "my room is clean" or "my code works" will soon be revealed as a fallacy, with repercussions to follow. Be sure to provide the rationale behind required tasks. If people understand what is in it for them, they will usually happily comply with the real intent of the request.

Be careful not to overregulate to cover up so many bad situations. This just results in people spending all their time complying with rules rather than getting their job done. Just as all work and no play makes Jack a dull boy, having to rigidly comply to a bulky process can take a lot of the joy out of a software development effort, while adding relatively little value to the overall reduction of program risk. Rules are best derived based on challenges that have cropped up in the past. In this manner, the list of rules will be relatively short, and you can be sure that they are applicable to the culture. Although it can be valuable to base these rules on an overall framework, start from the existing culture rather than from that framework.

You wouldn't want to throw all of Dr. Phil's recommendations at your child up front, and you wouldn't want to burden your software team with an exhaustive best practices framework either.

 Probably the most important thing to consider when putting rules in place is to include the team in the creation of the rules. Be sure that the rules apply to everyone in the organization, and that any allowed deviations from the rules are agreed upon in advance. Participation brings a sense of ownership and genuine buy-in, and an assurance that the system put in place will actually work. Expect that the rules will need tweaking over time, and build in to the overall project life cycle the opportunities to revisit the effectiveness of the rules and evolve as necessary.

> To be most effective, guidance is best done in a collaborative environment where we all contribute and understand the value of the rules we are constructing.
>
> I've found that thinking of process as a means of proactively facilitating the successful interaction of the team has been much more powerful than trying to mandate my own view of how things should be done.

Directed Versatility

Somewhere along the line in the advancement of software development practices, I think we may have made a wrong turn. In our analytical zeal to categorize and compartmentalize all we do into self-consistent models that we can then use to describe "the correct" approach for software development, we have lost the big picture.

We often fall into religious arguments about the relative merits of different frameworks, life cycles, approaches, and tools. We have all debated the relative usefulness of the waterfall model, or the "new benefits" of object-oriented approaches, or the latest "light versus heavy" issues. We get immersed so deeply in these arguments, we become so polarized that we forget that we have a job to do. We forget that we are here to solve a customer's problem.

All these models, all these approaches have their genesis in attempting to solve a problem. The problems have been very different, however, and although there is often some overlap in the solutions that have been modeled, it's pretty clear to me that there is no single solution for any problem. As a model or framework becomes more broadly applicable, its detailed usefulness gets watered down. The generic models are not directly applicable to any problem, and the specific approaches cannot be broadly applied to a wide range of problems.

 Those who exclusively embrace a single framework, life cycle, approach, or tool are constraining the space of problems they are capable of solving. Not all woodworking problems are solved with a hammer, and power tools are a great way of making a pile of sawdust in a hurry. Continuously strive to expand your toolbox. There will never be a single "correct approach." Versatility gives us the capacity to solve a broader range of problems and the flexibility to solve problems in a broader number of ways.

 That said, there is still a common thread of understanding to be discovered in solving any problem. Who, what, why, when, how, and how well are all questions to be resolved for any problem, in software development and elsewhere. Each is necessary, none is sufficient, and most models address each of these in a different way. Unfortunately, the what and how elements are often shortchanged in software development. We need a clear understanding of scope throughout, and a disciplined approach to the solution space that does not start in a code editor with "begin…end."

We often quickly blast past analysis and design in our headlong rush to solve the problem. It's like taking a raw piece of wood to a table saw and saying, "Okay, let's see, I think this chair will need four legs…maybe if I cut here…."

We need to address all the questions above, but need to understand that there is not an explicit order to them. Continuous refinement on all paths will allow us to solve the problem. Although some questions such as the why and who will more naturally reveal their answers sooner, we need to press on all fronts throughout the project. I like to compare it to pressing against a large opaque sheet. Some areas will give way under our pressure before others. It is in our best interests to make advances wherever we can and to ensure that our solution remains consistent with the problem we are trying to solve. The broader our toolkit, the more leverage we have in progressing quickly to the solution.

We will never be able to decide in advance which tools will be appropriate for all of our upcoming situations. Although we can, and should, think strategically about what our needs will be on an upcoming project, we need to remain flexible to be able select the right tool when the time comes.

Continuously strive to address all the key questions of a problem. An approach directed at resolving the who, what, why, when, how, and how well questions enables us to solve problems more predictably.

Real Programmers

For some, it is a serious badge of honor to work in a place that rewards long hours at the keyboard, all in the name of effort.

The effort is often endorsed and expected by management. If you pull it off, they will expect more next time around. If you blanche at the notion of such a culture during an interview, you might as well look elsewhere. Phrases such as "Who's in for pizza?" fill the evening air. You're sitting on a million lines of code, and you don't have time for "no stinkin' documentation," because there is still more code to produce.

Back to my screen, hand me another Jolt Cola. This is where *real programmers* work.

Gimme a break.

There is still too much emphasis on the construction phase of software development both in industry and academia. (Yes, we continue to roll out graduates who have little appreciation for the value of analysis and design or concern for product maintenance.) If these shops have any group called QA, it is product testing at best, or superficial product signoff at worst.

The scenario just described exists in many shops today, some of which are currently riding a wave of success.

> Unfortunately, it is inappropriate to assign a causal relationship between success, attitudes, and work ethic. It is dangerous to assume that even more of the same is what is needed to sustain the peak. These companies will likely join others that have ridden that wave but are now bewildered that the approach has not sustained them. Ask any surfer: A wave is neither controllable nor sustainable.

Laziness or Focused Creativity?

There is a great deal to be said for simple, elegant solutions to problems. When the design is right, the implementation follows cleanly. It can be quickly confirmed to be correct, understood by others, and easily modified if the need arises. There is improved likelihood for reuse because the code is well factored. Creation of a good design brings you to straightforward implementation with few surprises. The risk has been reduced, and the schedule becomes predictable. (Sorry, you'll have to look elsewhere for the adrenaline rush.) An elegant solution to a problem that involves a minimal amount of code can bring real joy.

This is not to be confused with the pain relief after a particularly difficult debugging session.

Elegance in software development rarely comes from long sessions in front of a code editor. Recognition of this is a key quality step that an organization can take. Developing a sustainable and controllable culture for continued production of elegant solutions is no accident. A strong quality-assurance presence in an organization will recognize and enforce the value of the analysis and design phases: not just the duration, but also the appropriate focus.

I'd say that Thomas Edison wasn't thinking about quality software when he said, "Genius is 1 percent inspiration and 99 percent perspiration." The genius in quality software lies not in the perspiration of intense coding and debugging sessions, but in the inspiration of a great design idea that has come to light. One of the strongest positive influences a QA group can have on organizational effectiveness is to ensure that there is reasonable effort up front for analysis and design activities. If you are about to code something up yourself, take the time to think before putting fingertips to keyboard: Can I save myself some time with a little focus here?

Shortcuts

In this *Name That Tune* world of software development ("I can build that product in...three months!"), we simply don't have the time to do all the things we know we should be doing to get the job done right. With most of the industry saying that insufficient resources is a key problem, and more than enough competitors out there that will gladly undercut your bid to get the job in the first place, it is critical to bid aggressively and to take shortcuts to ship product if necessary.

 Which shortcuts we take will often make or break the project.

I'd say that the vast majority of us enter into our work with the intent to meet or exceed the specification—that is, at least our interpretation of the specification, which often has wide tolerances built in to it (or more correctly, wide tolerances were not taken out). We all want to do well; we want to do the "right thing." It is not our nature to intentionally take shortcuts that undermine our results. We may even start out doing all the things we would want to do in a perfect world, but soon the schedule pressures catch up with us, new tasks get piled onto our queue, or something that we thought would be simple turns out to be much more difficult than it seemed.

Left to our own devices, each of us will take the shortcuts that are most expedient for our own value system, even if they are not in the best interest of the project as a whole:

> *I'm sure that little tweak won't affect anything else in the system, no need to go overboard to test that.*
>
> *I don't think I need to bother documenting that design approach, it's apparent to anyone reading the code.*
>
> *I'll just copy that code from over there, it's pretty similar to this, and I'll get back to cleaning up those comments after I get it working.*

Yes, we've all been there, and we've all been burned by our decisions.

Often these shortsighted decisions at the personal level scale up to the project level, with corresponding impact:

> *We don't have time to clarify what the customer needs up front. We've got to get this thing shipped!*
>
> *We've lost all our time for system testing because the coding took so long, we'll build more time for test in the next release!*
>
> *For that kind of money, we can go offshore and put five times the number of developers on the project. That will more than make up for any overhead we might have.*

Most of us have been there, too.

When looking at the breadth of things that should be done (given adequate resources), it is important to perform a reasonable prioritization to cull the low-value chores out and save time to meet your constraints. This should be done explicitly, at the project level, not left to the whim of individuals throughout the project. Good work packages have a clear description of scope as well as constraints, degrees of freedom, and completion criteria to reduce the risk of individual interpretation and arbitrary shortcuts. Look at reasonably trimming the scope, too, but be sure that the product still fulfills the vision for what is needed.

With the appropriate triage of process steps, you can ensure that there remains reasonable control and oversight to keep the risk tolerable. Chances are that if you are not developing a safety-critical system, a full traceability matrix will be more bother than it is worth. Test to make sure the requirements are met, but full path coverage testing for most systems will be less critical. If you were careful in building your specification, be at least as careful at keeping it current.

Think prioritization *and* balance.

Some shortcuts are too dangerous to take. Be absolutely thorough in change management; otherwise, schedules will become meaningless. Keep rigorous configuration control; otherwise, you might never be able to reproduce what is out in the field.

 Most of us start with the intent to do all the right things, possibly even documenting that intent. For people as well as projects, at the end of the day it is our actions that define us, not our statement of intent. Remain vigilant to the constraints and the goals of the project, and take explicit care to ensure that the only shortcuts taken are the ones least likely to jeopardize the outcome. If not carefully managed, each individual will take shortcuts based on personal priorities, and if something doesn't get done, then it was not a priority, regardless of what might have been stated up front.

Process Ergonomics

As we define the way in which we develop software within our teams, we soon find out some approaches are more effective than others. One of the problems that trap many of us is that we fail to consider the factors surrounding our definition that will impact the humans who will be living with this information.

We neglect the ergonomics of the process we define.

We cannot merely assume that people will automatically adopt any approach we propose. There is inertia in anything we do. For any of us to change our habits, we need to clearly understand the value to us for doing something different. The definition of the proposed approach is not the end; the adoption of the approach needs to be carefully managed over time. This definition is not the starting point either; the team skills, needs, and perceptions need to be factored into the building of an appropriate approach. The definition we provide is merely a part of a balanced overall solution.

Ease of use is one of the most important ergonomic factors to consider. Although it may feel satisfying to produce a massive magnum opus that declares in gory detail the approach to be used for developing software, there is little chance that it will ever become a bestseller among the team. There may indeed be tremendous value between the pages, but it is imperative that it is accessible, both for initial training and for ongoing reference by the group. What is much more important than the content of a massive tome is an extremely brief summary of the key practices critical for success.

If you can't produce a one-page cheat-sheet of the approach, there is probably more distilling to do (one standard written page, not one poster-sized sheet). One great way to distill the approach for the masses is the use of checklists and forms, and to evolve these atomic elements with specific refinements based on experience as the team progresses.

Another approach is to take what is envisioned as an all-encompassing approach and to break it up into a staged deployment. Rather than change the world in one step, prioritize and select a very few components to change. This will reduce the culture shock and the risk of pushback that often comes with overwhelming the team with too much change. The remaining elements can be kept in your back pocket to introduce when appropriate (or as opportunities arise). Besides, there is a good chance that your initial changes will provide you with insight that will modify or invalidate the secondary changes anyways.

Ease of learning is also important to consider. The greater the distance between the proposed approach and the status quo, the more emphasis there has to be placed on ensuring that the team truly understands the differences, and why these differences make sense from a business perspective. Standardized approaches and notations for conveying information are critical to ensure a common terminology to support learning. That said, beware the allure of simply taking a defined approach "out of the box." Ensure that the group understands how the principles of the approach are relevant for their needs.

Many attempts at defining or changing a defined development approach fall down through lack of adoption. This often occurs when we fail to appropriately focus on the life cycle of the information we collect and use on projects. It is not uncommon for reasonable specifications to be produced, but to have them neglected as the project progresses, either because they have fallen out of date, or because they cannot easily be found and accessed, or both. It is critical to identify the location and format of the information we use to build our products and to ensure that it is easy to find and access as required.

 Indeed, it would be quite reasonable to define as a specific requirement for the project that specific documents be maintained and stored in a specific location, in a specified format, for a reasonable timeframe. This would be a quality attribute in the area of maintainability—not all requirements have to be realized in the executable code of the system. Treat this requirement as part of the overall completion criteria alongside the functional requirements, and you are more likely to have access to this information when you need it.

The best way to build a reasonable defined approach for the organization is to involve the eventual users of the approach itself. Not only will they have the best insight into what will work, but also their involvement will bring a strong sense of ownership that will compel them to embrace the approach.

Be careful to build or refine your process with the ergonomics of your target group in mind. The likelihood of real adoption and value provided through these efforts will increase dramatically.

Size Doesn't Matter

We're all familiar with companies that act in accordance with their size. There are the big ones that are saturated with bureaucracy, small ones that are informal to the extreme. Companies can be so huge that you'll never meet all but a small percentage of the staff ("Oh, you work at Microsoft—do you know Eloise?"), and others small enough that you know how their kids are doing in school. You might even coach the CEO's daughter in hockey.

Occasionally, however, we run into a group that behaves quite incongruently with their size.

Still Small in Attitude

I worked with a company that was relatively large by some standards, but still exuded a number of start-up-like behaviors.

In running 85 people through technical training over 3 days, it was the founders and senior management who were some of the most engaged participants in the learning, drawing out the quieter ones in the room and working to ensure that the event was as valuable as possible for everyone.

Despite growth through acquisition, there was a real family feel in the room and a strong sense of alignment toward a common goal. They still saw themselves as a small shop, and I didn't sense any of the typical "I was told to come to this training and I don't really care" nuances that are often a part of large-company training. Wonderful.

Contrast that to a group I worked with a few months earlier, with perhaps 30 employees overall. The group acted very much out of proportion with their size. (Just how many levels of hierarchy can you have in a 30 person group?)

Strong silos had been built up between teams, resulting in interfaces that were clearly dysfunctional for the group as a whole, and senior management was too busy to take an interest in what was going on. With plenty of individual vested interests and infighting, it quickly became clear that there would be significant challenges to bring in any change there.

Indeed, the company has recently closed its doors.

This is not to say that all large-company behavior is bad, all small-team behavior is good. Certainly many of the systems that are put in place in the big shops contribute to consistency of deployment and take advantage of opportunities of scale. The leverage that a Microsoft or Google can have on the industry can be huge (and despite the whining from the masses, largely positive). In small shops (insert your threshold of large versus small here), the ability to get things done with little overhead and the strong sense of belonging and camaraderie that comes with knowing everyone involved in the operation can be powerful. Being small and flying under the radar can also be a significant bonus.

There are often islands of humanity as teams within a large corporation bond together, but there will remain a big-company feel for much of what is done there. What we need to do is to understand the contribution each of our behaviors makes to our overall success, and to recognize when we are acting too big for our britches or thinking small-time.

If you catch yourself blaming the defined process as a reason for not doing something that makes sense (or vice versa), you have suddenly gotten way too big and bureaucratic. If you find that other things are more important than understanding the motivations behind the actions of others within the group, there might be a problem. If your best reason for doing something is to suggest that it's just the way things are done around here or everyone else does it that way, it might be time to break the mold and find a better way to get things done.

If you don't think you can attract the talent that the big shops can draw, it's time to recognize that most employees count compensation well down on their list of priorities. If you're dubious of your ability to influence the world, recognize that it's not always the biggest companies that change the world.

Don't get hung up on the size of your company. Focus on the value and appropriateness of your actions. You're as young as you feel and as big as you act.

A company can be simultaneously small thinking and big world stodgy, or it can be warm, personal, and extremely influential. Size really does not matter.

Persistent Consistency

One of the baseline goals for software development organizations, according to the Software Engineering Institute at Carnegie Mellon University, is predictability and repeatability of project successes. Unfortunately, most organizations have not yet achieved this. Although SEI statistics show greater than 90 percent of organizations are at least this mature,[1] this data is based on a very small, highly biased sample of organizations mature enough to be interested in (or even aware of!) the institute and their Maturity Models (1,804 worldwide through December 2005).

The SEI advocates discipline in the traditional software engineering taxonomy that includes project management, quality assurance, and related elements, but I believe one of the understated critical practices for achieving predictability and repeatability is persistent consistency, in all dimensions.

Effective communication is necessary to achieve project goals, and the lines of communication to be managed grow significantly as a function of team size. With this in mind, consistency of communication at all levels is imperative.

Within the team, consistency will promote promptness and openness of dialogue among the team. Interaction with the team needs to be consistent with their performance against expectations, not on individual moods or allegiances. Consistent communication will promote an environment in which there is no hesitation to discuss issues and clarity about how to address them. With issues raised to the team level as soon as possible, the greater resources of the team can be applied to the problem to find the optimal solution.

 It is widely acknowledged that dependence on heroes in development organizations is a significant business risk. (What if that hero decides to walk with all her undocumented knowledge?) Even if that risk of departure does not materialize, there often exists an ongoing problem, as these heroes are allowed the luxury of cutting corners ("Bob's code doesn't need to be peer reviewed"), setting a dangerous double standard that erodes team morale. Consistent quality performance expectations across the team will eliminate this problem. The heroes should be setting the appropriate example for the rest of the team and leading a consistent approach.

 Consistency in application of practices is required across the lifetime of a project, too. All the value provided by a mature approach at any step of the project can be quickly undermined by shortcuts taken later in the game. This is a classic example of the weakest-link syndrome. The best specification you can initially muster degrades rapidly if potential changes to the spec are not managed accordingly downstream. A perfectly reasonable Gantt chart becomes a piece of abstract art days later if the actual performance is not tracked to the same level of discipline and changes managed into the schedule.

 Consistent discipline in review and application of changes to the system is important. Avoid the tendency to hastily throw in any change, no matter how trivial it may appear, in the name of urgency. A better approach is to identify a fast-track stream for clearly identified time-critical issues that allows expediency and is supported by mechanisms that ensure that diligence is completed shortly thereafter.

If you are not planning to maintain consistency through-out the project, in communication and application of practices, don't waste your time up front with a shallow attempt at best practices.

You may just as well dive into code-and-fix mode right now. You'll need all the time you can get if you ever hope to get something worthwhile out the door!

Summary

For guidance to be successfully applied in a team environment, it needs to be practical, applicable, and carefully deployed with consideration of the value provided to the recipients. Merely telling people what needs to be done simply will not work in a software environment.

Above all, guidance needs to be provided at a level where it can be consistently applied. This may mean that we need to explicitly identify the exceptional conditions under which our guidance would apply. It does not mean, however, that individuals should be exempt from the guidance, or that we stop doing these things under schedule pressure.

How Is This Relevant?

Practical guidance. Is the guidance reasonable for the project context? Has it been appropriately adjusted given the relative risk and importance of this project? Can this guidance be reasonably applied within the constraints of the project?

Consistent application. Is this guidance generally applicable to everyone on the team? Is it enforced throughout the project life cycle, even when schedule pressures loom?

> **Shared ownership.** Has this guidance been derived through participation with all stakeholders? Are all perspectives reasonably considered?

References

1. Software Engineering Institute, Process Maturity Profile, Software CMM 2005 End-Year Update, March 2006. http://www.sei.cmu.edu/appraisal-program/profile/pdf/SW-CMM/2006marSwCMM.pdf. The latest results from the CMMI appraisals are not significantly different.

PART FIVE

Stakeholders

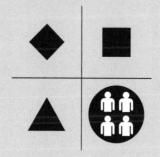

The primary goal of an organized team is to work together to solve a novel problem for a broader range of stakeholders. The coordination we build into teams allows us to do this in an effective, efficient manner.

As we start to address this challenge, we must first establish who our stakeholders are and identify the specific goals we are going to try to achieve for them. We then need to work with our stakeholders in a collaborative fashion to empathize with them and agree in detail what needs to be done.

After this has been achieved, we can then proceed toward solving our challenges. We need to be effective at monitoring progress, adjusting to change, and continuously rearranging our priorities so that we can make it to our desired end.

CHAPTER FIFTEEN

Customers

In determining who our customer is, we need to recognize that everyone involved in the construction or consumption of the product acts as a customer at some point, and all these voices need representation. Although the end user may have the primary voice, others need to be heard.

In this chapter, we consider the importance of understanding who needs to be involved in the decision making on our projects, and note that they all need reasonable representation throughout the project.

Who's Our Customer?

Business 101 suggests that one of your first steps to success is to clearly identify your customer through market analysis and segmentation. The more concretely you understand who your customer is, the more you understand their needs, the better equipped you are to provide a solution that fulfills those needs and allows you to build a successful business. Generally, this focus is on external clients, those who are expected to bring revenue in to sustain the organization.

 In recent years, the notion of a supply chain has become prominent. Companies such as Dell have excelled through a deep understanding and rigorous management of the entire chain through to us, their happy consumer.

 We in software rarely think that deeply. Our customers are simply the people who use our software, no? Indeed, it can be a challenge to find organizations that even make the distinction between the purchaser and the user of the system, or to identify several classes of users and segment the functionality accordingly. To think through and identify all the user classes for a software product is a critical step in allowing you to identify all that your product needs to deliver. Imagine the devastating effects of deploying an ATM machine without considering the needs of the user class that services the equipment.

A key leap that more companies should consider is to review the supply chain for their product as a way of identifying new user classes. Many companies have managed to produce a great deal of functionality for the end user within their vertical market, but find that each new installation is an excruciating process filled with long hours and heroic efforts to get the system going. While the purchasers of the product get all the focus when initially identifying the functionality of the system, their own implementation group is left in the cold. The development team considers the purchaser only, and assumes the installation is a trivial part of the entire supply chain, even though history has never borne this out.

 As large systems evolve over time, they may reach a point where the cost of implementation far outweighs the cost of development for a new installation. If the internal implementation team is viewed as a customer that could in effect pay by reducing the cost of implementation (along with reducing risk and increasing end-user satisfaction), there can often be a compelling business case built for defining a project where the client is strictly internal. Building an infrastructure that allows a flexible, managed implementation to a wide variety of external paying customers can be a sound investment in the company's future.

Understanding the entire supply chain of your solution can be quite revealing. Managing that entire chain is critical in optimizing value.

Focus on identifying who your most important customer is for your software products, and you are likely to find an entirely new class of functionality that can truly differentiate your product from the competition.

The End User's Advocate

Getting a great product out the door requires a great deal of initial activity to ensure that the right product is built. There has to be a solid understanding of the market needs being addressed, which has to be thoroughly analyzed and specified to the point where the development team can go forth and build the desired solution. To deliver in a timely fashion, that specification needs to be the based on a credible schedule. Progress needs to be closely monitored and changes need to be managed through to project completion.

Before the product can go out the door, however, you need to validate that the product will truly meet the end user's needs. Some companies take it as a given that whatever they build will satisfy the end user's needs. They are often surprised by the feedback they get from the market (which is sometimes no feedback at all, because the customer is off looking for someone else to better resolve their problems). Others exhaustively test against the specification to ensure that what was built is what was expected to be built. They generally receive fewer surprises from the field related to features that don't work properly, even though they are still susceptible to omissions and errors related to addressing the original market need.

An important aspect of exercising the product that these companies have missed is the practice of ensuring that the delivered product actually meets the high-level needs of the end user. In an ideal world, if project artifacts were derived from their predecessors properly, this would be a no-brainer. The project needs map down to the specification, which maps through the design to the implementation. But in real life, there are just too many translations and implicit assumptions along the way. Has the spec actually been validated thoroughly against the needs or just signed off based on its thickness or because the reviewer had much more pressing issues to worry about? Has the product evolved from a solid spec that addresses client needs, or has it been driven primarily by schedule pressures or the latest interesting technology choices?

There are plenty of side roads the building of a product can take, any of which can distract us from actually addressing the end user's needs. The final validation of the product before release must explicitly address this concern. Although it is good and important to ensure that the product has been implemented as specified, it is critical to step back to the original problem and identify whether the product solves the problem—in a quantifiable form, if possible.

If the intent was to optimize workflow in some manner, does the product measurably reduce time, improve accuracy, or facilitate deeper insights? If the intent was to improve the user experience, can we unambiguously state that we have a more enjoyable product, or that it is more compelling to use?

There are two key ways of making this happen. The first, something that any organization could do, is to initially specify quantified goals for the system, which will determine whether the end user's needs are met. Construct tests to validate whether the initial needs are indeed met. Use these tests to supplement the standard suite derived from the functional requirements and use cases.

The second approach is to ensure that the people performing the final checks on the product can accurately and reasonably act as an advocate for the end user. In many organizations, the product champion is leveraged initially to gather the voice of the customer in the analysis phase. They should also be used at the end of the day to ensure the user's needs are met. I think a big part of what makes the titles from Electronic Arts successful is the fact that everyone in their testing teams, indeed most people in their development teams too, are avid gamers themselves. They epitomize the best in end-user advocacy. They know what will work well in the market because they are actually part of the market themselves.

Do everything in your power to ensure that you have addressed the end user's needs before the product goes out the door.

Getting It Straight from the Horse's Mouth

It has been said that "one only needs two tools in life: WD-40 to make things go, and duct tape to make them stop." Clearly, this person was not asking for a software solution to his problem!

To have an understanding of what is really needed for a software product, you need to go right to the source. Managing requirements from the end user's perspective is critical. This is not simply an up-front activity. The voice of the customer must be heeded throughout the product life cycle.

Initially, at the conceptual stage, solicit client input in a manner that allows you to understand which features they need the most. Drill down to understand how the features will impact their business processes, with a goal to optimize these for the client. Use cases can be an effective communications vehicle, but few clients can build formal use cases without coaching. You'll need to either educate the users or, more likely, act as the scribe to collate the information yourself.

Afterward, while you need to constrain the freeform generation of new ideas (you now have a defined feature set to move forward with, right?), there is still value from constant client interaction. In design and implementation stages, user collaboration is valuable to constantly refine and prioritize your feature set. It can provide huge benefits in helping the development group understand how the product will be used. In the alpha and beta stages, the focus is on feedback for product refinement and prioritization of issues. Post-release collaboration and feedback remains important, too, because this information is critical for letting you measure your product effectiveness. It also sets the stage for new feature solicitation and refinements for the next round of development.

It's not just when but how to engage the client, especially if you have a large user base. Survey the user community. Beware of the tendency to emphasize the latest voice (or to pay too much attention to the squeaky wheel). Collect all the information in one place, and devise a mechanism that enables you to prioritize properly and select a comprehensive and consistent set of features to put into production.

Find a way to engage in a dialogue. The communication has to be in both directions. And although qualitative discussion is good, it can be improved significantly with a quantitative scheme to prioritize features. This can be a voting mechanism for users, but don't forget the internal concerns such as the cost of implementation and consistency of product vision.

Finally, please don't make commitments until all internal stakeholders agree that expectations can be reasonably met!

Not only do you need to do the right stuff, but also the right amount of stuff to allow the development team to put it together properly.

When developing software, get information straight from the horse's mouth, and do so in an objective, controlled manner.

Driving the Expectations Bus

It has been stated that *customer satisfaction* is proportional to *your performance* and inversely proportional to your *customer expectations.*

 If the equation was indeed mathematically correct, you naïvely could try to maximize customer satisfaction by minimizing expectations, but I doubt this would be a practical approach to achieving excellence, as you flirt with the dangerous "divide by zero" condition. Instead, what is required is a disciplined approach to effectively managing customer expectations throughout your projects.

Often in driving a project, the team takes the process focus inward to ensure that the proper steps are in place in an attempt to maximize the performance in the equation, and then wait for the customer to set their expectations for them. Unfortunately, performance itself is dependent on how well expectations are managed. It is interesting to note that most process frameworks that exist today are evolving to recognize that inward focus is insufficient to ensure project success.

One of the key considerations for expectations is that you are often dealing with more than one type of customer. It becomes a delicate balance to ensure that all (sometimes very different) expectations are properly managed. Even if you have a project that will be run by yourself, and the end product will only be used by yourself, you have two types of customer: the one developing the product, and the one using it.

 If you can manage to provide satisfaction both while creating the product and during its use afterward, you increase your chances at achieving overall excellence. Most projects have more than two types of customers. A little consideration will easily generate a reasonable taxonomy, with an understanding of the expectations of each type.

❔ For some projects, the significance of managing expectations can be huge. There can be a very large number of different customer classes, each with unique expectations for the outcome. Clearly, one of the critical success factors for these projects is the effectiveness of driving the expectations of this extremely diverse set of customers.

Managing the expectations of all clients (internal and external) will have the snowballing effect of reducing surprises and interruptions, and will foster a project environment with higher motivation, both of which will lead to higher performance.

By taking charge of improving expectations instead of letting it float or trying to minimize it, you will gain the effect of overall improvement, because expectations are one of the primary drivers of the performance numerator in the satisfaction equation.

Summary

We need to be completely clear who our customer is for our projects and ensure that they are adequately represented throughout the project.

With that understanding, we can carefully manage expectations so that there are fewer surprises as the projects come to completion, and we can ensure the right people are available to make considered decisions along the way.

How Is This Relevant?

Variety of customers. Do you understand the range of customer perspectives that are important for your projects? Does this list include both internal and external stakeholders? Do you have reasonable representation for each class of customer for your product?

Who makes decisions? Are the right people at the table for making decisions? How are they informed when they need to be involved? Have you ever had to make decisions on their behalf and regretted it later?

Engaging our customers. Do your customer representatives invest enough time in the project? Do they have the respect of the community they represent? Are their decisions binding?

CHAPTER SIXTEEN

Setting Goals

With representation at the table by all the distinct stakeholder groups, we can define the clear goals that put structure around what we are trying to achieve. This gives us a line in the sand that we can use to determine whether potential changes fit our goals, and allows us to clearly and specifically identify what success means to us, in a number of dimensions.

In this chapter, we try to clarify what this critical initial step of solving a problem entails, and describes how these goals need to remain relevant throughout the project.

Goals and Mandates

It's easy for people in an organization to want to get better, particularly when they are experiencing the pain of poor practices. However, simply having a goal is insufficient.

It is difficult to discern between a genuine goal and a mere wish—unless, of course, the same goal has been around for years, with no progress made toward achieving that goal. In that case, all you have there is a wish.

It is virtually impossible to achieve improvement goals without a concerted effort.

Organizations often get worse over time without managed controls. To sit idly, wishing for better times, or worse, to actively complain, is to give entropy the chance to decay the situation.

As an organization scales up in size, the situation gets worse. A lone voice for change can easily be drowned out in a sea of discontent. A few isolated attempts at changing things fail miserably, and layered on top of the existing pain is the belief that trying to fix things is a waste of time. It's not a comfortable place, but it is familiar, and it takes significant effort to overcome the inertia that can keep you where you are.

 The first step for change is to have clear goals. Choose your goals carefully, and be as detailed as possible. Are you clear on your motivations? Are you just interested in a fresh coat of paint to provide the illusion of effectiveness to a potential suitor, or are you genuinely interested in long-lasting change for the group? Clarity here will define the sort of effort and results you can expect, as well as the magnitude of resistance you are likely to see, and the type of improvement activities you should work on.

After you are clear on your goals, you need to define a mandate for achieving those goals. A mandate empowers people to actually take action toward the stated goals, by providing clear authorization from above to make it happen. Who is going to do what, with whom, when, and how will we measure it to ensure it helps us move toward our goals as expected? All of these need to be addressed in an action plan that addresses the mandate that has been set for the group. Without the coordination of a mandate, arbitrary efforts are unlikely to complement each other toward achieving a goal.

It's important to note that the mandate need not encompass the entire organization. It's dangerous to try to set a mandate that is broader than your sphere of control. In a large organization where there is little coordination between groups, it can be more practical initially to emphasize a mandate within your group.

 Call it a "make lemonade" mandate. Even if your group is not being fed the right stuff to do your job properly, there are different ways you can deal with what you are getting. There is often an opportunity to make significant improvements on a smaller scale. Tighter internal controls, realistic scheduling, and stronger feedback loops with external groups will settle some of the chaos internally and send a message to others that improvement is not out of reach.

Small successes can increase your ability to influence a broader mandate, too. However, championing the cause for the entire organization involves a more significant set of risk and reward issues to deal with. There will be much greater inertia, and there is a greater challenge in crafting goals and a mandate that all can work toward. If done correctly, however, the results can be staggering. A well-crafted mandate with clearly defined goals, driven to completion, can bring an entire organization together and literally turn it around in a very short time. It can be useful to leverage a significant organizational event to bring the entire team together. An example of this would be a major client success or key corporate milestone.

 Avoid using reorganization as a driver for change. As Gaius Petronius, a Roman general noted, "We trained very hard, but it seemed that every time we were beginning to form into teams we would be reorganized. I was to learn later in life that we tend to meet any new situation by reorganizing, and a wonderful method it can be for creating the illusion of progress, while producing confusion, inefficiency, and demoralization." It seems some things never change.

It's all well and good to express a desire for change. It's an entirely different matter to actually be proactive about achieving your goals. Complaining about the status quo will get you nowhere.

It takes willpower, discipline, and a clear mandate to make positive change happen.

Defining Success

Just as it is rare for software projects to define in advance what success means to the project (in terms of scope, cost, time, and quality), it is also rare for the company as a whole to clearly define what it means to be successful as an organization.

As with software projects, that lack of a predefined notion of success often allows for the flexibility of artificially declaring success by selectively pulling out data that defends your case. More important, it prevents you from explicitly driving toward a truly successful conclusion along the way.

Luck and rationalization overwhelms planning and discipline; success is in the eye of the beholder.

Although complete success can rarely be captured in a single dimension, there is always a strong tendency to simplify wherever possible, even to the point of absurdity. We're all familiar with quarterly earnings announcements from public companies, and the trend of private companies to follow suit with their informal earnings reports, but only when the results are positive. It is always amusing to see the press releases from companies that gloat about earnings growing significantly from the previous year, but we never see the releases announcing losses. The external perspective, unless disclosure is legislated, will always be glowing.

That focus on the single monetary dimension can be extremely misleading. Usually with this focus, success is achieved at the expense of other important factors. Are employees adequately supported in their careers? Are they reasonably compensated and rewarded for their efforts, or are they simply expendable resources along with the computers and furniture in the building? Do the perks provided by the company genuinely improve their quality of life, or just make it more convenient for them to stay at work for longer hours? How much turnover is there? Is that turnover reasonable and healthy for both employees and management?

For clients, is the emphasis on providing a shiny new technology or on providing a true solution to the client's needs? It is one thing to be technology focused (we're a wireless shop, we do .NET, and so on); it is entirely another matter to have a primary focus in solving client problems. Is there a reasonable history of repeat clientele, or does the business have to constantly struggle to find new clients from a shrinking pool of prospects?

If there isn't anything that can be done directly for the client, does the company try to force-fit a solution? Does it freely acknowledge that it indeed is not all things to all people? Being a success with a client doesn't necessarily mean that you can do anything. However, everything you do can be directed toward providing a stronger, broader solution for your clients, whether this means a strong network for referrals or more comprehensive internal offerings.

Does the business do anything to give back to the community, or is the meter always running? Is it even clear what the community is for this business? Volunteer work, contributions to local associations, and pro-bono services all support the broader environment and reflect well on the business, but with a single-minded focus on earnings, all these activities often take a back seat to billable time or shipped product.

What a company sees behind closed doors as a measure of success is much more important than what is contained in its press releases. When the façade of statistics is removed, how does your company measure its own success with regard to its employees, its clients, and the community it lives in? Only when this is clearly defined can plans be put in place to actually turn this into reality.

Aligning Priorities to Strengths

Generally in software projects (or projects in general, for that matter), the intent is to build something that meets the client's needs much better than the competition. Whether it is innovative features, lower price, latest technology, higher quality, or to win the race to market, one aspect usually stands out beyond all others.

 It is good practice in the first stages of a project to be clear what these differentiating factors are for the product. Whether the competitive landscape is the external market of existing projects, a completely new field that you are about to make the initial foray into, or the internal inventory of existing software in an IT shop, it is valuable to be clear as a group why you are going down the path. As Geoffrey Moore has indicated,[1] clearly specifying the product, the competition, and the primary differentiator in a quick vision statement can create a compelling constitution for the team.

With the uncertainty inherent in software projects, it is also a strong practice to identify up front what your priorities are, so that when the inevitable time arrives in the project when you need to make trade-offs, you have clear direction as to potential flexibility. Whether you work with a framework of cost, features, quality, schedule, and staff or some other taxonomy, it is important to understand which of these is driving your project. Few projects recognize quality as an explicit driver, usually resulting in implicit degradation of quality despite the team's best intentions. Although you might want everything to be top priority, it is worth recognizing up front (when things are less frantic) the varying degrees of flexibility across these elements, so that decisions can be more easily made later.

 Whereas few groups successfully identify both of the priorities and strengths for their projects, even fewer groups align their project priorities to their product strengths. If you were racing to get your product out the door ahead of the competition, possibly to demonstrate features at a trade show, time would reasonably be your driving priority. Unfortunately, there are too many projects for which the differentiator is not time based, but the priority is still an extreme deadline. How many project teams are attempting to build a safety-critical system or implement a cutting-edge technology but are constrained to work to unreasonable schedules, often artificially imposed with the intent of motivating the team? The result usually has the opposite effect: a demoralized group, failure to meet stated priorities, and a product whose differentiating factor has been compromised.

Be careful to align the compelling business differentiators in your mission statement with your project priorities.

Done early, this is a great sanity check for your project to ensure you are heading in the right direction.

Are You Sure You Want Quality?

It is a popular pastime to suggest that quality is important for your software projects, given the bad press the industry has had and the pleasure we gain from bashing the software we use on a daily basis. What does it really mean to focus on quality as a priority?

First and foremost, to truly have quality as a focus for your software project, you need to be detailed about what *quality* means. If you don't have a clear description of quality in terms that can be independently verified at the end of the project, this emphasis on quality is little more than hot air.

Generally, quality means different things to different people at different times. As I type on my laptop here, what are important to me are things like reliability (remember the days when Ctrl-Alt-Del was a standard procedure?) and usability (out here on the deck it is quite bright, it's nice to be able to crank up the display brightness). In other situations, I might be more interested in interoperability, and when buried in code, the focus turns toward testability, modifiability, or reusability.

Be careful what you ask for in terms of quality. As with many things in life, your product can't completely satisfy everyone. There are trade-offs between the various facets of quality, and satisfying some aspects of quality can only come at a very high price. Tuning a system for that last ounce of efficiency may mean that you sacrifice the maintainability of the code, for example.

If you are interested in the high availability that is built in to mission-critical systems, you will automatically narrow your options of operating systems, while increasing the cost of the hardware platform and complexity of the architecture. The simple statement that a system needs to be available for all but perhaps five minutes a year (which is not unheard of) can more than double the cost of the overall system all by itself.

If you want data integrity, you are best served to build in the checks and balances that help ensure that data integrity will indeed be maintained, and trapped as soon as possible if integrity is compromised. You need to proactively drive this quality at all levels of construction and testing, driven by a design and architecture that will provide the required infrastructure. This effort takes time and resources that needs to be planned for. Attempts to retrofit an existing system to add in stronger integrity can be more expensive and riskier than to start over.

There can be an extreme cost associated with building quality in to a system, but this can pale in comparison to the costs you may run into if you neglect quality altogether. You can't ask for high quality and constrain the team with schedule or cost constraints that don't allow them to do the job. Living in a code-and-fix world can dramatically increase schedules beyond what was anticipated, and the likelihood that you have done enough *fix* to deal with the *code* is relatively low. Delays and poor client satisfaction become even more costly because they are generally unexpected. From the quality perspective, you definitely get what you pay for.

On the other hand, working with clear, established quality goals can be a significant cost saver. Most projects that place an emphasis on schedule over quality generally find that they are usually late and end up shipping challenged software anyways. In emphasizing a constrained schedule, they fail both goals. With an emphasis on quality, however, there comes greater awareness and certainty of progress, often resulting in more reasonable schedules, too.

Be careful what you ask for in terms of quality, but be sure to ask for it, and be sure to be clear on what quality means for your projects.

The Slippery Slope

Rarely in software development have I seen a coherent, clear statement of the vision for the project. Who is the target audience? What is the value that this new product provides for the user? How is it differentiated from the competition (or the status quo)? What are the driving factors for success (and where are our degrees of freedom)? How do we know when we have succeeded?

Without such a vision, it is difficult for the team, with constant bombardment of pressures from different directions, to keep their eye on the big picture.

Odd Jobs

A few years ago, we finally got tired of tackling random jobs around the house: paint the basement floor this week, attack that shed out back the following week. None of this ever led to a sense that completion resulted in a better place to live. We had, just as in many software projects, lost sight of the overall vision of what we were trying to achieve.

It was time to inflict some project management on the situation. We stepped back, identified what our primary goals were for a renovation, brainstormed a list of anything we could think of that might need doing, and then pared down that list based on (among other things) whether these activities were aligned with the achievement of our goals.

The result was a plan of attack that allowed us to make a coherent set of changes bundled into a project that we closely managed, and we essentially reclaimed a great deal of space in our home.

We had agreed on the big picture up front. Instead of working with our own very different priorities and destinations in mind, it served to keep us in alignment throughout. With that clear vision in place, we avoided falling down that slippery slope.

We often fall down a slippery slope without realizing what is happening until it is too late. Work is done that doesn't really fit with the other elements of the project. The developers may work with quality in mind while management feels schedule pressures. Or the final product just ends up far less compelling than the original discussions made it out to be. All of these are symptoms of a poorly communicated and managed vision for the project.

To work properly, a good vision needs to be more than a hastily concocted set of buzzwords. It needs to be a well-considered description that will rally the team to collaborate in producing a winning product. It will serve as a benchmark for determining whether any potential change should be reasonably included in the project, and it will act as a reference to identify relative priorities and authorities right up front. Clarifying these things early, well before trouble starts, allows for effective decision making that can be more difficult later when everyone is buried in his or her own issues.

Although the requirements specification is the central source of all information that drives and coordinates all future work on a project (from the plans to the implementation and test artifacts), the vision statement and surrounding information comes first. This sets the stage for building the right specification for the job. In an ideal situation, all effort on a project should be in alignment with the single vision.

The Big Picture

I find myself in a situation right now where I have a large strategic project on the go, in addition to the tactical engagements and the day-to-day operations around here. It is a significant undertaking, and will probably consume the bulk of my time over the next year. Fitting everything in is a difficult task. There is constant juggling of priorities and adjustments that need to take place to achieve my goals.

Big deal. Welcome to my world, you might say.

True, we all juggle a large number of activities on a daily basis, some of us more effectively than others. What I find interesting at this point with a large project is that there is an inexorable draw into the details of the tasks, an attraction to deal with the minutiae before getting a handle on the bigger picture. It takes a great deal of conscious effort to step back and gain a handle on the overall issues.

Just like what happens in many large software projects, the sheer enormity of the effort, along with the multitude of interesting or challenging areas to focus on, can drive us down into the zone where we focus on the details prematurely.

 No matter the size of the project, there is value in stepping back and understanding the big picture. What success looks like, what *done* really means, and what approach is reasonable to allow you to get there. For the smaller efforts, or for the tasks that you are intimately familiar with, this can be a quick, trivial exercise. For those efforts that are greater in scope or more novel, it can be a difficult thing to do, but much more critical. For endeavors that span longer times or incorporate more risk and uncertainty, the effort of getting a handle on the big picture never really stops. This picture should constantly be refined with all the discovery that takes place along the way.

For many large projects, there is some effort applied to building the big picture to a point where a go/no-go decision is made. This may be as refined as a detailed spec and a correspondingly detailed Gantt chart, but more often the spec has holes in it, and the Gantt chart is little more than an exercise in fitting known tasks into a committed time period. Most "war rooms" I've seen are completely out of date, and not enough teams use the spec through the entire life cycle. There is an initial snapshot, but no current understanding.

Some project teams are strong at managing the big picture throughout, but they are relatively rare based on my experience. It is a difficult, labor-intensive job to continuously manage the overall project and to ensure that all resources are effectively working on the appropriate elements of the project. Most projects will descend into chaos sooner or later in a variety of ways.

In many projects, prototyping is a great way of answering questions at any point in the life cycle. Often, even seasoned developers will claim that they are prototyping to discover nuggets of information. These prototypes, however poorly constructed originally, expand to become components of the finished system. The prototype becomes a skunk works effort that is not related to the big picture. No expectation of schedule. No clear definition of completion. Any initial good intent is usurped. The potential value of the prototype is overcome by the chaos introduced through the delivery of a sloppy implementation.

In other projects, typically through lack of oversight, there will come a time when the team realizes there is much more work to do than there is available time. Instead of stepping back and strategizing when it is most critical, the team will pull out all the stops to get things done. Crazy hours, focus on bugs rather than scope, and burnout are rampant. If you haven't been there, count your blessings.

To avoid that descent into chaos, that nebulous phase best described as "and then a miracle happens," where heroic efforts battle against rampant uncertainty, characterized by hope rather than technical estimates, we must all see the big picture and keep it current.

So, what is this big picture, anyway? To my mind, it is the best possible understanding of the overall goals, scope, plan of attack, and areas of uncertainty and risk on the project. Although it is nice to build pretty Gantts and thick specs, it is far more critical to ensure that the entire team has a consistent common understanding of the big picture throughout the project life cycle, which is a much deeper effort. Gantt charts, documents, status reports, and other sundry items are tools to facilitate this consistent common understanding, but are insufficient in themselves.

We need to communicate in the most effective way possible, and that generally means a variety of approaches. Whiteboards, digital cameras, videos of design presentations, outliners, and mind maps are a few novel techniques you can add to your list of potential tools for communication. Take some time to consider the most appropriate techniques for collaborating. What information is critical to maintain throughout? Constant feedback among the team is critical to ensure that information is correctly received, and nothing on the project—the scope, the plan, the approach, the implementation, the understanding of risks and uncertainty—is sacrosanct. It is all open to debate, discussion, and refinement.

Even for a team of one, the big picture is essential to maintain. I don't have a crisp recollection of the things I decided yesterday without some form of record, and nobody likes having to discover or decide things twice.

Take the time to understand the big picture, and keep it current on your important projects. It is your most important investment.

Up Front or As You Go?

One of the key issues in the debate about how to develop software effectively is the relative merit of up-front analysis and design. Whereas some people are quite vocal about leaning toward one way or the other, others are less vocal, and take the third option of never bothering to really do either one.

I'm not sure they are even aware that a debate is going on around them.

In one camp, let's call it the traditional camp, there are strong arguments for doing the analysis up front. There is risk involved in proceeding with design or construction until it is clear what you need to build. This is the venerable waterfall model taken to its limit. For well-understood domains with limited uncertainty, there's a lot of merit in this approach.

In the other camp, call it the agile camp, the argument goes that you should quickly identify the scope of the system, just enough to give you a framework to move ahead. Spike a quick architectural overview, and dive into the code. Heck, while we're at it, let's stomp on the old waterfall model further by pulling the test before the coding phase! There's value in discovery, and there's no better way of discovering the challenges we are going to face than by getting on with it.

Back to that third option, which, to the untrained eye, looks a lot like the agile camp. It is unnerving how many organizations dive into the code before understanding what they are trying to build or how it should be structured. For many people in the industry, it's all about the construction phase, and life is a big code-and-fix party. (Bring your own pizza, life is not an option.) We'll be done when somebody says it's okay, when we run out of time, or when we find someone to buy it from us. Declaring completeness usually means that we then start to focus on fixing the features we've thrown together in front of the customer.

The distinction really needs to be made between this third group and the other camps, both of which advocate the construction of a strong product. Each of the first two can be a valid approach for different projects, and there are many shades of gray in between (none of which look like that third option).

? The key is to understand the nature of what you are building. Recognize the trade-offs for whether you front-end load the project with deep analysis and design or distribute the effort more evenly across the project. To simply neglect analysis and design is not a valid option.

If there are areas that are relatively stable and can be started early, or if there are areas that could use a prototype to help the discovery process, dive in. He who hesitates is lost.

If you have low tolerance for rework and the relative luxury of schedule slack, you are probably better off doing the analysis up front to the best of your ability. Look before you leap.

It is impossible to reasonably declare completeness until you have a complete understanding of what you are building, and that implies a thorough analysis has been done.

Whether that is reflected in a stack of signed-off specifications or a stack of feature cards and a happy onsite client is irrelevant. The choice is do it up front or do it as you go—but do it.

Summary

Clearly defined goals, agreed upon by the diverse range of stakeholders, are a critical starting point for a project.

When we take the time to resolve these in a specific, measurable fashion, they serve several purposes. They are a clear guidepost against which we can measure any potential changes to determine whether it would be appropriate to include them in the project. They also serve to make us accountable for the project, by defining what success means to us.

Without clearly defined goals, we could artificially declare success on our projects, but remain disappointed with the results.

How Is This Relevant?

First steps. Do you identify specific goals for your projects? Do representatives of all stakeholder groups agree on these goals?

What is success? Is success identified in a number of dimensions for your projects? Does it include specific measures for time, quality, scope, and cost? Are these balanced appropriately so that the most important goals are prioritized?

Knowing where we are headed. Are these goals used as a reasonable basis for definition of scope? Are they used to determine whether changes are appropriate to include in this project. Are these goals reviewed over time to ensure that they remain appropriate?

References

1. Geoffrey Moore, Crossing the Chasm: *Marketing and Selling Disruptive Products to Mainstream Customers* (HarperCollins, 2002).

CHAPTER SEVENTEEN

Specification

Thoroughly defining what we need to build is a difficult task to accomplish, but still much easier than the alternative. A good specification is the basis of everything that follows on a project: the schedule, the implementation, and the validation.

In this chapter, we look here at the arguments for putting the effort into this specification. Some projects lend themselves to building this understanding up front; some are more evolutionary in nature. It is inappropriate to expect that we will ever have a perfect specification of the product, regardless of the nature of the project. What we are looking for is enough to move forward with reduced risk.

Accidental Specification

Do you work on projects that might accidentally get to their destination?

Accidents Will Happen

You are driving along, in a rush because you are late. The traffic certainly has gotten worse now that the kids are back in school, and…oh yeah…you had better remember to…augghhhh…you've hammered the brakes a bit too late, and you have hit the person who has rather aggressively pulled out in front of you. Great! There goes your schedule!

The good news is that nobody is hurt, damage is minimal, and even your cell phone still works (which is surprising given how hard it slammed into the windshield when you let go of it). What is going through your mind as you hastily exchange details so that you can get on your way? There is probably some embarrassment over not watching where you were going, although that's not stated. More likely, there is some anger that the other person jumped out of nowhere and you ended up with intertwined license plates. What the heck was he thinking?

Actually, he was probably thinking along similar lines. Before the event: places to go, people to see, and the traffic is terrible. Afterward: maybe I should have been more careful, that other person could have given me more room. You get back into your cars and drive away. Although more careful for a day or two, you soon fall back to the old habits of not really paying attention to the rules of the road.

When we are behind the wheel, we are part of a larger system, whether we are aware of it or not. We rarely think of what we can do to help ensure that the overall system thrives, and that our contribution is a positive one. The rules of the road are there to help the system work more effectively, but many drivers see rules as a nuisance, something that stops them from achieving their goals.

Others drive as though they aren't aware the rules even exist.

I've been on software projects where most people charge along with a similar neglect for what their system should be doing.

In a frightfully large number of software projects, the specification—a clear, complete description of what the product should be—does not exist. The team rarely coordinates to the point where there is a common understanding of the vision. People are focused on an idea of what they need to work on, usually passed along by someone who carries that vision in his head. They rarely understand the context around their contribution.

As team members build their parts and then try to put the system together, there are all sorts of software fender benders:

"I thought you were going to send me this data element."

"Why did you implement it that way?"

"How could you possibly think that would work!"

The lack of shared vision appears quickly, often, and sometimes with heated debate and bruised egos. Unfortunately for most software projects, it often happens when there are only a few weeks left in the schedule. It's rush hour, and all the freeways are clogged.

Only after accidents or misunderstandings do we really think about the rules of the game, whether it is driving to a destination or building a software product. It is all too easy to forge ahead to where you think you need to be long before you are truly prepared. Software projects still get completed, but they rarely resemble the original vision. Few teams are fully aware of that vision from the beginning. Too often, the journey resembles a demolition derby more than a staid commute.

 Is your entire team playing to the same understanding of what they need to build, or will you be building your specification as you navigate the upcoming series of accidents?

Keep It Real

I'm working with a company right now that has significant problems with requirements development.

Or so they think.

They certainly have what would appear to be all the classic symptoms of trouble in this area. Projects end up being significantly delayed. Resources are cannibalized from other projects to pick up the pieces (hence delaying those projects, sometimes before they get started). Key resources on the team spend a great deal of their time answering the same questions for different people, and feel bogged down. E-mail is the primary communication source for changes that occur during the project, and we all know how effective that can be for maintaining a clean audit trail!

With a little bit of poking around, however, they have some real strengths to build on. They have a great handle on the competitive landscape. They set objectives for their projects based on specific quantified factors relative to their competition. They take the time to identify composite personas for their different user classes to ensure that they have a common understanding of their client and can reasonably gather the breadth of critical use cases. They are even starting to manage all their projects in terms of a broad strategic portfolio rather than unrelated projects with no leverage between them.

They spend a great deal of time up front defining the requirements, yet they have the symptoms of requirements problems. Where's the disconnect?

The disconnect lies in the minds and attitudes of the team members themselves. Most of them approach requirements as something to do on a project before you get started actually building the product. They have two modes of operation. They start out chilling their heels with requirements work in the early stages when the pressure is low. At some point in the project, an imaginary switch is turned on (could this be another project stealing some critical resources?), and suddenly it is time to get busy.

At that point, all that requirements work is cast aside, it's time to get the real work done. Build some prototypes, evolve them into the final system, and switch over to fixing bugs as a means of getting the project completed. Changes are made on-the-fly in a scramble to get things done, and the overruns begin. Eventually, a product is shipped, and the whole cycle starts again after management rewards the heroes who saved the day on this challenged project.

The team needs to appreciate the true value that complete, consistent, commonly understood requirements can provide them. The requirements need to be kept real, throughout the project.

It appears that this group is not alone in their approach. I've seen a number of companies that put significant effort into developing a set of requirements, but then fail to leverage their full value. Often, this leads to the perception that the whole requirements effort is a waste of time, is overhead work. The cycle can spiral out of control, and teams fall into the code-and-fix approach to getting their work done.

On the positive side of this challenge, we have the opportunity to frame potential changes in the context of work that is currently being done. All the effort that is in place now provides powerful insight into the problem space and structure into defining an effective solution. So, change in this context does not involve a great deal of additional work, which is usually the greatest barrier to change.

Indeed, in this situation, we need to weigh the cost of everyone discovering and solving important issues independently against the cost of managing an infrastructure that allows people to actually find the information that has been collected up front. The arguments for change become much more compelling as we get people to recognize that the information exists and that improved mechanisms for finding and maintaining this information are available.

The requirements effort is fine here. It is the knowledge management that needs to be addressed, and the habits and perceptions surrounding the initial efforts on the project. We have to refine the problem from trying to put a reasonable requirements development process in place to helping people appreciate the value in the work they are already doing. Although still a challenge to resolve, this is a much more precise area to focus on.

That work they are doing up front is the real effort that drives project success.

Reference Points

Whenever you head into uncharted territory, whether it is a trip across the country or a lunch with a friend at a new restaurant, we always try to identify where we are or where we are headed by using familiar reference points.

The greater our common familiarity, the more detailed and precise our reference points can be. I surprise many people in the

United States by explaining that the weather here in Vancouver is much like Seattle. Closer to home, I can just identify a particular Starbucks as a reference point for locating that new sushi bar that a friend and I need to find for lunch.

One would think that the reference points used by people on the same team, working on the same project, would be quite detailed and precise, but this is often not the case. It is unnerving to hear the number of people who don't regularly use a specification or design as the basis for developing an application—perhaps because it doesn't exist at all, is incomplete, out of date, can't be found, or because they can't be bothered to look or have been burned in the past!

When people get together to build a house, it would be unthinkable to do so without a reference point to work from. For a house, which has roughly the same order of complexity as many software projects, this reference point is a broad set of drawings and other information that is established in advance. It is kept current with "as-built" annotations along the way, even though there is much less novelty involved in building a house. The multiple views all tie together consistently, and whether it is a plan view, plumbing or electrical detail, landscaping, or other perspective of the house, each has been developed in the context of the others.

We have this consistent set of views for a house because we can all appreciate the cost of building House 2.0.

It just doesn't make sense to develop a product without a set of reference points to keep the team synchronized in the midst of uncertainty and discovery. Starting with a strong metaphor, through the development and evolution of user stories, the reference points for the project grow and strengthen with time. The fact that they are not collected in a formalized document is more often than not an advantage in the world of constant change.

 Those who might suggest that the code is the only real reference point for their software systems are, to my mind, just plain wrong. Although some projects will actually be deemed successful without the initial common ground and direction being laid, they almost always arrive at their endpoint through a great deal of confusion, restarts, disappointment, and missed expectations. The declared success is frail, and usually arbitrary.

Even for projects involving one person over a long time (as many of my "hobby" projects tend to be), there needs to be a place to capture information that can be referenced later. What I'm trying to build, what's been done, what's left to discover, and the rationale behind my decisions need to be documented so that I don't have to go through the painful discovery twice.

For any project, no matter the size, the team involved, or the timeframes you are dealing with, there is great value in deciding up front which reference points are going to be needed to keep the team headed to the same destination. With an understanding of what needs to be captured and where it is going to be stored, we have a higher likelihood of using it throughout the project. We know where our compass is.

As the information is being built up initially, retaining and managing it in a planned location and format reduces the risk of loss and makes it easier to cross-reference against other sources for consistency.

Focus on identifying and detailing those reference points to avoid having the team scattered in all directions. This makes it much easier to converge to the same endpoint as expected.

The Cone of Specification

Have you ever been on a project where there is a stage that can be best described as "and then a miracle happens?" For many software projects, that stage occurs very early, and magically, the team is off coding the product. If you were to ask them to describe the big picture for the project, however, you would probably get as many different answers as there are team members.

Information is successively refined from the initial idea to the point where we have enough information to allow the team to build the product. It doesn't all occur in a single magical moment.

Specification isn't a single monolithic activity that times out because the schedule says you need to hurry up and start coding.

Initially, all we have is the genesis of an idea, best defined as a potential solution for a real problem for an identified user. Being clear on the vision of the product is critical to align the team and the thinking around this idea. A specific identification of the need, the target market, the basic approach, and the key differentiators from either the competition or the status quo will serve as a solid sounding board for all that follows. Skimp here and you reduce the likelihood that the nifty idea actually solves a problem, or even holds together as a cohesive package.

Often, there are more ideas than there is time and resources, so the ideas need to be refined to the point where you can make rational decisions about which are most feasible or attractive to the business. We need to generate enough information for a business case, so we drill down to identify the major features of the system, the business constraints in which we will have to operate, and the expectations we have about the value of the system, both to the end user and to our business.

Don't mistake a list of features for a full specification. Although it might be enough to prioritize some actions at a high level, it is far too insufficiently detailed to guide a development team and expect a complete system. Miss this stage and you are likely to blow out your budget and schedule, fail to implement key features, run into major architectural surprises in the eleventh hour, and fail to meet your customer's expectations.

All you really have at this point is enough information to decide whether to move forward with a project. From here, you still have the bulk of the specification activity to deal with. This effort is meant to provide enough information to allow you to reasonably estimate effort, and to specify the expected behavior and properties of the system so that the team can forge ahead with little risk of surprise when you try to converge later. Skip this step and you are almost guaranteed to have a challenging integration stage, significant downstream issues with interpretation of how the features are to be implemented, slipped schedules, feature creep, compromised architecture, and poor delivered quality—assuming you even make it that far.

When are you done with the specification stage, how do you know at the end of the day that you have achieved your goals? You can ask a number of questions:

- Are you confident that you can send the team off on their activities with little risk of surprise at the task level, let alone at the overall product level?
- How do you know your product is good—is *goodness* defined?
- Can you credibly estimate based on this information, or are you just targeting?
- Do you have the same understanding of *goodness* as your customer does?
- For that matter, who is your customer, and what problem are you solving?

Real completion is not a matter of timing out, it is a matter of making sure all the appropriate steps are in place. Each one of the previously described steps, if not adequately covered, can be the seed for failure in a project.

Although it is possible to deliver even after skipping a few of the previously described steps, your chances for success will diminish significantly if you fail to respect them.

All the steps provide information that clarifies the solution space and in turn reduces risk. The information gathered at each step could reveal that the overall idea isn't feasible at all. The earlier you know that, the less money you will waste heading down the wrong path.

Keeping One Step Ahead

Ah, the perfect software specification. The Holy Grail of software development.

A perfect specification is a complete, clear document that everyone uses as a basis for defining his and her work on a project: the design, construction, testing, and validation activities required to put the product together. It facilitates reasonable planning and estimating, ensures that you have captured the intent for the end user, and…does not exist in this universe.

For any reasonably sized product to be built, the effort for producing a perfect specification far outweighs the value that you would gain if you were to somehow manage to achieve that goal. There isn't enough money in the budget or time on the calendar, and the customer is likely far less interested in the document than in the product that will actually solve his problems. Business moves much too quickly to allow any specification to remain perfect for any length of time. There will always be pressures for change, both internally and externally.

What you really need to do is have enough information to stay at least one step ahead of the team. Not perfect, but sufficient specification.

The specification provides guidance and common understanding, but at any point in time, you cannot look at the detailed specification in its entirety. When you have an understanding of the overall scope of the system, you have the opportunity to prioritize where you fill in the details. In any product, some areas of the system are more straightforward to specify. These are less likely to change and can be started with lower risk. Other areas that are highly risky should be specified and implemented sooner to mitigate that risk. Specify these to a point where the team can reasonably progress forward and you have bought yourself a precious commodity: time.

Certainly, there is value at all stages to look at the breadth of information available to check for consistency, completeness, and opportunities for optimization and reuse, but to wait for a complete specification before diving into some areas is usually not the best use of your time. It is critical that the team, usually the most expensive resource on a software project, is being utilized as effectively as possible throughout the project. You need to provide the team enough information to allow them to move forward in a planned manner.

You are laying the stepping-stones for the team to get across the pond, not paving the pond. There is a good chance on many projects that you will get to the end without having filled in all the holes you originally thought you would have to deal with. Discovery and changes along the way have made many of the original issues obsolete, and you have actually saved effort. The refined understanding you have from the partial implementation will simplify your job for the rest of the system and will validate the original intent internally and with the customer.

You need to stay at least one step ahead of the team, but you can't keep them waiting forever.

How Much Is Enough?

Anyone who has worked on reasonably sized software projects knows that it is impossible to craft a perfect specification.

There is the trade-off between spending the time to polish the final details that will never be complete and getting down to actually making progress toward the finished project. Too many unknowns can only be resolved with further investigation into the design and implementation areas. The business continues to evolve as we work to complete the project. There is a good chance that your customer will give the specification only a brief initial glance, ensuring that you will have refinements to make downstream.

How do we know that we have done enough work on the requirements to move on?

It has been said that software development is really an exercise in knowledge management. We start out in the abstract space. As we progress, we gain more information about what it is that we are building, how we are going to build it, and whether we have built it correctly. At the end, we have (hopefully) answered all our questions and solved our problem. The software itself is just one stage of the overall discovery process.

Whether you can comfortably move on beyond requirements as the primary focus will depend on a number of factors:

- **The criticality of the project.** Are you building a life-critical application or a simple jig to be used once?

- **The number and distribution of people that need to be coordinated for the project.** Is this a one-person task, or are we dealing with a large globally distributed team?
- **The duration of the project.** Will this be put together in a week or two, or will the life of the product span years or decades?
- **The degree of coupling of different components.** Can one well-understood area of the system progress while the others are still relatively vague?
- **The business constraints of the project.** When does it need to be completed, and how much can we afford to spend?

All these factors (and likely more) will combine to drive a distinct comfort level for that project. You can progress beyond requirements only when you have built up enough understanding to give yourself reasonable assurance that the current unknowns are not likely to burn you more than you can afford. The end of the requirements stage should not be a predetermined date that you arrive at. Instead, it should be a result of the careful balancing of a number of factors, which determine that your analysis is sufficient to move forward. To arbitrarily set a line in the sand, after which requirements are no longer addressed, is to ask for failure.

In the real world, I've found that even if there is a formal signoff or review to mark the end of the requirements stage, the demarcation remains quite fuzzy. There is an ongoing juggling between analysis, design, construction, and verification as we move forward. Just as Michelangelo saw his completed sculpture in a raw piece of stone and simply removed the chunks that were not part of his final masterpiece, building software is an ongoing effort to get to the endpoint by working at whatever level of abstraction "gives" the most at a given point in time. Early on, the big chunks can be roughed out, and the overall shape of the final product begins to emerge. This rough work needs to be done for at least some areas before we can progress to the detailed work.

We constantly bounce up and down the levels of abstraction to assure ourselves that we are still on target. We may need to dive into a prototype to understand the feasibility of an implementation. We may need to clarify user interaction with storyboarding. We can't reduce the uncertainty in the estimates and schedule without actually doing some of the work, but we must continuously bounce back to our original vision to be sure we are actually solving the right problem.

We've done enough requirements work only when we can safely move forward without worrying about having to paste huge pieces of stone back into place. Few of us have an infinite supply of stone or time to create our masterpieces.

Summary

The specification of your product is your most critical intellectual property and should be treated as such.

Almost every organization I have ever worked with would benefit from a more conscientious effort in building and maintaining their specification. Although most critical, it is often the most neglected component.

We need to appreciate the value of clarifying our understanding of what we need to build. This needs to be the basis for all of our work, and needs to be kept current and commonly understood throughout our projects. Anything less is an invitation for missteps, which can be costly.

How Is This Relevant?

Basis for everything. Do you use a specification as a basis for your schedule, implementation, and validation of your product? Is it considered a contract for work, or more like a wish list of possibilities?

Evolving understanding. Is your specification kept current as your project progresses? Are problems with the specification corrected throughout the project?

Persisted communication. Has everyone contributed to the construction and validation of the specification? Has it been written by a narrower team (or individual) and thrown over the wall? Do all participants use it regularly to ensure they are all working in a coordinated fashion?

CHAPTER EIGHTEEN

Prioritization

I have yet to see a project where there are adequate resources and time to accomplish everything that we would like to. Using our goals to provide ongoing, balanced guidance of what is important to us, we need to strike a balance of what can reasonably be accomplished within our constraints, to provide the best solution possible.

In this chapter, we look at the necessity of prioritization and some of the costs we could incur if we fail to prioritize our efforts throughout the project.

Getting Started with the Right Foot Forward

On any project, at any point in time, you could spend your time on a variety of activities. Most of us, most of the time, are probably working on suboptimal activities, and at the beginning of a project the cost of inappropriate focus is highest. Decisions have a nasty habit of snowballing throughout the project life cycle, especially the ones that weren't made early enough.

Focus on the important rather than the urgent. Steven Covey got it right. Most of us spend much more time than we should working on tasks that seem to be urgent, giving us little or no time to focus on the tasks that are really important. How many of us have the Pavlovian tendency to check our e-mail each time we hear that bell? I know it is one of my worst habits, although I'd like to think I make up for it by ruthlessly keeping my inbox clear and all correspondence appropriately sorted.

Emphasis on projects is often the same. We have a tendency to work on the things we see as interesting, leaving the difficult decisions as long as we possibly can.

Strategize up front to determine what the important activities are for your project. Clearly identify what the endpoint looks like (in terms of features, time, cost, and quality). Identify the major milestones and stumbling blocks along the way. The high-risk issues and difficult areas of the project are best tackled earlier rather than later, so there is sufficient time and flexibility to change direction should things not work out as expected. If one of these issues happens to become a showstopper, you have the ability to kill the project and redirect the resources where they can be more effective before you waste too much time.

Build a tracking and reporting system that allows you to focus on extraordinary events. If you are starting a project, construct the schedule at the level where you can gain prompt knowledge when a task is about to go off the rails, but not so detailed that you spend a lot of time managing the schedule in the planning tool rather than actually running the project. Use status reports that focus on the issues that need attention, instead of repeating the same drivel every reporting period. Don't be afraid to sit down and determine what that critical information is, instead of just reporting the same expected status tens or hundreds of times throughout the project.

Focus on all potential changes in the same context, and ruthlessly protect the goal rather than the current path to that goal. The plan is merely a way of structuring your approach toward the goal, and will change dramatically over time as you discover greater insight throughout the project. At any point in time, your current activity may become redundant or counterproductive. Only a clear understanding of the overall goals and true impact of any proposed changes will allow you to ensure that you are working on the important issues.

Identify up front what is important, what the end looks like, and how you are going to progress. Tracking your project will go a long way toward helping your team focus on the appropriate activities.

> I've yet to see a project that would not have benefited from a better identification and understanding of the most important activities.

Strategize Before Prioritizing

 If you've spent any time in the software industry (or taken on any other project, for that matter), you know that there is rarely enough time to get everything done that you would like to. It quickly becomes clear that prioritization of your activities and overall scope is important if you want to achieve any sense of accomplishment.

Prioritizing the potential scope for a project is critical for a couple of reasons. It allows you to order your efforts such that the most important elements are accomplished early, providing the flexibility to cut the "nice to haves" if necessary as the schedule tightens toward the deadline. You are likely to leave some of the originally intended scope on the sidelines, and prioritization reduces the likelihood that one of those neglected features was necessary for success.

Before proceeding down that prioritization path, it is useful to step back and explicitly identify the appropriate strategy to take. With a commonly understood rationale behind the prioritized scope, everyone can work together with a consistent understanding of what *important* means in your specific situation. Depending where you are with your product, there can be a combination of strategies that are determined to be critical, each driving you to a very different prioritization scheme on your way to completion:

- If you are in the early phases of an iterative development cycle, you may need to validate architectural or design elements to reduce risk of the overall implementation and provide a solid basis for growth. In doing so, you might choose to downplay many of the observable features of the product and focus on the critical infrastructure that holds everything together.

- If you are determined to take the product into a trade show, your strategy may be to ensure that your differentiating features are clearly apparent, even if they have to be presented with well-rehearsed scripts and artificial back ends.

- If you are bringing the product to market, you will want to ensure that all the features are ready for prime time, and that the features released hold together with no loose ends.

- If you are looking to stabilize a product that has been less than polished in the marketplace, you will want to step back and identify root causes for the major issues and resolve them rather than apply bandages and perpetuate your problems. In this case, design and analysis are prioritized over new features.

Select an explicit strategy for your situation before you delve into the prioritization process.

With an explicit strategy in place, the *important* elements of the product that is embodied in the vision (you do have an identified vision for the project, don't you?) can be married to the *urgency* of the business constraints.

You will certainly improve both your product and your sense of accomplishment.

Juggling Priorities

It's easy to suggest that any project—given scope, schedule, cost, and quality—must have one absolute priority at any given time. That priority will certainly differ from project to project and can change within the same project at different points; if people on the same project are placing emphasis on different priorities as they approach their work, however, you can expect problems.

 That's the theory, but many real-life situations don't appear so cut and dry. Although there are a few projects where it can be relatively easy to make the choice (hopefully the focus for life-critical systems is quality above all), most projects are not easily categorized. It can be difficult to understand how to manage the apparently conflicting priorities that seem to want to pull the project apart. What is often happening under the hood, however, is that the superficial focus on one of these dimensions is actually degrading performance in the other areas much more than it needs to be.

The most often cited critical factor for a project is schedule, which comes in several forms. There are appropriate schedule priorities, such as the need to meet external demands driven by the tax year, Labor Day, or the holiday retail season. If you miss those deadlines, your window of opportunity has vanished (and as it often turns out, so has the project manager).

Unfortunately, there are also inappropriate schedule priorities, those that are artificially dumped on the team, often with the intent of maintaining pressure. Whether it was dates promised to a client at a trade show or some other fictitious concoction, trying to live to a target without regard to the technical feasibility is never a good thing. If there were technical considerations beyond the use of a dartboard in selecting a schedule, be sure to communicate this to the team so that they understand that they are not just the victims of targeting.

Quality comes in as the second most cited priority. What often happens is that the priority is specified early on, but when push comes to shove on the project, quality is sacrificed in the name of getting the product out the door. The key with a quality focus is to explicitly define precisely what *quality* means for the product being built. This will allow you to determine whether you have succeeded. It will tell you early what sort of infrastructure you need to build alongside the product to verify that quality. It is a feeble façade to cite quality as the critical project factor but then to ignore a test infrastructure, defined quality requirements, or specific testing activities as a means to that end.

There is often a perception that a quality priority will cost a great deal more money and time. In reality, companies need to consider the "cost of nonquality" they are experiencing in the systems they are building today. Because most organizations are running with huge inefficiencies, a significant cost savings can easily be realized internally quite quickly with a little focus on tuning the right activities. A reasonable focus on quality (perhaps not to the level of life-critical systems) would actually develop a better system faster and cheaper than what they are capable of today.

Cost and scope are rarely cited as absolute priorities on projects, so the best way of looking at these are as tools for managing the key priorities, whatever they may be. Certainly if cost is paramount, it makes sense to not be extravagant, but it is important to consider that simply cost cutting is rarely an effective approach. As with everything, it is important to understand the overall value proposition.

With scope, the challenge often comes when the stakeholders suggest that everything is the highest priority for a system. Few systems have all the functionality that is critical for the next release. A little diligence in feature prioritization can go a long way toward making life easier. Implementing the critical features first provides flexibility for projects that truly are schedule constrained, and allows you to truly validate these features if you are prioritizing quality. A critical feature may be part of the core architecture, a differentiating feature in the marketplace, or an absolute must-have based on externally driven factors such as business rules. As push comes to shove on your project (have you ever been on a project where it hasn't?), you still have the option of dropping the lower-priority features and delivering a reasonable product.

 If your project is like most, quality and schedule are often both high priorities. It's got to work, and it's got to be available. If that is the case, take the time to understand in a quantified fashion what that really means for you. Develop an understanding of your flexibility in all four dimensions that will make it easier to satisfy your goals. There are usually some options available for having your cake and eating it, too.

Leveling and Prioritizing Scope

Few projects have the luxury of having more resources available than needed for the production of everything that is desired, to the degree of quality that is needed. Although we can (and often do) fool ourselves by neglecting quality and cramming everything into our constraints, a more reasonable approach is to prioritize the scope so that we are more likely to complete what is needed and can choose what to do with the rest. We could relax the schedule to get everything done, defer the functionality to the next release, or acknowledge that it really wasn't that important after all.

If we choose to do this, there are a couple of steps to take (refer to Karl Wiegers for more information on this approach, and access to a supporting spreadsheet[1]). The first is to collect all the scope together at the appropriate level.

Working with high-level business requirements, we have the advantage of dealing with a relatively small number of items. At this point, the scope is naturally bundled into nuggets that hold together. We are less likely to orphan dependent components. On the other hand, we lose the fine granularity that allows us to select specific aspects of a business feature that could otherwise be deferred to a later release.

We could just as easily work at the level of use cases, which gives us more elements to deal with, but allows us to continue to focus at the level of the end user and we can be more selective in prioritizing our scope.

You would need a pretty good reason to prioritize requirements at the detailed functional level, with the massive number and the increased risk of breaking up the cohesiveness of the selected scope.

After you have decided the level at which you want to work, the next step is to eliminate those requirements that clearly must be part of the current release. Core functionality and those features that essentially define the product need not be considered. Don't waste your time including them in the prioritization; reduce the number of elements to deal with.

When prioritizing, be sure to consider the perspectives of all the different stakeholders. A reasonable and straightforward approach is to consider the needs of the user community and the development community. These are both valid positions, often at odds with one another. From the user side, there may be a high cost if a component that would normally be expected in this product class is removed, just as there can be a high cost if a feature that is a strong differentiator from the competition is dropped. From the development side, a feature that is expensive to implement would be lower priority than one that is easy to implement, if their value to the client is equivalent. We need to consider the risk of implementing this feature, too. This includes the uncertainty in the magnitude of effort and the likelihood of perturbing the existing architecture.

Other models can certainly be used. You may want to consider the degree of impact on the existing business processes made by the proposed system and overall life cycle costs. Or, you might choose to select between alternative implementations of the same feature, varying by technological approach or degree of fidelity.

Whatever model makes sense for the situation, decide in advance, and use a spreadsheet to do the calculations for prioritization. Separating the prioritization model used from the actual data to be evaluated is a strong practice to reduce (or at least focus) the debates that could arise. It gives all the participants an appreciation for the different perspectives that are represented.

Remember, too, that you have degrees of freedom when you consider the quality attributes at the feature level. Do you want to implement the feature as a reusable component? Are there other quality attributes that you can use as levers to provide flexibility, such as testability and maintainability, security, and perhaps even usability? A less-usable system could be compensated for through more training, for example.

It is really all about maximizing your flexibility as you adjust scope to give the best overall product that will fit inside your constraints. Choose the right level, select and agree upon a model in advance, and your prioritization exercise will yield strong results.

The Cost of Delaying Cleanup

We've all seen the curves showing the cost of repair for a defect as a function of how long it has been latent in the system. Statistics show an exponential increase in cost with up to a hundredfold difference between defects caught early and those left lurking in the system. We all know, however, that statistics can be used, as essayist Andrew Lang notes, "As a drunken man uses lamp-posts—for support rather than illumination." Perhaps we can look for some illumination in the underlying mechanisms for this cost.

Once software or a supporting document gets placed into the developmental baseline, additional product will start to be built on top of it. The longer it's in the system, the more the entire structure is likely to depend on this supporting base. When the original issue is found and fixed, the rest of the structure can come falling down in a cascading Tower of Babel, increasing the scope of change. The increased cost here is likely exponential as a function of latency time.

As an element moves on in the life cycle of a project, it will often transition to other teams to be further refined—analysis models to designers, code to testers, and so on. The costs to repair defects increases as more people are involved and further coordination is required. Here we likely get a step-function increase each time someone else is involved with an element.

A similar driver, whether or not additional people are involved, is whether an element is part of an earlier stage activity (requirements or design, for example). If so, its span of influence is typically much wider than that of downstream elements (code or test cases, for example). A problem with these early-phase artifacts can affect a high percentage of the system. Here we get another phase-based step-function of cost as we transition to a new phase.

One of the greatest jumps in cost occurs if the client finds the defect. The costs of fixing the issue as described previously are often outweighed by the costs of re-release, patches, and softer costs of lost credibility. This jump alone, an enormous step-function at product release, accounts for the lion's share of what is typically shown as an exponential curve.

 What does all this mean? All these contributors are compelling evidence for the need to capture as many defects as possible in the phase in which they were injected into the system. Many companies focus exclusively on functional testing to confirm their product works. This is way too late in the cycle. It is cost intensive if done to any degree of completeness, and just plain misses many early-phase defects altogether. Defects can indeed be found earlier, in documents, code, or any other element that is created.

 Another significant cost that isn't captured at all in these exponential curves is the cost of lost flexibility. As time marches on, your options for dealing with a defect will diminish. A scope defect found early can be easily managed in a variety of ways, but one caught close to delivery can often force you down a very forbidding path to recovery. One not caught until after delivery can spell disaster. A test strategy based solely on exercising the product at its completion is not a strategy at all.

Summary

An ongoing balancing act takes place as we wrangle a project to completion. Prioritization has to take place at all levels, throughout the project life cycle.

We need to be clear, at any point in time, which are the most important things to focus on. This can only be done with representation from all stakeholders, and can be done much more efficiently if we first step back to determine how we are going to judge what is important and what model we are going to use to rank our information.

Without prioritization, we may end up building the wrong thing, spend too much time and resources doing it, and end up with a product that disappoints our stakeholders. We can easily all lose.

How Is This Relevant?

Organized decisions. Is prioritization done in an organized fashion? Are all relevant stakeholders represented? Is there a clear model that you can use to separate the politics out of the decision making? Are elements prioritized against higher-level information, such as specific goals?

Reduced chaos. Are your projects currently characterized by chaos? Are people working on elements that will never be delivered, or not working on elements that the customer would want?

Increased quality. Are activities that would generate higher quality, such as planning and testing, prioritized as important? Does active prioritization result in a stronger product? Does it reduce stress and rework with the team?

References

1. Karl Wiegers, *Software Requirements, 2nd Edition* (Microsoft Press, 2003).

CHAPTER NINETEEN

Change

If a project is the novel creation of a product, it follows that we cannot reasonably define the final solution up front. Projects are rife with discovery, and we must acknowledge that change will occur. Although we still need to understand the project in as much detail as possible, as early as possible, we still need to accommodate change.

This chapter examines the various internal and external drivers of change here, and explains the necessity of managing all potential sources of change in the same context. Change management is not a replacement for avoiding up-front planning efforts, but is the complementary ongoing activity that preserves the initial investment.

Volatility Demands Versatility

With large projects that are well understood, it is common practice to perform a reasonably thorough analysis of the problem space to provide a corresponding thorough understanding of what it will take to produce a solution. With smaller projects, or with projects that are not as well understood, however, there is often a reluctance to spend the time to gain that clarity. Suggestions that "we don't know what the end product will look like" or "this is a research project" become excuses for ignoring early-stage analysis and diving into the solution space. As the lack of certainty increases, so does the reluctance to bite off this critical chunk of effort. We have all seen the results.

When a great deal of uncertainty exists, fostering increased clarity becomes paramount for success. Throwing your hands in the air and proclaiming that we must live with huge unknowns simply gives you license to meander along, relying on luck to bring the project to closure. In any project, no matter how uncertain, there are elements that you can focus on to proactively drive to a successful conclusion.

Focus on the Known

At the very least, if you don't understand the reason for kicking off the project, you really don't have a project at all but a collection of activities that may or may not end up in something useful.

Capturing this underlying reason can bring clarity on its own. Call it a vision statement or a metaphor depending on which development camp you prefer, but working through and understanding who needs the results and what makes your solution different from what is out there can really bring a team together. For any project, it is also important to identify the overall context: the surrounding systems that will interact with this product being built, the key stakeholders, and the primary drivers of the project. (Are you driven by time, budget, scope, or quality?)

It is alarming how projects of all types will fail because of a misunderstanding in one of these areas.

Focus on the Unknown

For projects where there is a great deal of uncertainty, knowing what you don't know becomes the critical element.

This information can take several forms. There are the unknown aspects of the context you tried to identify above. (Is there really a market, for example, or how many others are building the same mousetrap?) There are also the areas of the project where the scope is unclear, or where there is uncertainty in effort required for any activity. Finally, you may encounter areas of the technology that you are unsure of.

Unaware is far different from *unknown*. It is important to recognize that with a little brainstorming, forethought, or simply recollection of previous experience, many areas of uncertainty can be identified as specific elements to clarify, or as risks to the project that can be managed appropriately.

All of these elements become known placeholders for information, can be prioritized alongside the known aspects of the system, and can be managed to closure (with that added step of clarifying the situation in each case). The longer the unknowns remain that way on a project, the greater the risk they impose.

Focus on the Changes

With all that is unknown, it is clear that change is going to be a major factor in the project.

Change needs to be treated as a positive element on these projects, and versatility becomes as important as visibility in driving toward a successful conclusion. Indeed, with a strong understanding of what is unknown, uncertain, or risky with a project, change can be proactively managed. Those areas of uncertainty or high risk should be the initial areas of focus, with the intent of reducing the risk, removing the uncertainty, and effectively converting the project as quickly as possible to one that has relatively few unknowns and that can be managed to completion (or stopped before too much effort has been consumed) with confidence.

Initial efforts are focused on filling in the gaps of the puzzle rather than just doing the easy stuff and hoping that everything will fall into place.

Running projects with a lot of unknowns can be exhilarating or frustrating, depending on your perspective and your ability to manage the gaps. There is a great deal that we know about any project, and whereas traditional analysis focuses on managing the known capabilities of the system, it is knowing what is missing and managing the uncertainty that is important for many projects we deal with. Just because you can't construct a complete and trustworthy Gantt chart up front doesn't mean there is no value in proactively planning your project. There is no correlation between uncertainty and manageability. Projects with more uncertainty just require a distinct approach to the problem.

Managing Change Management

In chatting recently with a couple of peers about projects in general, an interesting example came up about a colleague who was managing the construction of nuclear power plants in the United States. I was initially surprised to learn that the single greatest process-related challenge they face is change management. I had assumed that the process would be similar to the cookie-cutter approach used for the CANDU reactors developed here in Canada.

It seems, however, that the ecosystem in which a project exists can exert a huge influence on how the project plays out. As you would expect, regulations surround the construction of nuclear power plants, which in general is a good thing. One of the ways these regulations manifest themselves is that the profit associated with these projects is a capped percentage of the capital costs of the project.

This incents the contractor to make the project as large as possible. One of the ways to do this is to go through the entire scope and design phases for each new project. (Disclaimer: This might be an oversimplification and is likely not the intent of the regulations, but appears to be one of the results.)

With new discovery in each project, you can imagine that the change management issues can be huge, because there is little opportunity to leverage experience from previous projects.

 Comparing this to software-intensive projects, it becomes readily apparent that the ecosystem in which a project exists can dramatically affect the level of change management required.

For those large systems that are bid and won because the vendor was "least-cost compliant" (they've satisfied all of the conditions requested, at a price that is lower than the competitors), it is often the expectation that the vendor will be able to recoup some of their losses (the lower price often means extremely aggressive pricing) through change requests, which will have steep prices associated with them. A massive change management effort can be expected on such projects. The vendor will be trying to squeeze as much money out of each change as possible, while the client tries to determine whether each "change" is really just a clarification of an existing requirement.

This is nasty business. Change management becomes a necessary evil in these projects.

For new systems where we head down the development path without a clear, consistent, complete understanding of what we want (or if not complete, at least accompanied by a clear understanding of where the uncertainties lie), we can also expect significant change management issues. For many projects, this is expected and a reasonable approach. The project becomes one of discovery. It is a rare journey where each overturned rock reveals exactly what we anticipated.

The agile approaches recognize and accept this by working to make change a positive element in the cycle. For companies that take this approach and truly recognize the implications, it can become a great ecosystem to bring client and vendor together to work toward common goals on a project. Change management that is expected and planned for is not considered a burden, but a natural link in the overall process to completion.

A third type of software project starts with a weak specification and does not anticipate change downstream. This is the naïve project. Each change comes as a surprise, further derailing them from their originally intended path, which was filled with targets and promises and a little bit of black magic to squeeze the expected scope into the available envelope of time and resources. Changes are often not controlled on these projects, or begrudgingly managed with effort that was not budgeted. Change is usually considered overhead, not contributing to the completion of the project. Unfortunately, on too many projects changes lead to unanticipated schedule slips and cost overruns, while in reality those changes are often just the manifestation of initial uncertainty.

The amount of effort we can expect in the change management is often a function of the business system that has been put in place around the project. Understand the drivers that you have for scope stability, and plan to spend time in the change management cycle accordingly. If you have the rare luxury of being able to clearly specify stable requirements up front, don't squander the opportunity. At any rate, if you are finding yourself surprised by the huge amount of volatility in your project, you should probably step back to see whether you have managed your change management expectations appropriately.

Off the Happy Path

Generally, when a company actually sits down to define the process they will use to develop software, what gets captured is the "happy path." This is the thread of activities and products that would be created if everything were to go as planned.

Unfortunately, I have yet to see any reasonably sized project (and few very small projects) actually go as planned. There is always going to be some deviation from what was originally expected. For large projects, this can involve a great deal of discovery. Poor planning up front can make the defined happy path as relevant as a street map from the wrong town.

Relevance is the keyword when it comes to defining a development approach that will add value for the organization. The more the defined guidance is applicable to a given situation on the project, the more it can benefit the team. Guidance is needed more when a project is falling off the rails than when things are going as planned. Indeed, a good measure of the strength of a defined process would be a combination of how well the project achieved its defined success criteria and how often the supporting process actually provided appropriate guidance about what to do in a given situation.

A valuable defined process, therefore, needs to identify both the happy path and potential "sad paths." If the standard approach is practical and commonly followed, it is safe to say that the number of sad paths defined can be minimized, but there is always need to identify what to do when things go awry. Project retrospectives are a great source of information about which sad paths should be clarified for your projects.

The change management process can provide a good example of what a defined sad path can look like. Although most items going through the process will follow the happy path of states, such as submitted, reviewed, assigned, implemented, validated, and closed (or something similar), there will always be pressure to short circuit or avoid some elements of the standard approach. If the client calls to say that they're dead in the water until they get a fix, it could make strong business sense to emphasize speed over standard careful process to get them running again.

A well-defined sad path for a change management process includes the following:

- Clear criteria for determining whether a proposed change could be accommodated on this path
- Explicit description of the steps in the happy path that could be shortened or dropped to expedite the change through the system
- Precise instructions of how the skipped steps will be recovered later to ensure that the overall value of the change management·process is not undermined

This clarity eliminates the challenges created by individuals working to get around the defined process at their whim. It preserves the integrity of the happy path approach while accommodating the problems that commonly occur on any project, well run or not.

Defining paths such as this in advance enables us to plan how we will deal with the challenges that we know we will face, before the crisis hits and the heat is on. A well-defined process certainly contains the fair-weather guide through the park, but also includes the survival kit with instructions, prepared in advance.

What Were We Thinking? CM as a Memory Jogger

Have you ever run into the situation where, months after you've made a decision, you find yourself back in a similar situation, or even worse, in a real pickle because of the decision you made? For the life of you, it is impossible to remember what you were thinking of in the first place.

Been there, done that. If only I knew then what I know now. Hmm... what *did* I know then, anyway? It seems like a lifetime ago!

Configuration management (CM) principles help the project out in many ways. Most of us recognize CM as a tool that helps us recover that file that mysteriously went missing, or back out of an implementation path that is even worse than the one we hoped to fix. Living in the here and now, while capturing and maintaining our information under CM, gives us the confidence to move forward, knowing we have the safety net if we take a wrong step. It helps coordinate the team, and if used well, helps avoid the deadly integration stages that you may never dig yourself out of.

We have also come to depend on CM to give us assurance that we can pull together precisely what is needed to build the system: all the stuff we need, and nothing extra. Done right, we know precisely which version of each file holds together to form a cohesive set. We can reproduce any set of information we have released without having to maintain a plethora of different versions. In some shops, CM has become a crutch that has allowed us to be very sloppy with our releases. (What's one more branch?)

 In many companies I have worked with, there is one capability in CM systems that is rarely used well: the capability of capturing the rationale behind any changes that are made to the system. Any CM tool worth its salt will allow you identify the reason for change. Indeed, I don't know of any commercial tools that don't support this. Whether it is freeform text or a reference to a change request number, this audit trail is critical for the strategic evolution of the system. At any point in time, you should be able to go back to any change that has taken place and understand who made the change, why the change was made, and how it was made.

 If you find that as you check in files you just click past that troublesome dialog box that pops up asking for a comment, you are performing a severe disservice to yourself and to the project. Very few of us can recall our rationale for all our actions even a week after the fact, let alone six months or more. It is impossible for others to decipher the rationale from empty comment fields. Without the knowledge of why changes were made, you are left at best to relearn the rationale, or at worst to misinterpret the rationale and inject more problems into the system.

When you have your project baselined, you have set up a commitment and expectations with all the stakeholders. Capture this baseline under a solid configuration. Manage change appropriately from that point on, and your commitment will be preserved.

Use your CM system to preserve the changes and the rationale behind those changes, and you have a built-in long-term memory for the myriad decisions made on any project.

It is much easier to retrace your steps with a solid audit trail than to use forensics to try to reconstruct your rationale after the fact.

Just One More

One more slice of turkey, just a touch more gravy, maybe one more chocolate for dessert. There is always temptation to indulge a bit more than usual over the holidays, and the seasonal vices can easily become habits. After all, what's wrong with just one more little tidbit?

Those who recall Monty Python's *The Meaning of Life* might understand the potential implications of a single after-dinner mint.

In the business world, as we look at all the projects we have on our plate at any one time, there can be a strong temptation to take on just one more. We need to be careful that we understand the implications of our decisions. Our portfolio plate has only so much capacity, and although we can make several trips to the trough or get a bigger plate, we need to make these decisions judiciously.

Pressures come within projects, too. For those who are developing software products, there is always pressure to cram more features into the next release, often to the point where they suffer from the indigestion of half-baked ideas afterward. For those who manage to juggle a number of clients concurrently, there is the pressure to maintain the pipeline and bring new clients into the fray as soon as they can be signed on. The team can easily get spread too thinly to truly satisfy any of the clients.

Then there are those who would like to think they are developing a product, but jump when a single customer suggests that they need yet another feature. In that case, they really need to ask whether they are actually a product company after all.

Project or portfolio, we need to manage a careful juggling act to gain the most satisfaction out of our efforts without overtaxing our resources. At any point in time, we have our current level of work on our plate, and we have a constant influx of potential changes. These changes can be internally or externally driven, such as change requests, problems to fix, new projects to take on. They should all be handled together in the same manner, and all potential changes, regardless of source, can vary in a number of dimensions, such as the following:

- **Necessity of incorporating the change.** Some changes, such as the discovery that our planned approach to implementing a solution won't work, must be dealt with, whereas others are completely discretionary. Deal with the ones that must be handled as soon as they are discovered; apply triage to the remainder.

- **Impact to existing work.** Our current expectation of who is doing what and when will be impacted by any change. We need to understand the implications to the timelines of individuals and to the higher-level expectations of milestones for existing projects, both positive and negative, factoring in the impacts of learning curves and recovery periods required after strenuous bursts. (They are just bursts, aren't they?)

- **Impact to portfolio value.** Not all change is bad. Although some changes can be disappointing, others can open huge new opportunities for the business. Be careful to maximize the overall value of the portfolio that is being developed. This will allow you to focus more appropriately on reuse opportunities, too.

- **Risk of incorporating the change.** Beyond the raw cost of the change, there are several dimensions of risk to consider. How much uncertainty is there in the estimates of work for the change? How does this change impact the stability of the existing product base? All else being equal, a lower risk change would certainly be more attractive to take on.

With principles such as "make hay while the sun shines" and "the customer is always right," we all have a tendency to bite off more than we can chew.

We focus on the allure of increasing the portfolio value while neglecting any realistic assessments of impact to current work and overall risk. Although we can get away with a little of this imbalanced perspective, it will eventually overtax our systems, resulting in mistakes, reduced efficiency, and failure to deliver as promised. We cannot escape the problems associated with ignoring the capacity of our systems and managing our intake correspondingly.

This all assumes, of course, that we have a current understanding of our capacity, workload, potential portfolio value, and risks to work with. In software companies, as in real life, most of us have only a glancing awareness of the relationship between how hard we push ourselves and our ability to sustain production. No change is so small as to have no impact, and even a single after-dinner mint can have disastrous results.

Summary

Change is an inevitable component of any of our projects. It will come from both internal and external sources and will continue throughout the entire life cycle. Projects can accommodate very large changes early on; but as time progresses, we are more sensitive to the impact of change.

Although most change is seen as negative, change can also have a strong positive impact on a project. We need to be able to recognize these opportunities when they arise.

All changes must be dealt with together so that we can appropriately triage them, with all stakeholders involved. In doing so, we can maintain the fidelity of the scope and schedule for the project, and converge to completion as expected.

How Is This Relevant?

Everything on the plate. Do you manage potential changes to scope alongside defects found in your product? Is the internal and external impact of these changes analyzed and balanced against the effort required to make the change?

All stakeholders. Is there reasonable representation from all stakeholder communities when change is managed? Are appropriate people called in to defend their case for or against specific changes?

Preserved fidelity. When changes are made, are all artifacts that are impacted by the change adjusted accordingly? Is the schedule adjusted? Is scope dropped if necessary? Are all original expectations tested to confirm that they remain valid?

CHAPTER TWENTY

Progress

The effort of defining our goals, expanding them into a clear specification, ongoing prioritization, and management of change takes considerable time. The value this provides is that it allows us to know how far along we are on the project, whether we are getting into trouble, when it would make sense to stop the project, and when we are really done. This knowledge is critical for reducing the uncertainty and increasing the predictability on our projects.

In this chapter, we look at the resulting value of all this work we put in project oversight, with a few specific issues that cause problems in the ongoing management of many projects.

Three Key Roles

 For any reasonably sized project, it is critical to recognize that there will always be different viewpoints and priorities, and that these conflicting views can each be valid in their own right. We need to be able to balance these perspectives in a manner that produces an optimal solution for all stakeholders over the course of the project.

Instead of seeking out a single individual, the traditional project manager, to juggle these often-conflicting viewpoints, it can be useful to consider three complementary roles that need to be filled to maintain a proper balance.

The first of these roles is that of the product champion. The product champion ensures that the users are adequately (and accurately) represented.

They carry the domain knowledge, and can clearly communicate the user needs to the development organization.

Although it can be useful to have some understanding of the software development world, the emphasis must be on the domain itself, the essential side rather than the implementation side. Initially focused on providing the depth of information required to develop the scope of the project, the product champion remains engaged throughout to ensure that there is no divergence of expectations as the project evolves.

The product champion provides the required domain information to the requirements analyst (often called a systems analyst or some similar term). Their primary task is to extract the domain-based information of the user needs and perform a translation to identify what the development team needs to progress with the project. The role here is to oversee the creation and maintenance of the shared understanding of scope.

The development community requires information in a drastically different form than most users provide. It needs to be consistent, explicitly testable, and so on. The requirements analyst needs to ensure that the information is captured in the appropriate form, and that the information is complete. Instead of focusing solely on the function of the product, emphasis needs to be placed on the fitness for use and ongoing maintainability as well as other quality requirements.

Finally, the project manager is charged with developing and managing a schedule based on the requirements specification, available resources, business constraints, and numerous other factors to bring the project home. Dealing with tactical issues as they arise while keeping an eye on the overall objectives, the project manager consults with the requirements analyst and product champion as required to succeed.

Each of these three roles is critical for project success. Each represents a different perspective that must be respected. Different people can carry the roles, by separate teams if the project is large enough, or by an individual that recognizes the need to carry three distinct hats around on the job. With an understanding of the distinct roles that need to be filled, an astute project manager can explicitly make the choice of having someone who may be more qualified to fill the two complementary roles, or at least, with higher awareness, better represent the needs of the stakeholders that might otherwise be neglected.

A Disciplined Approach

In managing projects, we often get to the point where we are fighting fires rather than executing on a well-choreographed plan to completion. We fail to recognize the big picture, let alone drive as a team to a common goal. And what ever happened to that original Gantt chart of ours, anyway?

Are We Managing or Parenting?

In raising two children who are now 7 and 11 years old, I've come to recognize a few daunting truths.

As parents, we are constrained to a window of about 15 years to set our children on a positive path, after which we will likely have minimal influence on them. If we fail to achieve our objectives, we may be dealing with the consequences for a very long time. We rarely have the luxury of clearly articulated guidance on what to do next for challenges more complicated than diaper rash or multiplication tables.

Baby sitters have an organized training program available, but you don't need any qualifications to become a parent, and the selection criteria is usually inappropriate.

In parenting, we don't have things like earned value to see whether we are on track. Our "team" seems to be working against one another more often than not. Often, our approach to dealing with the crisis du jour is determined by all manner of factors, rarely including a predetermined plan of attack. More often than not, it is a matter of survival rather than any notion of success against a goal.

Several aspects of parenting are generally part of the terrain:

- Few of us are given a game plan on how to be a parent, yet it can be one of the most important activities that we will ever do.

- Without a game plan, we end up learning by trial and error, and sometimes those errors can be costly.

- Some people find parenting easier than others, and some parents raise better kids than others (but there may not necessarily be a

> correlation between these two groups). There is a huge variation in both capability and performance.
>
> Come to think of it, that's not too different from most software projects and project managers I've seen over the years.

Project management has evolved as a discipline to a point where the elements above do not need to apply.

I came up through the ranks like many project managers in software development, and only after dealing with significant challenges did I discover the infrastructure that exists to support the discipline. If only I knew then what I know now! The benefit of experience is an expensive one, much more so than the disciplined training that is available. Although proper training will not guarantee success on projects, it will certainly raise awareness of the options available to deal with challenges, or prevent these challenges from occurring in the first place.

 Whereas both managing and parenting express ownership of the challenge, managing seems to imply a greater facility to stay on top of the problems that arise. It also suggests better team coordination that acts as a great preventative measure. Having explicit awareness of the big picture, and using that awareness as a sounding board for decision making, is a powerful approach that more parents could use to better achieve their goals.

We need to be careful to recognize when we are falling away from a disciplined approach and relying on our firefighting skills to bring a project home. Just as there are no criteria for becoming a parent, anyone can inherit a project to manage, but it is our actions rather than our title that determines whether we are a manager. On your projects, are you really managing or simply parenting?

Tackling Hard Problems

 Frighteningly often in software development, a team runs into a nagging problem that becomes a real thorn in the side. I've chased my tail around for months tracking down a nasty problem in the implementation of a serial protocol, and have seen many other teams face similar challenges.

It might appear as a dramatic drop in performance, or a system that becomes extremely unstable with a new build. Some systems evolve from a single simple implementation to monstrosities that have been cobbled together based on successive clients' needs, and each new implementation becomes more nightmarish than the next.

These hard problems all seem to have similar symptoms: The grief appears out of nowhere, usually at the worst possible time in the schedule. (Is there ever a good time for these challenges?) The manifestation of the problem is a surprise to most people (especially the younger ones), and the number of opinions about what might be the root of the problem is usually at least double the number of people present. The team throws all sorts of potential solutions at the problem, but it persists anyway. In most cases, the issue is pervasive and cannot be resolved with a simple coding fix. It is far more malignant. Been there? Some companies appear to have adopted this as the official corporate lifestyle.

Without a disciplined approach to solving the problem, it is unlikely that it will magically go away on its own, and there may be dire consequences for the project and the organization. Generally, the root cause can be traced back to one of two areas. First, there may be flaws in the design of the system that have been allowed to survive into the construction phase, and at some point, a flaw manifests itself in these surprising ways. Second, there may have been insufficient focus on the quality attributes of the system, such as maintainability, testability, or flexibility, which would have driven a design approach that took these into consideration. In either case, it is a deeply rooted issue.

When a hard problem such as this arises, it is important to tackle the problem diligently, until you are sure you have actually solved it. With a growing backlog of other things you should be doing (and absolutely no pleasure in chasing your tail on this problem), there is a strong tendency to change focus to other things as soon as possible. It's human nature. When the pressure eases somewhat, the tendency is to hope that something you did has solved the problem. Whew, that's over! Now let's get back to our other late tasks…and cross our fingers.

There is a better way, but it usually takes a cultural shift that can be tough to swallow. First, make sure that you can safely reproduce the problem. Identify up front a means of determining whether the problem has actually gone away, both as a final validation and as a way of ensuring that you can't artificially declare victory should the problem temporarily go into remission. Take an approach where you avoid any quick fixes that will often just mask the symptoms. Work with the design to truly understand why the problem appeared and how to resolve it so that it will not come back. If you cannot clearly explain how something you have done has eliminated the problem and prevented it from recurring, you are not done.

 Having to deal with hard problems is usually a symptom of a lack of discipline somewhere earlier in the project life cycle. Continued lack of discipline will not help you out of the fix you are in now. The better approach is to understand the true nature of the lesson, pull up your socks, and get real about solving the problem, once and for all. Persist until you know that a hard problem is really solved.

Risky Business

Risk, the possibility of experiencing loss or harm, is a natural part of any business venture, but we all have different approaches to dealing with it. We can ignore it or dwell on it, we can fear or embrace it, but no matter what we do, risk is always there. We're swimming in a sea of piranha-sized risks, with a few great whites hanging around to keep things interesting.

Often, businesses run with a vague background awareness of risks, focusing primarily on the intended path forward, until one or more of those risks creeps up and whacks them across the head. It may be a competitor that has just come out with the killer application that makes theirs obsolete, or they've run out of money before getting that next round of financing, or their customers refuse to cooperate with their hockey-stick revenue projections. Risks can surface from any direction, but they are usually predictable. Few businesses have been sidelined by a novel risk that no one has ever seen before.

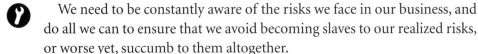 Some would suggest that "risk is a part of life" and choose to forge ahead without regard to the precarious position of their business. Preferring to deal with issues as they arise, they soon find that they are dealing with these issues on a full-time basis, and the business they are in is the business of staying afloat.

They are not dealing with risk, they are taking chances. Fine for a weekend in Vegas, but not the best way to drive a business. Although we hear about the few great success stories (that can often be distilled down to taking chances), there are many more stories you don't hear about that didn't turn out quite so happy.

There is a difference between risk adversity and risk awareness. Erica Jong said, "If you don't risk anything, you risk even more." Risk adversity reduces our flexibility, and in turn becomes a risk itself. Every move we make has some risk associated with it; we need to understand the magnitudes of the risks in front of us and make conscious decisions to move forward.

With awareness comes the ability to manage our risks appropriately: We can steer clear of them, we can take steps to minimize the loss, or we can choose to simply deal with them should they arise, but it is a conscious choice. We can even choose to drive our business by tackling risks head on and proactively dealing with those we are most exposed to.

We need to be constantly aware of the risks we face in our business, and do all we can to ensure that we avoid becoming slaves to our realized risks, or worse yet, succumb to them altogether.

Critical with a Capital C

Many software groups don't take project planning to the point of developing a network of activities assigned to individuals, with dependencies between one another based on the work products created or the people performing the work. Some have done this exercise in the past and found they are managing the Gantt chart and neglecting the project itself. Others have never ventured this far. All are missing valuable information. The term *critical path* is apt at several levels.

It's not easy to put together a realistic network of activities for a reasonably sized project, and extremely difficult for a large project. There is a great deal of early uncertainty in identifying which activities will be performed, who is going to perform them, and how long each of these will take. Gantt charts and PERT (Program and Evaluation Review Technique) charts just don't seen to have enough dimensions to capture all this uncertainty, and we're all aware that the network we build will probably not reflect reality by the time it is published. It will take effort to develop and maintain throughout the project's life, so the insight gained needs to make all that effort worthwhile.

Putting that initial network together can create tremendous value in itself. If done as a team, this activity allows everyone to understand the approach for putting the system together and where their contributions fit in the big picture. An opportunity exists for everyone to critically assess all the project elements from their different perspectives. The remaining risks and unknowns are collectively known. It can be a tremendous team-building exercise if done well, and will provide strong technical insight to help you determine your best course of action.

Managing the project network along the way preserves that initial planning investment, and provides even greater value in an ongoing fashion. A properly developed network will reveal to you the critical path of activities that is driving the project end date. These few activities are linked together without any slack time. If one of these slips, the end date of the project is in jeopardy, which in most cases is a very bad thing. Knowing this path allows you to narrow your intense focus to this smaller subset in the overall schedule. Other activities may become part of the critical path if they overrun, but generally, they can be less intensely scrutinized. With this information, you have a realistic picture of where the major skirmishes are and what is left to do at any point in time. You can chart a course accordingly.

Without this knowledge, focus on critical elements often falls on individuals, rather than a linked chain of work products. *"Bob's critical this week."* The notion of someone being the critical path, instead of acknowledging shared team accountability, is a dangerous one. The individual often has a number of activities queued up, and it might not be clear which of these is on the critical path and which can be reasonably adjusted. The personal focus can often generate a negative form of scrutiny and pressure to pull oneself out of this mess. Without knowledge of the flexibility available to others on the team, there can be a tendency to neglect opportunities for the team to pull together to resolve the challenge in creative ways.

Any project, at any time, has a critical path, and it is usually a collection of activities driven by a number of people on the team. It's not bad to be on the critical path. It's bad to not have the appropriate information available and leverage it to find the most appropriate solution as a team.

What Does Document Signoff Mean?

Often, especially on larger software projects, there comes a point at which the specification (or some other document that is produced) gets signed off. Usually marking the end of a phase in the development life cycle, the understanding by many across the team is that the spec is complete. Now the tasks of developing the actual product can begin.

A couple of real challenges with these notions fly in the face of practicality.

First is the notion of "document signoff." Have you ever experienced the situation in which a document has been signed off, and done so without a thorough review of its contents? With pressures to get on with the "real work," and with some documents requiring a large number of signatures, there can be a tendency for people to rationalize that others have adequately covered the issues, that the effort leading up to the signing ceremony has ensured that the specification is adequate to continue. Sometimes it's a simple ruffle through the tome to ensure that all is there at a superficial level, and then it's ink to paper. It is important to recognize the distinction between document signoff and informed consent. Your signature should actually signify that the contents are acceptable from your perspective, that they are an accurate representation of the best possible understanding of the scope of work to date. There is significant responsibility that goes along with the signature, but often the pomp and circumstance outweighs the diligence (with insufficient accountability attached to the responsibility).

Second, the ceremony of document signoff often gives the impression that the specification is complete, but this is unrealistic. For most projects, the specification (and the corresponding schedule, which is the embodiment of how you intend to complete the scope within the specification) should be considered live throughout the project and managed accordingly. With a signed-off specification, changes are handled in several problematic ways. At best, there are significant hurdles to driving change within the project. At worst, the scope changes, and the spec and corresponding published schedule aren't updated to reflect these changes.

It is vitally important to spend the time up front to capture your best understanding of the scope of work as early as possible. This will allow you to decide whether the project is viable at all, and will form the basis of the most realistic schedule for moving forward that you can create. All stakeholder representatives should agree that, to the best of their ability, the documentation of this scope is correct and current. Documentation signoff should accurately reflect this agreement.

 Signoff, however, should not be interpreted as the completion of the management of scope. Instead, it should be the beginning of ongoing management of scope and schedule. With external pressure for new features and internal discovery through design refinement and issues that are raised, the scope of work needs to be considered subject to change at any time, with appropriate management of these changes. Recognition that the cost of change will generally increase over the life of the project should drive you to start with your best foot forward, but rarely can a project successfully deliver precisely what was originally specified at that initial signoff point. All potential changes need to be adequately assessed for overall impact with the same diligence as the initial specification for you to retain that value of the effort put into that document.

For many organizations, the best way to convert to this mindset may be to treat all elements generated during the project (the specification, the schedule, the source code, and so on) in the same way.

Everything is subject to change at any time, but all changes (especially after the artifact is in broad use) need to be well managed.

Knowing When to Quit

Vince Lombardi said (probably before every big game), "Winners never quit, and quitters never win." But, life is not football, where the rules demand that you stay on the field for the duration of the game. Sometimes it makes perfect sense to step back and acknowledge that continuing the game no longer makes sense.

Although it is true that making a habit of not completing projects will result in failure to realize their potential benefits, it is also true that dragging dead projects (or too many projects) to their inevitable conclusion can prove much more costly to the organization.

I doubt that many companies would start a project that didn't make business sense. Although the usual driver is monetary, there can be other compelling reasons to take on a project, such as industry exposure, benefits such as improved quality or stability, and so on. It is generally an accepted best practice to identify your critical success factors up front for any project.

Few companies, however, take the time to consider the critical failure factors. These elements would kill a project should they materialize. Sometimes these are the inverse of stated success factors, but there can often be other factors that would make it most reasonable to stop the project. Better options may arise for the business, or the working relationship with the client may have stalled. Initial assumptions may change or simply have been unfounded in the first place. Your initial window of opportunity may have disappeared, or you might find that "you just can't get there from here."

When a value proposition no longer exists for the company or the client, your best decision may be just to move on. Some companies will go so far as to call project milestones "kill points," indicating that if the project no longer makes business sense, it is reasonable to kill the project and redirect the resources toward viable projects.

Some companies follow a more accidental approach. Without a managed portfolio of projects (all of which are high priority, of course), the list of things to do can get so long that the organization gets nothing done at all and simply thrashes. Trying to please all the people all the time, as the saying goes, is a losing proposition. Companies that spend a lot of their time fighting fires are usually not managing a portfolio at all. They are reacting to events, and they need to step back and differentiate between the urgent and the important. Although it might seem urgent to satisfy a screaming client, it is likely more important to stabilize the system so that all your clients don't start screaming (or silently heading elsewhere). If a project is merely urgent, it might be worth killing altogether.

An old Chinese Proverb sums it up much more appropriately than Lombardi for most projects: "If you must play, decide on three things at the start: the rules of the game, the stakes, and the quitting time." Consider up front the factors that would make it reasonable to shut down a project.

Done

Clearly, the definition of *done* varies tremendously, based on the perspective that you are taking. Given the myriad potential definitions for a term we use loosely and frequently every day, is it any wonder that we often fail to hit expectations with our peers when we try to agree that we have finished something?

 On projects, we often fall into the trap of failing to explicitly state what *done* means, and this ambiguity gets us in all sorts of trouble. Even with completion criteria for a simple development task, the interpretations can vary widely. Is it done when it compiles (and to what degree have the compiler warnings been turned off)? Should the software have been unit tested, and how thoroughly? Does it have to have been integrated into the overall system, or will a simple regression test suffice? What about the documentation and traceability for the module?

Pile up all these ambiguities for the individual tasks, layer on top of that the vague criteria for completion of the project as a whole, and we often find ourselves in quite a pickle. Although we could easily interpret this ambiguity as an opportunity to falsely declare victory whenever we please, all stakeholders rarely agree upon the victory, and the resulting debates can become quite heated.

Just as beauty lies in the eyes of the beholder, it is the perspective of the recipient that matters when we try to come to grips with what *done* really means. At all levels, from the entire project down to a single line of code or status report, our perspective of what *done* means for what we are building is much less relevant than that of the person who is receiving our work. We need to solicit an understanding of what *done* means as soon as possible, and iterate on that understanding if we have to.

We need to put in the effort up front to have an agreement with the recipient about what *done* really means. Clear completion criteria written in an unambiguous form (specific, measurable, attainable, realistic, and tangible; much as I detest acronyms, SMART works well here) is necessary for the detailed elements and for the project as a whole. The more that is left open to interpretation, the more that you can expect that interpretations will vary, with results that can be as innocuous as a little bit of the "back to the drawing board" armed with some clarification, to a huge failure to meet expectations on the overall project.

Take the time to agree what *done* means with the recipient of your work—unless, of course, you enjoy the debate about whether you have really done your job.

Summary

There is some effort involved in building an infrastructure that will allow us to track progress on our projects, but the value in doing so is immense.

We can more easily determine that we are remaining on track for completion, and discover earlier when we are falling into trouble (when there are more options available to us for resolving the issues). In being able to reassess whether it makes sense to continue with the project, we could appropriately redirect our resources to other projects if it makes sense, too.

Most important, being able to clearly track progress against our original goals enables us to determine whether we have achieved those goals. We gain the opportunity to objectively say we are done.

How Is This Relevant?

Genuine oversight. Do you really know whether you are on schedule to complete your projects, or is this more a function of hope? Can you determine in the early stages of a project that you need to adjust expectations, or do you tend to be surprised toward the end of the schedule?

Cutting losses. Do you have the information available that would allow you to determine whether it still makes sense to continue with your projects or to move resources elsewhere? Have you ever continued on projects after it was no longer reasonable to do so?

Really done? Do you define what *done* means in an objective fashion, in advance? Is completion based on a broad range of success factors, or more a function of schedule and defect counts?

PART SIX

Putting It All Together

Changing the way we work as a team is a difficult but critical challenge. When we decide that the status quo has room for improvement, it makes a lot of sense to think of this initiative as a project in itself. In constructing a novel product, there are initial goals, which in this case can be our refined approach.

We need to address a number of key issues to improve the way we work. We need to select an appropriate and practical set of adjustments, and we need to be sure that we are thorough in our implementation of these changes. As with any project, we need to have clear and measurable goals, and foster the initiative through the changes to completion.

Most of all, we need to remain honest with ourselves, remain diligent, and celebrate our victories as a team. In this section, we look at some key issues that affect improvement initiatives just as strongly as any other project we choose to undertake.

CHAPTER TWENTY-ONE

Pick Your Battles

It is important to recognize that we will not change the world all at once. We need to be careful to pick small, practical initiatives that will benefit the organization and ensure that everyone involved understands his or her own measure of value these changes bring.

In this chapter, we look at the need for reasonable guidance to the team. We focus on defining rules that serve everyone's best interest. We need to pick a reasonably sized project, and there is no time like the present to get moving.

A Critical Procedure

It might be a single sentence posted for all to see or a more elaborate page with precise instructions and details. It could possibly be accompanied by a humorous illustration or two for effect and it likely explains the dire consequences if you fail to follow the posted procedure. It isn't something left to chance, and is rarely passed along only by word of mouth.

Chances are, based on my experience, it is likely one of the first procedures established in your office (quite possibly the only one). It's the one most people have committed to memory by their second week on the job, and the one most stringently built into the fabric of the culture where you work.

That procedure has nothing to do with consistently getting good products out the door, although I am sure some would disagree.

> It's how to make a fresh pot of coffee: something you probably learned your first morning on the job.
>
> Even in shops that would like to claim industry leadership in software development best practices and procedures, ensuring that there is always coffee available is often more ruthlessly upheld and enforced than the practices that would ensure the customers have a consistent positive experience.

Appropriate Procedures

When there is a lack of reasonable guidance, we all have a tendency to focus on what is important to us personally. With any reasonably sized organization, most employees are at least several degrees removed from the customer and the pain they may be feeling, but everyone knows when he needs more java to keep producing more Java. Because of this, making coffee is what gets the grassroots emphasis.

When identifying and implementing procedures that can help ensure that the right product gets out the door at the right time, there are a few elements to ponder. As with any improvement initiative, you do not want to blindly incorporate a broad range of procedures with hopes that some will add value. Some probably would, but any benefit would be lost in the sea of less-beneficial paperwork.

Some elements in our workplace are familiar to us, the technical equivalent to making a pot of coffee. Even if we don't all do them the same way, there isn't a significant impact if there is slight (or even massive) variation. How we answer the phone or leave voicemail, how we decorate our offices are all areas which I have seen addressed with more rigorousness than necessary. To apply procedures here and to neglect the client perspective is to squander one of your few opportunities to build consistency where it really adds value.

On the other hand, there are many elements of the team dynamic where the overall product results can be improved significantly, by improving consistency and predictability, by reducing defects and overall technical risk. A strong build procedure can do wonders for product stability. Consistently managing defects or changes to scope can drastically reduce project uncertainty. Capturing how backups are managed is critical so that someone else can do them when necessary. Find the places where doing it wrong or inconsistently will hurt the most. Pick the spots where things absolutely must be done correctly, especially in an emergency. These are the places where you should first apply procedures.

Chances are there was at least one fire in your last project that probably would not have flared up with a reasonable procedure in place. These are often things done by the one or two "go-to" people in the organization capable of doing the job. These areas are prime candidates for formalized procedures.

> If your chairs and computers are more closely tracked than the products you produce for profit, if the ramifications of leaving an empty coffeepot are more significant than a disappointing user experience, it is time to rethink where consistency is best applied in your organization.

Rules

"Hell, there are no rules here—we're trying to accomplish something."
—Thomas A. Edison

I was a bit taken aback when I first read this quote, given my respect for all of Edison's achievements and contributions over his lifetime. To be able to come out with a major invention every six months is no small feat. It is hard to fathom this capacity for innovation in a place where there are no rules.

Edison's quote, however, is not the only place you will hear this sentiment. When I mentioned that I was going to write something about rules, the first thing out of my wife's mouth was that "rules are meant to be broken." It was not clear whether this was a reflection of the ongoing challenges of raising two kids, or an indication that I shouldn't try to enforce too many rules on her, or both!

Anywhere you turn these days, you will find signs of rules being broken, from minor traffic violations to capital offenses and everything in between. Ask any person who has broken a rule why he or she did so, and there is a good chance that the person

- Knew perfectly well that they were breaking the rule, and
- Can easily rationalize how that rule just didn't fit with their guiding principles at the time.

Although they might be full of remorse for breaking the rule (or more accurately, remorse that they were caught), there's no guarantee that the result would be any different next time around.

Rules are an overt attempt to force consistency on our diverse value systems. That seems to be the problem. We are using duct tape to build conformance, but all we do is mask a much more deeply seated issue.

In software teams, there have been numerous attempts to build predictability and consistency into the development process using rules. Frameworks and methodologies suggest that if you follow Step A with Step B (adding Step C as necessary), all should go well. Almost universally, however, for one reason or another, people find a way to miss a step or two, and the carefully constructed framework and its glorious product comes tumbling down.

We don't like to be constrained by rules. Rules are the equivalent of a belt done up too tightly after a good holiday meal. It feels so good to loosen them up a notch or two.

Dig a little deeper into Edison's achievements and we get a clearer understanding of his quote. One of the stories in the book *Virtuoso Teams* is about Edison and the evolution of his Menlo Park research facility.[1] Although there might not have been any rules to constrain the team or apparently restrict innovation within the group, there was a clear focus on the internalization of consistent goals and on hiring of the right people with interest in innovation and practical experience. There was also the explicit manipulation of the environment around the team to ensure they had all the resources required to accomplish their goals without constraints.

Edison's rules were there, but instead of being used to constrain the team, they were there to assist the team to do great things. They lived the right rules, the ones that facilitated innovative progress rather than enforcing predictable mediocrity.

This is as it should be with rules supporting software development teams. Although there is still a place for some strict rules in any organization, they should be centered on the practices recognized as critical for success and consistent delivery. The vast majority of the rules should be centered on ensuring that the team has the right structure, that they have the capabilities and resources to do the right things, rather than on stepwise procedures to be dogmatically followed.

Most software projects cannot be compared to a production line. We don't hire bright people so that we can constrain them. The rules we enforce need to be liberating for the group. (Liberation to be creative in a clear direction, not liberation to be anarchistic, of course.)

If we choose our rules wisely, we need not worry that they will be broken.

Decoupling Projects

We live in a world in which the pace and volume of information is growing exponentially. We have duped ourselves into believing that multitasking is an effective coping mechanism for this growth. We have four or five things on the go at any one time, while we deal with interruptions and…well, we all drop a ball or two from time to time. The problem, however, is that busy is not necessarily the same as productive.

As we move our perspective up from the task level to the project level, we can often see the equivalent mechanism impacting our efforts. We are juggling too many projects simultaneously. Although it is fine to have a number of projects on the go at the same time, it is critical that we clearly understand where one project ends and another begins. We need to decouple projects from one another to ensure that they do not disrupt each other. Finally, we actually need to finish projects, each to their reasonable expectations.

There will often be some relationship between projects. For an organization that selects and drives projects according to an explicit vision and business cases, the leverage between projects can be immense. Product roadmaps are often laid out as a series of sequential projects with successively more comprehensive scope, complexity, and components built at each stage. With a little forethought, chaining these projects can build efficiency into the operations as a whole.

Just as with developing code, however, where extensive coupling between modules will lead to excessive complexity and maintainability issues, inappropriately coupled projects can suffer dire consequences. Projects that differ significantly in almost any dimension—expected timeframe for completion, mission criticality (for the client or the organization itself), scope volatility, quality expectations, or key resources required, for example—can suffer from the dilution of priorities and goals if they are too closely intertwined.

When considering the relationship between concurrent projects in your portfolio, it is worth borrowing a page from coding and requirements development best practices. Maintain clearly defined interfaces between the different projects. Be careful to manage the evolution of that interface throughout the life cycle. Keep the interfaces as narrowly defined as possible. Monitor the contributors to these interfaces for early warnings of change. Finally, work to manage the relationship with external contributors to minimize disruption.

Here are a number of instances of excessive project coupling that can spell trouble:

- Projects that introduce significant new infrastructure (new tools or underlying frameworks) to a mission-critical project can be too disruptive. Culture shock and the technical risk of the change can potentially overwhelm the benefits and lead to project failure.

- Projects based on funding initiatives or the provision of key resources that dissolve before the completion of the project they are supporting can leave a team in a lurch as well, jeopardizing successful completion.

- Implementing process improvement changes can be disruptive, especially large-scale ones. It is generally acknowledged that significant change will tend to slow the first project it is implemented on, rather than speed it up. This flies in the face of the most common argument for process change.

Do your best to avoid complicating your life and your project portfolio. Explicitly focus on minimizing the interfaces between your projects, especially when you are running them concurrently.

Manage these necessary relationships to ensure they don't disrupt your projects. There will likely be enough sources of grief as it is. Don't add more.

Greasing the Wheels

Change is tough on anyone. We'll fight tooth and nail to avoid change, even if our current situation is untenable. Dealing with this human barrier is the key to driving effective change.

I've been working with a team where I had done "drive-by training" in the past. Back then, two days jam-packed with bullets of information hit the group, but they sat listless, and nothing really came of the engagement. There was no opportunity to facilitate effective change of any kind.

I got a call about 18 months later from the same group. They were now interested in change. They had found an internal champion and a budget, and asked whether I was interested in pitching in. Despite the previous experience, where I had sworn it just wasn't worth the effort, I now jumped in with both feet.

We gathered some numbers from surveys, but were careful to not read too much into them. At the highest level, there was a clear indication of pain across the team and a significant gap in perception between management and the technical staff. With management having a rosier perspective, there was concern that contentment could scuttle any real efforts, so we knew we had work to do there.

We listened to a lot of people: how they worked, the pain they were feeling, the suggestions they had for making things better. It was clear that everyone experienced significant pain, but everyone had a very different description of this pain. With different perspectives come different ramifications of the challenges. After a lot of cross tabbing and correlating, we started to see a picture developing. We had uncovered a root cause and could finally start attacking the real problem.

We went back to the people: face-to-face meetings to discuss the findings of both the strengths and opportunities within the team. We started to help them paint a picture of what a better world might look like. To do this effectively with the different groups, we ended up painting a gallery of different pictures: one where there was predictable closure on projects, another where there was less disruption and chaos. We painted a picture where projects could happily coexist without stealing resources, and the group as a whole could leap ahead against the competition. Everyone could relate to at least one of these visions.

We walked them down the path of how to get to these places. We had carefully selected the path of least resistance. We proposed little disruption to the way they currently worked. Indeed, what we suggested was an infrastructure that would allow them to do the things they wanted and needed to do in an unfettered manner.

We then ran a significant amount of…well, not quite training, more like acclimatization. We reinforced the concerns that the pain was universal, and walked them through the root causes we were trying to excise and the changes that would allow that to happen. Everyone had the opportunity to express their challenges, and in seeing the broad range of perspectives, different groups started to bond. We worked with almost as many managers as we did technical staff, to reinforce that managers had the critical role of removing the roadblocks that could get in the way (including some of their own disruptive behaviors from the past). We worked with their partners around the world, because the changes involved more managed communication across these groups, too.

There was universal support. There was a buzz around the coffee machines that went beyond caffeine. As the training progressed, there was an increasing demand for more. Lunchtime discussions were optimistic, and people looked forward to getting started. Criticisms were almost exclusively suggestions to go further with the implementation, but we were careful to ensure we could walk before we ran.

Compared to the reaction to the standard training 18 months earlier, this was a different group (except that it was actually the same people).

Eighteen months earlier, there was relatively little investment, and virtually no value gained. We were merely helping them spend their training budget. Now, there was significantly more investment, but there was also an overwhelming upside. This turned out to be a wise business decision.

The difference is that we didn't lecture or ramble on about what they should be doing. We listened, we coached, we solicited input, we facilitated. We helped the team find their own better place. We were greasing the wheels.

It's Never Too Late

It always fascinates me when companies forge ahead without a software specification or ignore the design phase of product development altogether. Although this approach might work for undergrad assignments that you will never see again, a commercial software product should have a life beyond the initial deployment, implying that you will be revisiting the product for bug fixes, feature refinement (with a fine line between these two), and additional functionality.

As a developer, there's nothing worse than having to go straight to the code to figure out how something works after the fact. I've had to do this myself many times, even on an air traffic control system. It is a safe bet that for those systems that have been developed without a solid specification and a reasonable design, the development team spends an inordinate amount of their time back in the code, fixing what was written before. Alas, some developers have never experienced the luxury of changing code based on information in reasonable specifications or designs.

The most energetic pushback to improving practices often comes from the team that doesn't want to invest the time to document the functionality or to go back and capture their design in the name of future refinement. Perhaps it is embarrassment or fear of the unknown. It can't be the joy of working in an environment of constant patching rather than easily adding in great new functionality, can't it?

It doesn't have to be that way. Whereas stopping the project, stepping back, and documenting your entire feature set or redesigning the system from the ground up only makes business sense in the most extreme of cases, there is plenty of gray between the darkness of the unknown system and the white of the perfectly documented product. In fact, I've yet to see either one. Some knowledge always resides in the minds of the developers, and some areas will never be precisely specified.

If you find yourself spending most of your time buried in the code, consider the following approaches. Take the time to understand those nasty areas of functionality that you are continually revisiting. Chances are that stepping back and identifying precisely what should be happening will clarify the intent, allowing you to implement what was intended, and prevent that same area from cropping up as a problem in the future. On the design side, take the time to design system-wide mechanisms such as error-handling strategies, information logging, data persistence, or other elements that are often implemented differently by numerous people on the team.

In either case, it is a safe bet that the time spent in clarifying the intent of the system will be more than made up in time saved, even in the short term.

Start putting some emphasis on the quality side. Take small steps geared toward reduction of your greatest pains.

If you genuinely believe that you don't have time to start capturing the intent or design of your product, perhaps it is time to start capturing the intent or design of a replacement system for that product.

There's a good chance you will end up building that replacement.

Summary

As we start to introduce changes into the way we build software in our teams, we need to be careful to facilitate it in a way that will maximize our success.

We need to carefully select small, cohesive projects that have a clear benefit for the group, and build our guidance in such a way that it helps the team understand the right steps they need to take. If people don't understand the benefit to them for following the rules, they will find ways to circumvent them.

In any case, it is important to take steps now to move in the right direction for improvement.

How Is This Relevant?

Reasonable guidance. Are you working with an appropriate set of procedures, the ones that are truly critical to ensure that you consistently provide value to your clients? Does everyone recognize the value in following this philosophy? Are your defined procedures ignored when time pressures arise?

Simple, cohesive projects. Are there simple changes you can make that will provide significant gain? Does each component of the project add value? Are you introducing comprehensive change that will dilute the results? Can you realize value in the short term?

Time to start. Are you working to improve the effectiveness of the team today? What steps can you take to get started? Do you recognize the cost of not making changes? Where are the greatest opportunities for change?

References

1. Andy Boynton and Bill Fischer, *Virtuoso Teams: Lessons from Teams That Changed Their Worlds* (FT Prentice Hall, 2006).

CHAPTER TWENTY-TWO

Flexibility and Rigor

As we start to understand the things we need to do to get our projects out the door, we can split these tasks into two camps: the things that must be done under any circumstances, and the things where we have some latitude on their implementation.

This chapter covers a few guidelines that we can use to ensure that our approach is visible, reasonable to follow, and supports the need to effectively and efficiently get our job done.

Guidance over Prescription

A consensus seems to exist among many companies that the way to ensure the success of software projects is to prescribe how everyone will do his or her job.

Policies and procedures. Audits and documentation. An excessively detailed schedule. If the project failed last time around, it's an indication that we either need more of this stuff, or that we didn't follow the rules closely enough.

Although this might work for assembly lines that produce widgets, few software development projects will benefit from such a rigid structure. It's great to have an understanding of how to do the work, but that understanding needs to transcend what is usually found in plans and procedures. The team needs to reach a point at which it is commonly understood why the work needs to be done in a certain way, and how to determine the best approach for attacking the work. What is needed is guidance, not prescription.

Most software projects are characterized by the ongoing discovery of information that takes place throughout the project life cycle. More details about the product or the environment give us better insights into how to best approach or change the remaining work, or to even change or stop the project altogether. A prescribed approach for the entire project rarely works well. We simply can't accurately predict the pitfalls we will have to overcome on our journey. As the situation evolves, we either find that we need to rethink our "best laid plans," or worse, we try to follow these original plans to everyone's detriment.

To be effective, we need to focus on guiding principles for getting the job done and an overall vision of what the product is all about. These rarely change. We can establish them early and ensure that everyone completely understands them completely. We now have in place a basis upon which we can make decisions with our newfound information as the project unfolds. Are we still in alignment with our overall project goals? Are we true to our principles for how we develop software here?

Once we have the guidance, we need to be comfortable with disciplined flexibility to get the job done effectively. We need to be able to react to information quickly. We should recognize that early discovery of information that is counter to our goals is good news, for now we can correct our course and advance. Communication is critical for the whole team, and the team extends beyond the developers to include the customers and other key stakeholders.

Policies and procedures do have their place. There are often regulatory issues to deal with. As the team grows, there does need to be some degree of consistency and common understanding, as well as a basis for learning just how the job gets done. It is important to remember, however, that most regulatory bodies merely expect you to be able to demonstrate that you do what you say you will do, not that you will do everything.

Their intent is not to slow you down, but to make you more reliable. If you go down the route of defining process documentation, ensure that it is just enough to support effective development. Too much will just bog you down.

The strongest process is not just a set of procedures that suggests that all the industry's "best practices" will be slavishly applied. Instead, it is one that allows the team to adapt to the situation in a disciplined manner.

Its emphasis is on collaboration and sharing information to facilitate a shared success. The few absolutes are the guiding approach for development quality and the information required to ensure that the vision and scope of the project are known and managed.

In the hands of a conscientious team, supportive guidance goes a lot further than rigid prescription.

Checklists and Signatures

The essence of consistency in a team environment is to ensure that everyone knows what the important tasks are and to make sure they get done.

Standard Operating Procedures

The standard operating procedure for driving your car usually does not include a thorough walk around to check all essential features before getting in and heading down to the corner store. We simply hop in and head out. Technology has evolved to the point where cars are quite reliable, and the root cause of the vast majority of problems we have on the road is driver error.

Take the same car in for service, however, or look through the owner's manual, and you will find a checklist of maintenance items. These things should be done against a prescribed schedule to ensure that mechanical problems we don't want to worry about remain unlikely.

For aircraft, even though the technology is at least as reliable as in cars, the magnitude of the consequences associated with a mechanical failure at altitude is generally much more severe. Despite maintenance schedules being more rigorously adhered to, all pilots, both commercial and the private pilots I have flown with, go through a rigorous checklist and walk around before taking off. It would be foolhardy not to.

There are all kinds of situations in which it is convenient to list the things you need to do. They could be one-off situations such as creating a grocery list, or repetitive situations such as following a favorite recipe or preparing an airplane for a flight.

Checklists are effective, concise memory joggers meant to help ensure that nothing falls off the plate.

In software development, many situations lend themselves wonderfully to the use of checklists. Whether it is a list of items that need to be considered when initiating a project, design paradigms to be aware of, elements to watch out for when coding (or reviewing code), test cases to consider, or steps required to build or release the software, a checklist keeps the key information all in one place.

When used as a supplement to a more comprehensive form of communication such as policies and procedures, checklists carry the essence that can be tacked on the wall and referred to repeatedly. They can also be maintained tactically to remain relevant.

Unfortunately, all these efforts of capturing and disseminating what is to be done count for nothing if there is a risk that the tasks are going to be neglected anyway.

Signing Off

Watch closely before you take your next commercial flight and you will find that a number of checks are required.

Up in the cockpit, the pilot and co-pilot are signing off their preflight checklist. The last thing the flight crew does before the door is closed is to sign off the manifest of the passengers onboard. Then, they go through their crosschecks and other preflight checks.

> Even most public washrooms will have a piece of paper by the door, initialed by the attendant responsible for keeping the place clean.
>
> The act of putting your name to a piece of paper attesting that you have done things can be quite compelling.

With software, however, we rarely see this.

Document signoff has often become an administrative activity. Many organizations (even those with fairly weighty defined processes) have very little accountability associated with activities such as checking in code or even releasing software. Although configuration management (CM) systems can be used to forensically identify the check-in culprit, few organizations have mechanisms in place to enforce a "standard" list of pre-check-in activities such as peer review and unit and regression testing.

This is interesting, because the ramifications of failing to follow the right steps in software development can often be more similar to the results of an in-flight failure than to leaving the toilet paper roll empty. The cost of putting simple accountability in place is much less than the cost of relaxed or uneven enforcement. An ounce of prevention....

It is all about stating what you are going to do and showing that you have done it.

Policies, procedures, and templates can serve to support the letter of the defined approach, and can keep most auditors at bay, too.

When you really get down to it, however, checklists and signatures can go a long way toward documenting and verifying that the intent has been properly achieved.

Real Design Issues: Diversification and Convergence

Lewis Carroll captured this dialog between Alice and the Cheshire cat in 1865:

"Would you tell me, please, which way I ought to go from here?"
"That depends a good deal on where you want to get to," said the Cat.
"I don't much care where…," said Alice.
"Then it doesn't matter which way you go," replied the Cat.
"…so long as I get SOMEWHERE," Alice added as an explanation.
"Oh, you're sure to do that," said the Cat, *"if you only walk long enough."*

In many software projects, even those that appropriately deal with some key design issues such as concurrency, error handling, and data persistence, there is often an important design phase opportunity that is missed. If design is viewed as a problem-solving activity, it is best to choose a solution from a number of possible alternatives by applying the concepts of diversification and convergence.

Strong Design in Action

I worked with a graphic design firm and had a chance to see their design process in action.

It was fascinating to see the effort spent by this firm in exploring the diversity of solution alternatives before narrowing the search.

This was actually done explicitly several times in the process of arriving at an optimal solution, with a toolset consisting of pencil, paper, and imagination. The results of this design process produced literally hundreds of design options that were explored and rejected for one reason or another.

Those alternatives that were cast aside were retained until project closure so we could go back to review the approaches we had considered.

The approach finally converged on a design that fit the original specified goals and could be used as a basis for the final implementation. The results were far superior to what would have likely been obtained with a linear approach.

In software, an approach is often selected after the project scope is specified, and we quickly move directly to the implementation phase. We are coding, so we're finally being productive, right?

As Glenford Myers noted almost 30 years ago, "We try to solve the problem by rushing through the design process so that enough time will be left at the end of the project to uncover errors that were made because we rushed through the design process."

Getting successful closure on software projects requires the appropriate selection of your destination, as well as the selection of the right path along the way.

Be sure to investigate several approaches for their relative merit, instead of choosing the first one that comes along.

Documentation and Common Knowledge

Documentation is one of the great four-letter words in the software industry, and often for good reason.

Most of us have at some point gone through a laborious exercise to create a document, only to see it whither, forgotten on the shelf. On the maintenance side, I've tried to add to an application by reviewing the design documentation, only to find that I had to review the source code to see what was really done. I've been involved in a project where the spec was created after the fact, as it was a deliverable item. I've also been through several projects where the requirements analysis phase involved far too little analysis and far too much paper.

What's wrong with this picture?

When I hear that dreaded *D* word, I prefer to translate it to "shared understanding," as that is the essence of why we would choose to document information in the first place. As with any task on a software project, we should be clear that there is an anticipated benefit for the effort of putting a document together. Instead of viewing documents as the product of an intellectual activity, documents should be viewed as the persistence mechanism for the information generated from that activity. If it is worth retaining, it needs to be captured and shared.

Instead of "we have a specification, so we're done with requirements analysis," it becomes "we have analyzed the user's needs, and our findings are captured here."

So, how do we do this? To determine whether it is worth retaining at all, there are several drivers to consider, such as the expected lifetime and volatility of the information, criticality of the information to the project, how the information is gathered or obtained in the first place, and who the recipients of that information are.

After we've determined that a piece of information is important to retain and share, a wide variety of documentation options are available: e-mail, paper trails, discussion threads, wikis and intranets, traditional documents, presentation decks, flipcharts and whiteboards, index cards, databases, and blogs. Even word of mouth ("Bob's got the donuts") can be a reasonable alternative for different types of information. Each alternative brings along different strengths and weaknesses.

One of the most effective approaches I've experienced was for the architecture for an air traffic control system, which evolved over a number of years in a large number of discrete elements, with a variety of authors and revisions for a large development team. There was no monolithic design document. We derived an evolving series of "ArchiNotes" that were each easily maintained and referred to as necessary.

Unfortunately, project teams often go for extremes. Documentation efforts can range from almost no documentation (the proverbial back of the envelope), which usually brings risks and rework to an unacceptable level, to ponderous documentation throughout, which can result in higher costs and maintainability issues.

Instead of continuing to create documents that will never be read, we need to find the sweet spot.

We need to determine what information needs to become common knowledge on our projects and then determine the best vehicle for making this happen.

Avoiding Evolutionary Complexity

Quite often, organizations developing products in a specific vertical market start out with the intent to produce a system that cleanly meets the needs of an entire customer base. Over time, however, they find that subtle nuances make each client unique.

Whether it involves different internal business processes, interfaces with different external systems, or just different user preferences, it often appears impossible to provide a one-size-fits-all solution in a specific niche.

Faced with growing variety of client needs, what happens next is a key point in product evolution. In the worst case, some companies jealously guard their rigid functionality and underlying implied business processes, constraining their clients and often losing business along the way. Other organizations opt to provide features that add to the flexibility of the system from the user perspective. In turn, this dramatically increases the complexity of the system for the development team.

As more options are made available to the end user in an uncoordinated fashion, the system will often reach a point at which the development team cannot anticipate all possible configurations, much less validate them all. As one organization put it, "Our system is so flexible we cannot possibly test it." Unfortunately, the results of that untestability have been readily apparent in the field, making them a candidate for the software equivalent of the Darwin Awards.

A more mature approach would be to acknowledge up front that there will be variability in user demands, and to design in the capability to manage this appropriately. With proper design, the complexity of permutations can be adequately managed. Focus on managed compatibility of the combinations and their interactions to avoid the possibility of unanticipated results at the client site. With these capabilities designed into the system, tests can then be devised and an associated test infrastructure, developed as required, can be used to thoroughly validate allowable permutations and confirm that the system correctly denies incompatible combinations. Any system deemed to be untestable to a point where it is a challenge to deploy has not been properly designed.

Indeed, for those systems that have already evolved to the point of being difficult to deploy and maintain, it can be prudent to take a step back and architect flexibility into the system properly. With the lengthy implementation phase (often a thinly veiled name for the phase of frantic struggle to make it fit at the client site) and costly maintenance phase taken into account, everyone benefits from a system that was properly designed to accommodate specific client needs in the first place.

Post It!

Quite often, the greatest advantage a small team can give themselves is to sit together in the same room. Close proximity is a critical factor in fostering strong communications among the group. Especially with small teams that are driving hard, working on projects with a great deal of uncertainty and change, a shared space should be considered a necessity for success.

Having the space, however, is a far cry from using it as effectively as possible.

This space has a huge advantage over the documents that might be passed around or artifacts such as blogs, wikis, or folders and documents on your server. The walls, windows, and doors are visible to everyone who passes through. They are in your face. They are visible without even having to look for them, and should be leveraged accordingly.

On any project, there is a collection of information that everyone should have access to instantaneously, in a form that can be shared, discussed, and debated without a lot of effort to bring it to the surface.

The vision for the project should be clear in anyone's mind. Why the project exists. Who the customer is. What makes this product different from what exists elsewhere. This serves as a basis for aligning the team and validating any proposed changes to the scope.

A list of the prioritized features for the project keeps people aware of the overall scope of work. Those that are definitely needed, those that would be great if there was time, and those that you can squeeze in if a miracle happens with all the other stuff. Keep it at a high level, either business features or use cases, so that it doesn't become a maintenance nightmare. With a few embellishments, such as the status and expected completion date, ownership, dependencies on other features and any current issues or concerns, this list becomes a powerful overall perspective of the project scope and status.

Tie to this list a list of milestones, commitments, and constraints that are shaping the project, and you will have a view of the box that you are trying to fit all this scope into. Don't try to merge the two sets of information together. Retain the scope with the most reasonable estimates to completion that you can. Avoid trying to arbitrarily fit them into the business constraints you have set. Expose the gap between the two and manage this properly.

Tasks that need to get done but don't register at the feature level need to be captured and tracked to completion, and this list could be effectively posted, too. All too often, teams will diligently have weekly (or more frequent) team meetings where the same things are discussed again and again. Keep these items on a managed list; don't carry them forward from week to week without closure.

Each of these pieces of information should be prominently placed where the whole team can see it as they go about their daily business. This could be next to the coffee machine, posted in the primary meeting room, or right next to the whiteboard that everyone uses. Choose a place where the team congregates. Keep the information current and relevant. Use it to drive the project, and it will be a major communication aid for the team.

Let it fall out of date, like so many six-month-old Gantt charts posted in "war rooms," and it will become invisible to the team.

Run your team meetings with all the relevant information posted and readily available. Use your wall space effectively, and your team will suddenly be meeting and discussing issues in the context of the project itself.

If you do this, the team will be much more aware of the imperative of actually getting things done.

Summary

We need to choose the right balance when guiding the work for our team.

Some elements of our work should be considered sacrosanct. These practices actually become more important as the pressure rises, even though they are often the first to be dropped on most projects.

Other elements can be considered more flexible. These are potentially valuable, given appropriate specific situations. It is always useful to build the capacity into the team to be able to leverage these optional skills, in case the situation arises.

In all cases, it is best that the team has a common understanding of which approaches are the most appropriate, and what the current situation is on the project. In this way, they will have the tools to make the best decisions under the circumstances.

Tactical decisions can support strategic goals only if they are intrinsically linked.

How Is This Relevant?

Balanced approach. Are your software projects run with a reasonable balance of activities? Are key steps skipped so that you can get to what seems important: coding and fixing? Do you follow the equivalent of the basic food groups in deciding what activities to perform? Or, are you subsisting on a junk-food diet? Does your project performance reflect this diet?

Practical focus. Are you defining expected practices at a level that will allow them to be applied to a variety of situations? Can they be easily followed? Are they accessible by the group? Do they provide guidance on how to select appropriate practices? Or, do they define a rigid set of actions?

Shared context. Does everyone have access to important information as they make decisions? Does this include process-based guidance and current project progress?

CHAPTER TWENTY-THREE

Progress Revisited

We need to monitor progress on the changes we make to our culture and processes. Although anecdotal evidence can be compelling in some cases, there is no evidence more compelling than quantified data.

This chapter elaborates on the need to take measurements to confirm our progress in what we are trying to achieve, explains that some of the most important measures concern the current costs of dysfunction, and suggests that measurement is for everyone.

Measuring as a Necessary Evil

Few industries view what constitutes a critical practice so narrowly as the software industry. In most software shops, developing and managing requirements is done when we have time. Estimation practice looks a lot like target practice, and project management is akin to herding cats, with little or no semblance of pragmatic, proactive effort.

Measurement is something that few of us do well in this industry. This unfortunately includes many of those who advocate measurement as a good practice. It is little wonder that the industry continues to be plagued by many of the same issues that were first raised decades ago. Those who do not learn from their mistakes are doomed to repeat them.

Our anecdotal recollection of past performance is often way off the mark. We all have a tendency to see our past through rose-tinted glasses. Our perspective of others, however, is often strongly biased in one direction or another depending on our experience with them. Even if these biases are not entirely justified, we hold fast to them. Anecdotal recollection is too arbitrary, too far removed from reality to be used as a basis for rational decisions.

We all know this, but we still don't measure.

In principle, most of us have a strong aversion to measurement. Taking the time to capture how big something was, how long it took us to do something, or how much it cost is the kind of closure that few of us take the time to do. We're far too busy forging ahead with the next task on our list to deal with this triviality.

Layered on top of that is the fear that this information will be used against us. I've seen timesheets used to insinuate that some people were not pulling their weight, or used to drive more work in less time as over-time is conveniently neglected. I've seen inspections decay into discussion of local sports teams because the people know that any issues found would be reflected in annual performance appraisals. In some organizations, the fear of measurement is quite justified.

For these reasons, measurement is the last thing that most of us would want to spend our time doing, but we need to gain comfort with the value that measurement can bring.

Take the time to consider where measures might add some value. Identify the activities where there isn't a clear appreciation of how long they take or how much they cost. Repetitive tasks are good. Think of elements that you perform again and again, or that could be captured on a weekly basis to identify trends over time. Think about how you might capture some of these measures. Consider what to count, where to store the results, and when and how they might be used again.

There is a very strong chance that after a very brief period, within three to five measurement cycles, you will gain new insights that will surprise you. Over longer periods, you will be able to use this information to predict future outcomes with more accuracy.

Done right, measurement is not evil at all. It is an absolute necessity. I capture a variety of data points on all aspects of the business to drive operations that I would be lost without. Yes, sometimes the data has not provided great news. There have been strong urges to bias the results to sweeten the deal, even knowing that I would only be lying to myself.

I have learned, however, that even bad news in the form of unbiased, defendable data is extremely powerful in allowing me to make reasonable decisions in a clear manner. Measurement has become a core practice for driving a business that has spilled over into multiple areas. For me, the loss of being able to effectively measure and base decisions on this insight would be a far greater evil.

Tactical and Strategic Metrics

When putting together a practical collection of measures to track your project, product, or process, it is important to recognize that you need to balance short-term tactical measures with long-term strategic measures to gain a complete picture. Although it is valuable to know whether you are going to make this week's deliveries as promised, it is equally important to know that the project is not headed for the proverbial cliff.

Start with some short-term measures first. They will generally be more localized, easier to measure, and will provide the quick feedback that will make it easier to start and sustain a measurement program. You might find value in knowing what the likelihood of completing your currently assigned tasks on time is, or by how much you expect to blow out your initial estimates, or how all these tasks roll up to determine whether the project will be completed on time at all.

Strategically, the change in tactical measures over time will reveal trends that can provide a different level of insight. Are we improving in our ability to estimate? Is the number of open defects diminishing as we approach our proposed delivery date? Do we see the definition of scope stabilizing over the life of the project?

Many strategic measures are derived from the change in tactical measures over time, implying the need to carry these measures forward in some sort of repository. Often, this infrastructure is built in to requirements management or issue-tracking tools, but spreadsheets with pivot tables or simple databases will do in a pinch for tracking trends in measures such as estimates versus actuals. Remember to avoid going overboard with the tool support. Focus on getting value out of the numbers themselves. Spanning multiple projects, we can gather information about the effectiveness of the business as a whole.

For any metrics program, it is important to take a disciplined approach to identifying what to measure instead of just measuring what is readily available or searching for numbers that justify your cause.

In any case, no single measure is sufficient for a complete understanding of where you stand with your current approach. Be sure that you know enough about the tactical and strategic issues to be able to make informed decisions.

Inconspicuous Consumption

It was always interesting around the turn-of-the-century frenzy to visit start-up companies, primarily to witness their unique versions of unbridled spending. Aeron chairs for everyone, projection TVs with game consoles and leather sofas to recline on, and beer fridges that were always stocked despite prodigious use. There was a gold rush in progress, and it seemed that the flow of money would never stop.

A few years later, it did stop. The furniture delivery trucks that blocked the streets in the tech parks were replaced with trucks picking up the same expensive furniture. This time, however, it was for fire-sale auctions of assets for the same, now cash-strapped companies.

The era of conspicuous consumption was over, at least for the time being.

Many of those high-roller companies no longer exist, at least partially because of their extravagances. The investors who bankrolled this excess have become much more timid, and much more conscious of how their money is spent—that is, for the visible expenditures that they track, anyway.

This cycle will continue. It is still safe to say that this conspicuous consumption is not the largest source of unnecessary costs in most shops, and probably never was. While being careful to avoid creature comforts that might peak out at 5 percent to 10 percent of their overall costs, almost every company I have worked with has no idea how much money they are burning due to inefficiencies in how they work.

Even with increased accounting demands, the focus is generally constrained to tracking and accounting against traditional line items: specific projects, activities, and so on. There remains little visibility into the cost of inefficiency, and this needs to change.

The Way Things Are

When I talk to groups about the cost of their inefficiencies, I get a range of responses from "we actually do pretty well here" to "we're dying here with the waste and rework."

Despite the range of responses, all of these groups have two things in common. The first is that they don't actually know what the cost of this waste is. They don't actually measure it. Usually, they don't even have a common definition of what would fall into that "waste" category.

The second thing these companies all have in common is that they don't recognize this waste as a massive opportunity for improvement that is entirely within their sphere of control.

Little is being done to manage and reduce these inefficiencies. They are often seen as merely a by-product of running hard toward an ever-evolving goal, with an ever-changing team.

Do the math.

Rework is one possible dimension to measure the inefficiencies in your organization. Studies have shown that for software companies, rework comes in at the 30 percent to 40 percent range. I've measured it to be close to double that in some companies, and others in this line of work have similar horror stories. If you don't know what these numbers are in your organization (that is, if rework has not been an area that is top of mind), there isn't any reason to believe it is less than the 30 percent to 40 percent average in companies that know they are being measured. Let's be optimistic and suggest you are running with 30 percent rework, dealing with stuff that you thought you had washed your hands of.

We can't expect to eliminate this. From my experience, with a little consideration (especially if it is the first time you tackle this issue), it should be easy to chop this number in half—not by adding resources, but by doing more of the good things you are currently doing, and fewer of the things that are contributing to waste.

In this little thought experiment, we have gained 15 percent of our time and resources back, maybe more. If we annualize that, we would be looking at an Aeron chair and game console for everyone in the place, a cruise to Hawaii for the entire team over Christmas, and still have enough efficiency left over to get more product out the door. This doesn't even take into account the opportunity of being able to tackle other projects. If your organization is really feeling pain, the math here only becomes more compelling.

We all look at the obvious extravagances in some companies and cry "what a waste," while unbeknownst to us our own inconspicuous inefficiencies, such as rework within a project cycle and maintenance costs that are not accounted back to the original project, are far more wasteful!

To mature as an industry, our accounting practices need to look at all the dimensions of consumption. If we do our job right, we can easily find greater value in legislated accounting requirements that will open up vast areas for improvement right under our noses. This can also alleviate the problem of having to go to the very tight open market for additional resources. We win on all measurable accounts, and the softer issues such as morale improve, too.

Not Too Big, Not Too Small

There is a time for following a clearly defined approach to software development, and there is a time when you should reconsider all the pomp and circumstance that is expected of you. The tough part is figuring out which time is which.

Sometimes you will find yourself being asked to do something, but you won't be able to figure out how this contributes to your goals. It might be some paperwork that routinely gets filed, never to be seen again. It might be a formal specification that gets superseded with e-mail and telephone calls. It might be a design model that doesn't provide any new insight. Especially after a company has become very large (with the perceived need for a correspondingly weighty process) or right after having been severely burned (where there unfolds the hysteresis of "we have to do everything right, at least for the next few months"), defined approaches can be dreadful overkill at times.

A defined approach is not something to do blindly just because it says so in a binder or is posted on a Web site. Policies should serve to ensure consistency in the proper application of best practices, not to replace the application of gray matter in the form of good judgment. If you think that what you are being asked to do is overkill, put up your hand and ask. If you can't get a reasonable answer about why you should perform that task, maybe it wasn't important in the first place.

Don't take for granted that the defined approach is always right. Even under ideal circumstances, sometimes some steps are a waste of time. Cut where appropriate.

For most small companies, most of the time (and even large companies some of the time), there is usually a need for a little more of that pomp and circumstance, a little less of that "wing-and-a-prayer" approach to getting software out the door. This is not because there is no clearly defined approach to follow (which is often the case). It is that there are so many ways to seriously injure your chances of delivery at a moment's notice. This can be anything from not having everything under version control, to not regression testing, to not understanding what you needed to build in the first place, and all sorts of pitfalls in between.

Having the practices documented rarely solves the problem. We're notorious for not reading the manual in this industry. If the manual tells us to do things that we don't like to do, or if nobody is checking in to see whether we are following the manual, we've wasted time putting it together in the first place.

The problem lies in the lack of appreciation for what a reasonable approach does for us, both in the trenches and at the senior level. Even if we have been burned more than once, we're quick to blame external circumstances for the problem and lapse back into the same old bad habits. Often, we're told to cut corners when deadlines loom. We create a "damn the torpedoes, full steam ahead" scenario, without realizing that the torpedoes are ours.

Chances are, if you are prevented from getting something done by a mishap (either yours or someone else's) or you are taking a technical leap that is too broad and difficult, you need to step back and figure out which corners have been cut that shouldn't have been. Your preferred approach is probably too small. Add where appropriate.

The right size of your development approach can make for a nice, predictable ride to product delivery, with the excitement coming from the rush of creating new capabilities rather than from the "surprise du jour." That "rush," however, rarely happens when the overhead required to get there puts you to sleep.

Be as picky as Goldilocks when you are looking at your approach to software development. It is a delicate balance. There is no substitute for actually thinking about what makes sense in your situation.

We have known for years that there are practices that clearly and measurably reduce overall effort and risk on software projects. Many of these things support the successful completion of projects of any kind. Clearly defined scope, a realistic schedule, checks and balances, objective validation, and clear communication are a few of the prominent practices that fit most projects.

Many software shops look at the commonly acknowledged "best practices" in the industry with disdain. They can't seem to afford the time to deal with the pomp and circumstance of requirements analysis. The design? Well, that is just embodied in the code, right? They ruthlessly guard their code as personal property and ship when the compiler says all is okay. (Thank goodness we can tune out those pesky warnings.) They don't have time for all those overhead activities. They have tight deadlines, after all. If these things were so important, they would have spent more time on these in school (rather than the languages, databases, and operating systems), wouldn't they have? These things just slow us down from getting the job done. We're doing just fine, thank you very much. Quality is someone else's problem.

Huge amounts of rework and poor quality are killing software companies, even today.

Some software shops recognize the true value of applying reasonable practices. Yes, there is a cost of doing these things. Although some should be considered mandatory on any project, many simply aren't worth it for trivial little tasks, and some aren't even worth it for larger ones. If you really want to develop industrial-strength software, due consideration of how you build your software is critical and worth every penny of the investment. This is not overhead; this actually speeds you up and reduces your overall risk on projects, when applied appropriately for the given situation.

There is no time like the present to acknowledge what Fred Brooks suggested over a quarter century ago, that there is plenty of room for improvement in most software development shops. Although some teams are recognizing this and becoming more effective over time, many are still mired in the goop of their own dysfunction, wondering why they can't get things done. Some are doomed to extinction because they refuse to recognize they have a role in their own predicament, and will never take the steps to address their challenges.

Summary

We all hate to measure and will find all sorts of justifications for not taking measurements, but we can only really be sure if we have the precise data.

If we take the time to carefully select what we measure and are careful to ensure that we are not using the data to artificially justify our arguments, we will find that the insight provided will far outweigh any inconvenience in collecting the data.

Perhaps the greatest value comes from measuring the current cost of dysfunction, because this defines the pool that we draw from in our improvement efforts. Raising awareness in this area can significantly improve our ability to rally people to our cause.

How Is This Relevant?

Cost of nonquality. Do you have measures for the costs of not doing the right things? What is your average amount of effort devoted to rework? How much does your scope change over the life of a project? Do you slip schedules? Is your customer happy?

Variable data. How much variability do you have in your project success? Can you correlate this variability with specific causes such as new versus maintenance projects, degree of technology innovation, or differences in who is running the project? Is this a tolerable level of variation?

Appropriate practices. Are your practices appropriate for your team size, the culture of the group, and the importance of the products you build? Are there best practices that you could adopt that would provide a net benefit to the team? When did you last consider these questions?

CHAPTER TWENTY-FOUR

Change Revisited

Managing change is a part of any initiative we are involved in, but what are we to do when our initiative is change itself? We need to be careful to facilitate change in the team by taking small steps and helping everyone understand that the change represents an opportunity for improvement.

This chapter examines the approaches that we can take to prepare the team for change by identifying key opportunities and raising awareness of the challenges with the current approaches.

Realistic Planning: Planning for Change

Most would agree that project planning is a critical activity: having an understanding of what you are about to build and why, who's on the team, and where, when and how these people will do their job is key to getting a project started in the right direction. Any project manager will tell you that. Any seasoned project manager will also tell you, however, that your original plan is out of date by the time it is posted.

Why bother, then?

You might have experienced successful project planning sessions, in which everyone involved gets together to discuss his or her perspective on how a project should play itself out. This is often done in a place fancifully called the "war room." Although a great motivator and team builder, the initial buzz is often lost soon after the planning session is completed. The plans that have been made here don't reflect the current activities in the least.

Projects such as this have a life of their own, with little resemblance to those aging Gantt charts that were created at the beginning of the project or any updated versions. Chances are that this project will take longer and cost more than expected, even after cutting some quality corners and eliminating features that required too much time to complete.

Change on a software project will come in several forms, both internal and external. For every ounce of effort you put into your original planning session, you will have to put a pound of sweat into making sure that you still meet your original objectives after addressing all the changes that arise. The original plan is merely the first step on the journey. There will be bug fixes (preferably sooner as well as later), pieces of the technological puzzle that just won't fit as originally planned, and a constant pressure from the outside to change the scope (which should not be ignored).

Running a software project isn't like taking a drive down the coast with the route clearly laid out by your automobile club. It's more akin to an off-road adventure to a lake you've never been to, after a heavy storm has washed out roads and knocked over trees. You can make it if you are prepared to make numerous mid-course corrections along the way, and if you are properly equipped to do so. There is even a good chance you can get there with all your original goals intact.

Don't be so optimistic as to think that your project will play out as it was originally planned. Change management is simply the continuation of that original planning session. Only now there is more refined data to work with as you move toward completion.

It is naïve to think you can succeed without a generous helping of adjustments to the original plan.

Out with the Old…

It's been stated in many different ways that change is inevitable, and that change is resisted by all of us. We don't have the time to learn new things. We can't afford to do more things. We've tried that "change thing," and it just didn't work. It is easier to embrace the inertia of our current practices, dysfunctional or not. The devil we know drives the vast majority of our actions.

Change is a double-edged sword. Indeed, as we start out doing these new things, we tend to do them relatively poorly and inefficiently. If we have never consciously designed a system, for example, our first designs will be fraught with problems. The learning curve can be a painful experience, but we learn best by doing.

Along with all these learning pains, however, comes a silver lining. Assuming we have selected the appropriate changes, what we have are not additional things to do but a displacement of activities. Literally, we need to make time for the new practices, because we cannot introduce more hours to our day. In some shops, the simple practice of spending less time at the office can have a net positive result. In all cases, it becomes an "out with the old" approach to allow for "in with the new."

The trick to change is to ensure we are optimizing the effectiveness of our practices, not merely adding more things to do. Diving straight into the code without thinking out the design and architecture (or even considering what the scope should really be) is highly inefficient, even if it appears to be productive on the surface. Placing appropriate focus on early stage efforts will not eliminate the need for developing code, but the activity will become a lot more efficient. You will find yourself able to focus on the implementation details instead of discovering the design on-the-fly.

The sad truth, however, is that many organizations have perfectly adequate defined practices and life cycles but never seem to be able to get a project out the door. When we think of change and process improvement, we normally think of changed practices. The "out with the old, in with the new" strategy is certainly a critical component for success here. Unfortunately, a defined approach is insufficient. We need to consider change in other dimensions, too, such as the dimensions of behaviors and attitudes. From this perspective, we find another crucial and often neglected side of change.

In some cases, the "out with the old" will end up applying to people as well as practices.

As practices are changed or as existing practices are finally enforced, there will be a disruption to the comfort zone of the team members. Some will learn to adjust and recognize the value to themselves and to the team as a whole. Others will find that they are no longer comfortable. They may grouse about the changes. They may even consciously try to undermine the changes to get back to their previous comfort zone. Eventually, if the changes stick and discomfort persists under the new approach, these people will often move on. Even if they were team leads or strong influencers within the group, if they cannot fit within the system that the team is working with, this move is probably best for everyone involved.

To have an agreed upon approach is one thing. To follow it even when the pressure is on is quite another. People take different approaches to the application of best practices. This is a concern that needs to be just as consciously managed. For an approach to work, it needs to be consistently applied. There can be no opting out for the sake of tactical convenience.

I'm not an advocate of cleaning house before giving people a chance to show reasonable attitudes, but I do advocate laying down clear laws and sticking to them. There is no room in team-based software development for individual approaches that jeopardize the integrity of the overall system.

Nobody should be immune to check-out/check-in procedures, nobody should be exempt from peer reviews, and nobody should be allowed to go dark, period. If people consciously subvert the system (as opposed to reasonably debating the merit of the system itself), their next task should be to find a new job.

This, like working fewer hours in a day, may be all that it takes for some organizations to dramatically improve their performance. This is simply plugging the holes in the well-structured but leaky boat.

When we manage change, we need to consider the approach as well as the application, acceptance, and evolution of the approach by the team to ensure success.

Categorizing the Future

It is critical to plan for change, which is inevitable on any reasonably sized software project, and most projects that are not so reasonably sized. It is important to realize, however, that not all change is good change. As we consider all the future work on our plates related to projects, we can identify three categories:

- Current known work
- Potential new work
- Rework

We must recognize the need to deal with these through diligence, flexibility, and discipline.

The first and hopefully most significant category is "current known work." Plan it out. Schedule and track it. Be sure that you have clear completion criteria. In doing so, you have a fighting chance of reducing the amount that comes back to haunt you as rework: from software bugs to bad requirements. Accept that your work will not necessarily play out as planned. If it becomes apparent that you are struggling against a dead end, it is often time to step back and rethink your strategy.

In most projects, there is internal and external pressure to change the scope of known work. This is a primary source of scope creep when managed poorly. Acknowledge it and understand the relative value of this compared to the current work on your plate. Ignore it and you risk failing to satisfy your customers or missing industry trends. Only if it makes business sense should you build it in to your current known workload. It is easy to continue to change things and suddenly find yourself without a real business case for what you are doing. Scope change pressure is like the weather. You can't influence it, so your best approach is to adapt to it tactically.

Rework is that stuff you are not aware of now but will appear because of not having done your job completely or correctly sometime in the past. When it arises, you need to look at it as potential change and deal with it as you would any scope change. The key distinction here is that it is within your power to influence the amount of rework that hits you. Industry statistics show that the average amount of time spent in rework is more than 30 percent. I've worked with many companies that think that this number is low for them!

If you are constantly being surprised with rework, you are not doing your job well. Deal with problems as they arise, but deal with the causes of the problems, too.

To paraphrase Saint Francis of Assisi, "Lord, grant me the serenity to drive current work to completion, the courage to accept the changes that will strengthen my business, and the wisdom to do things in a manner that will minimize needless rework."

Opportunity Knocks

For software, there is much emphasis, if not enough execution, on early project planning.

If no planning is done, a project can meander about for quite a long time before arriving at some destination, and victory can often be artificially declared. As people start to understand the value of planning, there can be a tendency to plan in excruciating detail, and then jealously guard that plan as the righteous path to completion, despite all the uncertainties that were present when the planning took place. If there was so much we didn't know when we started on our journey, why are we ruthless at protecting the intended path instead of finding the best approach? Most projects are more akin to bushwhacking expeditions than trips down the interstate.

A project plan is one possible path to a known destination, but is really only a means of understanding the reasonableness of getting to that end. Without a plan, you are only wandering. However, even a detailed plan is nothing without a clear understanding of your goals and destination. Flexibility in planning and tracking is valuable. A plan does not deserve protection; it is there to be consumed. It is merely a tool to assist you in getting you to your destination.

There is a great deal of guidance on how to stay on track and how to deal with problems as they arise, but relatively little on how to ensure the track you are on is the right one. This is probably due to the fact that problems tend to arise frequently, and dealing with these downsides as they appear is necessary to avoid outright failure. We are careful to make corrections to our intended path, but rarely consider alternatives that might take us to a totally different destination, even where the overall value may be significantly greater. We put in place change control boards and only allow adjustments that realign us to our target. It is rare that we reconsider our targets in light of the new information in front of us.

Not all change is bad, but it requires a particular mindset to take advantage of the opportunities that may arise at any time. Instead of trying to control change, we need to manage change and recognize that change is often good (and sometimes necessary). A change management board should be charged with looking at all the information on the table and deciding the relative merits of different destinations and simple course corrections. Instead of protecting the current course, protect the notion that the goals with the highest returns should be achieved. Is this potential change a threat to be wary of or is it an opportunity to seize? This is a much larger mandate with greater responsibility, but it also holds much more potential for the organization.

When an opportunity presents itself, it can be so rare an occurrence that the natural tendency is to struggle to retain the status quo rather than to truly leverage the new opportunity.

There is always a cost to change, but there can often be a greater cost to not changing when it makes sense to do so. If we only look to set and define our goals when we initiate new projects, we shut down almost all the opportunity we have to advance beyond the limits of our initial parameters. This is especially true if we are stuck on the same project for too long.

We need to be vigilant and always listen for that knock at the door.

Tying Process to Reality

Step into the middle of many, perhaps most software organizations these days and you will find a huge discrepancy between the defined process and what actually goes on in the software projects themselves.

Quite often, those who are charged with defining the process for the group will fulfill this task, but they fail to create anything that can be reasonably used to help the organization. You can complete the exercise but still fail in several ways.

First, let's clarify the term *defined process*. It's an extremely rare organization that actually has a clearly defined, commonly understood explanation of how a project should be completed: roles, responsibilities, deliverables; supported by checklists, templates, guidance, policies, reviews, and audits. In some ways, it is sometimes better that this is rare. More is not necessarily better.

There are those groups that provide no guidance at all on how to complete a project. Whether or not there is a definition of what the product needs to do, the whole notion of what steps should be taken, what information should be captured, what form the information should take, what completion really looks like and how everything should tie together for delivery is left open to interpretation.

With this ad hoc approach, the best intentions at the beginning of the project often fall by the wayside as deadlines loom. Interpretations of what is a reasonable approach changes dramatically in a never-ending cycle: from "we resolve to do it right this time" to "we'll dot our i's and cross our t's later" to "we've got to rush to get it out the door" to "I told you we should have done it right last time!"

Some groups have all this process stuff because they have qualifications to maintain and the standard drives what will be in place. It should be made clear, however, that the past performance (in this case, the attained qualification) is not a reliable predictor of future performance. Just because it is written down by no means implies it is the right stuff to do or is actually being done.

There are those who have purchased a packaged process and have managed to somehow deploy it to the group in a practical fashion.

Some have taken a few pieces that add value and have reaped strong benefits. Others have dogmatically foisted the whole thing (which is often larger than practical if it is to be generally commercially viable) on the team like a pair of cement overshoes. They have saved time in getting an industrial-strength, consistent "defined process," but have often missed the point.

The real goal in tying process to reality is to provide guidance to the team on what needs to be done to increase the likelihood of successfully delivering their products. For all but a few groups that do the same thing over and over ad nauseum, this needs to be more than a set of static definitions and procedures. There is no one size fits all even within a single organization, and don't even entertain that notion for the industry as a whole.

The key to tying process to reality is to define it in a practical, accessible form. A thorough definition of what should be done is useless in a collection of binders that are only opened under duress. Here are a few pointers to help you build up a process definition that can actually be used by a group to reduce delivery risk:

- **Introduce changes gradually.** You don't want to overwhelm the team with change, so pick the areas that are going to provide the most return for the least cost. Introduce the change and then give it time to be institutionalized before introducing more. Don't worry; there will always be opportunities for additional changes later.

- **Respect individuality.** Projects vary in size, duration, risk, criticality, novelty, and countless other factors. Provide guidance on how to tailor the "defined process" for each project based on the factors that arise in your group. Help define the critical terms *completion* and *success* on projects.

- **Deal with the early stage and oversight activities first.** These have the greatest cascading impact on the overall project, so improving these areas provides the most value. (Someone said once that all project problems start in the first few minutes of the project.) Focus on solid requirements over coding standards, practical change management over document templates.

- **Emphasize problem solving.** Few people go to the manual for guidance when things are going according to plan. It's when things are not going according to plan that they need help. Consider how to manage change, and how to manage risk with practical decision support tools. Determine who needs to be in the loop for decisions, when corrective action needs to be taken, and what should be done.

- **Focus on high visibility and communication throughout.** Almost any issue I have ever seen on a project can be traced back to a lack of shared understanding or decisions made without sufficient information (which, paradoxically, was often actually readily available). Documentation is not just creating documents, it is persisting a common understanding, and the information contained needs to survive as long as it is relevant.

- **Leverage technology.** There are many opportunities to support communication online beyond just storing huge documents in a repository. Break them up, hyperlink, incorporate graphics, and enforce workflows. Share information as openly and efficiently as reasonable.

- **Keep it lightweight.** Binders collect dust. Checklists and other memory joggers are much more likely to be used. Capture the key elements in a concise form, even on a single sheet of paper (perhaps the change control workflow, key sources of project information, and minimum requirements for task completion, for example), and they are much more likely to be followed.

Building a process that is tied to the reality of the operations of a group is not easy. Treat it as a project and respect the product of this project as one of the most important things that a company will ever produce.

Make it practical, and it will be valuable and useful for your group.

Take Small, Measured Steps

There are all sorts of reasons for software teams to not get better at what they do. We've tried and failed at that stuff before. We can't afford the time to do more stuff. It is going to cost us more money. Whatever the reason, the barriers to change are generally high enough that the team will continue to muddle on, and perhaps get their product out the door at some point. It will likely be a bit late, cost more than hoped, and do less than anticipated.

Drill down into most of these barriers and you will find that they are actually rationalizations. Without really knowing how much time is wasted on a typical project or how drastically the scope evolves, most people will have a rose-tinted recollection of how well they are doing. If not measured, time spent in rework will seem negligible compared to the "difficult," but more easily quantified costs of agreeing on the scope of work, or building a credible plan, or heaven forbid, considering the impact of change as the project moves on. Actual data will tell a different tale. Without it, however, the team easily remains complacent and inefficient. Inertia is powerful.

Occasionally, teams are forced to change their habits. Whether they need ISO certification to get into Europe, are diving into a CMMI-based initiative, or are finding that they suddenly need to be compliant with Sarbanes-Oxley, the team that was comfortable with doing things as they always have suddenly finds they have a great deal more to do beyond what they thought was developing software. Accountability and traceability appear to be the necessary ugly stepsisters to repeatability. A lot of the joy can be removed from the creative endeavor of building software if you are not careful.

Often, the focus in these initiatives can be to achieve compliance rather than to make the team more effective. The considerations of effectiveness and efficiency are rarely a primary driver, despite the original intent of the authors.

You just don't go out and run a marathon after spending years spent eating chips in front of *Seinfeld* reruns. Most of us wouldn't think of even trying such a move. For many of us, the inertia that keeps software teams muddling on is the same inertia that keeps us in front of the tube rather than watching our weight.

For the few that improve, the small gradual changes that reinforce the value of the program work best. For most of us, being able to run a marathon is a little ambitious, so we set more moderate goals such as minding our intake and building up our physical activity. Just being healthy can do as much for longevity as training to be an elite athlete does.

With software teams, a similar approach works well. Pick a few small things to do differently from what you are doing now. Usually the best things to do are early-stage activities such as capturing the scope and putting together a reasonable schedule. Keep both of these current by considering each change before saying okay, and throw in a few simple measures to confirm things are working. How much time is being spent on rework? How fluid is the scope? How close are you to meeting your targets? Avoid overkill. Focus on a shared understanding across the team. Chances are you will find that your projects will run much more smoothly, and you will have the numbers to back it up.

Don't get yourself caught in the situation where you will have to make a huge leap to satisfy some externally driven regulatory body or certifying agency. Recognize the internal value for becoming more effective at the activities that are core to your business. Start today on the continuing path of getting better.

Properly selected, gradual, measured changes can reap huge rewards early.

Raising Awareness

Change is difficult to bring into any organization. We all have our set approach for getting things done. All of us do at least one thing in a horribly inefficient fashion, but we can't be bothered to change our ways. Inertia is extremely strong, and we all have so much on our plates these days that we apparently can't afford to take the time to step back and adjust our approach.

If it is tough for an individual, the difficulty increases dramatically as we try to extrapolate up to team-based practices. Any organization, software or nonsoftware related, has their set way of doing things. It's usually not what is documented in the process manuals (for those companies that have actually produced, or bought them). Even if you belong to one of the few shops that has a defined approach that is the same as the institutionalized approach (you actually do what you say you are going to do, even when schedule pressure is immense), adjustments may be reasonable, but are extremely difficult to inject.

Often, people bring in their own pet approaches from previous assignments for getting their job done. In many shops, their approach is a potpourri of techniques and tricks that eventually get a product out the door, albeit usually late and with disappointing quality. The overall approach grows with a patchwork of individual contributions, and the team as a whole fails to benefit from any synergistic efficiencies.

The first step to bringing change that will reduce risk or improve efficiencies in an organization is to raise awareness that there are gains to be had. Few organizations have measures in place that reveal the cost of the current approach. Anecdotal recollection is such that even a week or two after the most painful project experience imaginable, the team quickly forgets the pain and falls back into the old habits that caused the pain to begin with.

Without clear measures of dysfunction (rework, costs of poor quality, or failure to meet schedule, for example), it is easy to rationalize away anything *more* on the next project. After all, if we were late on the last project, why would we want to do anything more next time around? Without clear measures of dysfunction, any request for more time planning or specifying the system will sound like you are suggesting that the sky is falling.

First, you need to overcome people's refusal to acknowledge the problem. After you have caught the group's attention by exposing the true cost of the current approach, the next step is to raise awareness that there might be a better way.

It never ceases to amaze me how few people in this industry are aware of the many "best practices" that have been established for years. It can appear easy to breeze through the survey courses that touch on these topics in school, if you are exposed to them at all. Most students wait until the last moment to do their projects because they are busy ignoring the very practices that are described in these survey courses. Take that experience into the industry and work at a firm that practices a similar approach to the way you used to get your term projects done, and you have reinforced an approach that leaves the industry in the sorry state it is in. Here, you need to overcome the ignorance that there can be a solution.

Merely mandating changes won't work. People need to clearly understand that the current approach is expensive, and then they will be open to the notion that there are alternatives that might be more reasonable.

Select the changes carefully after raising awareness, and you are well on your way to actually bringing positive and lasting change into your organization.

Summary

In any organization, there are opportunities for change that can drastically improve the performance of the team.

As with any change, it is important to only adjust what is necessary to avoid culture shock. We also need to take care to ensure that everyone understands the rationale behind the change, and the value it brings to him or her.

There are many barriers to overcome in the process of managing change, and they all must be addressed head on.

How Is This Relevant?

Time for change. Have you built time for change in to your schedules? Do you recognize all the pressures for change, both internal and external? Are your initial project schedules built with the expectation that they will evolve over the project's life?

Change as opportunity. Have you been involved in changes that were presented as opportunities? How did you react to these changes? Was this different from just being told to do things differently? What opportunities for change are presenting themselves to you now?

Awareness of need. Does the group recognize the need for change? Are the concerns quantified in an objective form? Is this awareness presented to each participant in a way that is most compelling for him or her?

CHAPTER TWENTY-FIVE

Constant Vigilance

A good start on a project is insufficient for success. We need to be constantly vigilant that we are still moving in the right direction, because any small change can put us on a path that takes us far from our intended goals.

In this chapter, we discuss the challenges of keeping a project on track and the perils of wandering from our intended course. Finally, we recognize that the primary reason for any success we achieve is the team itself.

Blinkers

As thoroughbreds race toward the finish line, they are single-mindedly focused on that end, showing little concern for the pack around them.

Look closely and you will find that most of them achieve this focus with a set of blinkers: half-cups built in to their headgear that blocks their peripheral vision. Blinkers eliminate the extraneous clutter of issues around them that just aren't important.

Step back a bit and you will realize that the blinkers are actually part of a broader system. Thoroughbreds also come equipped with a jockey. The jockey is a device that compensates for the blinkers by watching the surroundings and making appropriate tactical decisions while the horse races toward the finish.

The end goal is certainly critical, but the tactical roadblocks must be taken into account, and the jockey deals with this very effectively.

In business, it is interesting to see how many executives drive with their blinkers on. There is a razor-sharp focus on the end goal (even if that end goal is not clearly defined), and nothing is allowed to get in the way. Admirable in principle, but often that end goal is not achieved because of tactical issues that were apparent but ignored.

All the events, all the information uncovered along the way toward your end goal has the potential to refine your understanding of the reasonableness of your approach and hence the likelihood of achieving your end goal. Initially, your goals are high-level ideas of what you would like to achieve. These are gradually fleshed out through better understanding of your approach and your environment. Some of that understanding will support your goals (strong market demand or a breakthrough in technology, for example). Some will cause you to reassess your goals (a new competitor or the discovery of critical internal inefficiencies). This external information is used to make appropriate decisions along the way so that you can achieve your goals. Hundreds of decisions will have to be made, and when you first start out there is no way to safely decide. You actually start out unaware of all the decisions that will have to be made down the road.

It is interesting to participate in business plan competitions as a mentor. We get to see all sorts of ideas and work with a wide variety of entrepreneurs at all stages of starting a business. Over the years, it has become easier to see who is going to do well overall. Although there are certainly elements such as market demand and intellectual property that provide an advantage, one of the key "intangibles" that makes a difference is how well the team listens to advice.

Changes made at the business plan stage are much less costly than experiencing the problems in the implementation stage. Teams that can accept advice as information that helps them adjust their plans will do well overall—both in the competition and in business in general. Those that react to criticism by staunchly defending their approach rarely make it to their end goal.

Information that is ignored is done so at the potential peril of the business. Bad news needs to be dealt with, and good news can be leveraged to your advantage. Neglecting information will not advance your quest for the end goal. Nobody enjoys a precise, risk-free path to success from the start.

Being willfully ignorant is not the same as being focused.

Critical Introspection

I ran into a colleague at a networking event where we had an interesting discussion about their current attempts to rein in their development challenges by adopting an agile approach. I provided some of my observations from working with other teams: mostly caveats, given the low success rate I have seen with most groups. After a spell, we decided it would be interesting for me to drop by and chat with the team about their approach in more detail.

A couple of weeks later, I sat down with several of the key people involved in the initiative. They explained why they were motivated to make such a change, which aspects of Extreme Programming (XP) they had taken on (they were migrating an existing product, so it was clearly not a Greenfield effort), and their observations of what had happened to date (they were just completing their second sprint).

They had just completed a brief internal review of progress to date, and already their positive notes from their experience outweighed their suggested deltas. (When was the last time you ran a retrospective and had your successes outweigh your challenges?) None of the suggested deltas were overwhelming, while many of the positives were quite strong indeed. They were making careful steps, taking into account their culture and the state of their product and approach.

At the end of the session, the group asked what they could be doing better.

Unlike many situations in which the challenge is to prioritize and sanitize the results to avoid overwhelming the group with too many issues that they could improve on, the problem here was to find a way to further optimize their approach. They had acknowledged that their approach in the past was imperfect. They were following the path of carefully introducing change, and were using feedback to ensure that their intervention was helping rather than hurting the cause.

In my opinion, the most important contributor to their success was not their adoption of a specific approach to software development, but their critical assessment of both their internal situation and the potential value and pitfalls of the approach they were considering.

They were starting slowly, carefully monitoring their progress and checking their vital signs along the way.

They were adapting the textbook approach to their culture and product, with a strong emphasis on up-front requirements gathering and prioritizing, because the product was well understood.

The responsibility lies with the advocates to ensure that the medicine is appropriate for the symptoms and that it is taken properly, with sensitivity to any adverse side effects.

Unfortunately, as with many grand elixirs before, the message is often being disseminated in a way similar to a doctor who has prefilled his prescription pad for a strong antibiotic, and every patient who sees him gets one of these prescriptions. The solution does not fit every problem, although in the case just described, it does fit nicely with appropriate adjustments.

Regardless of the approach you want to adopt, use your noggin. Carefully monitor your needs, deployment, and possible side effects, and the odds of success improve dramatically.

Knowledge Decay

Here's an example of knowledge gone awry, starting with a statement from a client:

"We used Extreme Programming for the prototype. You should see an Extreme project in action. Nobody's really sure what is going on, and there is no documentation. It's quite chaotic."

After hearing this, I decided to ask Martin Fowler, Agile Alliance signatory and co-author of *Planning Extreme Programming*, for his opinion, which he gave:

That comment sounds to me that they weren't doing Extreme Programming. It must have been its evil twin: stupid programming.

The release and iteration planning work in XP means that everybody does have a good idea what he or she is doing because everybody is involved in the planning process.

Release planning gives a long-term view across one or more releases between the team and the customer. This plan is subject to constant, but controlled change. (The plan is there to control the change.) Iteration planning charts everybody's tasks out for a full iteration (one to three weeks). Every member of the team takes part in building the iteration plan, which does a lot to help coordination. The practice of daily stand-up meetings (ten minutes) helps maintain visibility for everyone.

Done properly, XP involves a lot of planning, done continuously with everyone involved, and a lot of visibility. (And by the way, XP does not say not to do documentation. It just has no mandatory documentation steps other than the acceptance tests, which are preferably automated.)

Thanks, Martin…well stated.

Particularly in software development, information is growing exponentially, and personal awareness of the cutting edge can't possibly keep up. There are a number of reasons for the decay of knowledge:

- There is the phenomenon of information loss associated with repeated verbal communication. (Remember passing stories to one another around the campfire?) This includes issues of hearsay and conjecture to interpolate gaps of knowledge, instead of diving in to find the original pearl of information.

- Shortcuts are perceived to be an easier way to complete the picture, but we bring our own biases and experiences with us, making it inevitable that we will color our "complete" understanding in ways that the originator never intended.

- Assumptions often miss the mark, and we are generally optimistic of how deeply we understand the information we have received.

Whether we are part of a large multinational corporation, a global phenomenon, or just two people sharing information, consistent knowledge is a very difficult thing to achieve and maintain. Integrity of the original information can only be determined through feedback from the recipient and iterating until all the nuances are shared and understood consistently. With no feedback, interpretations cannot possibly be managed adequately, and knowledge decay will take place.

We need to be diligent in our gathering of information and even more careful about the fidelity of our assertions to others.

Where Does It Hurt?

The benefits of staying healthy and in shape are clear to everyone, but the effort that we put into our fitness varies tremendously.

From those who are extremely fit athletes or meticulous about what they eat to the slovenly couch potatoes or those who sue fast-food joints because of their obesity, we generally reap what we sow. Although there are cases of extremely fit people passing away in their prime, statistics overwhelmingly indicate there are benefits to taking reasonable care of ourselves. With a little consideration, everyone can find the right balance to maximize his or her quality of life. We don't all need to train for marathons, but we shouldn't subsist on fast food either.

So it is with software development organizations. Although we all know that doing the right thing is good for us, we adhere to that mantra in varying degrees. There are the extremely mature shops that get the job done on time, every time (and have real lives, too), and there are those who can't seem to get projects done at all (and are quick to blame external circumstances for their own malaise). Yes, all sorts of market conditions can shut down the strongest shops without warning, but again, it is pretty clear that software groups can do many things to "take care of themselves." Any shop has room for improvement, and the quality of life in the development world is to a very large degree within your control.

A critical component of any health initiative is an external perspective. Most of us understand that an annual visit to our doctor makes great sense, not only as a general health indicator but also for the battery of tests that we just aren't equipped to perform ourselves. How are my cholesterol levels? Why am I so tired all the time? What is that lump, anyway?

In software, the questions are similar: We feel the pain, but we often can't put our finger on the root cause. Why can't we ship on time? Why do we ship so many bugs? Why can't we retain our staff? We can guess, but in most cases it takes an external perspective and broad experience to make the right call.

A good external resource won't talk down to you. They ensure you understand the merits of doing something before asking you to take the plunge. They won't over prescribe or put you on a program that is beyond your means. They take the time to understand your particular situation, and don't have a stock solution for your problems. They work with you to identify an approach that works for you and refer you to others if the situation warrants. They are genuinely interested in your quality of life. All of this is true for software development groups, too.

No organization can perform a complete and objective self-assessment, and few are equipped with the expertise to safely diagnose and prescribe a path to better quality of life.

Backsliding

Almost anywhere I go, I hear stories about individuals or companies that do great things, only to have that greatness backslide over time, often to a point where that great performance never really happened.

In one organization, I worked with a wide range of people on their personal effectiveness. One point that was consistently mentioned at the end of each session was the concern that these newly developed good habits would disappear. For many of their peers, this had already happened.

One division of a large company embraced formal software inspections. Their experience was so overwhelmingly positive that it is commonly used as an industry benchmark for the value of formal inspections. In speaking with some of the engineers involved in the study, they indicate that they don't really do that anymore: "Well, you know, we had a reorg…" is how the story starts.

A lot of companies that change the way they do business often find themselves falling back into their familiar old habits.

It's not a software team syndrome. It is part of the human condition to quickly lose what has not been conditioned and reinforced in favor of what is familiar, regardless of the consequences.

In *Leading Strategic Change,*[1] the authors suggest that change is a cycle:

- We start in a state where we are doing the right thing and doing it well. This is the proverbial status quo.

- Something happens (market conditions change, for example), and we find that while we are still doing the same thing, and doing it well, it is no longer the right thing to do. In software, I would modify this to suggest that while in the status quo state, some disastrous event or astute introspection reveals that we actually weren't doing the right thing in the first place, but we were oblivious to the problems.

- We change our behavior, and initially the new practices are not being done well, although they are the right things to do in the new situation. In software, this is where we learn to see the value of appropriate application of best practices.

Here we need to ensure that there is strategic continuity in what we do. We need to constantly reinforce our belief that the new behaviors are the right ones, through demonstration of our new successes, however small initially. Until we start to see those new successes, we need to focus even harder to ensure our efforts don't fall off the rails.

We need to strive to truly institutionalize our changed behaviors. More than demonstrating simply that we can do it, more than even showing the benefit, we need to get to a point where it becomes rote. When it becomes rote, we need to continue to reinforce the practice, to make this reinforcement part of the practice itself, part of our culture. We need to constantly recognize the positive efforts in the group and share the positive experiences as a standard part of doing business. If we don't, our improved practices are at risk of being neglected into oblivion.

Oh Please! Credit Where Credit Is Due

I attended an event where people from two companies had a chance to speak about their success. They were the winner and runner-up for awards in the Team of the Year category from a local trade association.

One presenter identified an explicit focus on maintaining their culture and involvement at all levels as key to their success, but the same emphasis wasn't present in the second presentation.

Instead, when it came time to talk about how they overcame their challenges on the road to their incredible success, they identified two factors in the same breath: adoption of agile practices and incorporation of CMM Level 5 processes. I was very disappointed.

In my opinion, their success was due to the fact that the team worked together to accomplish great things (hence the name of the award). The emphasis should have been on the "we did great things" part of the presentation, rather than the dreadful namedropping.

No specific approach, no defined methodology has ever (or will ever) played a key role in the accomplishments of a successful team—for that matter, neither will any purchased tool or leveraged consultant that is introduced into the equation. They are at most bit players, catalysts that can serve to enable the team to do great things.

Both presenters were proud of their accomplishments, and rightly so.

One has survived being purchased with their unique culture and values intact, while managing massive growth and success in the process. The other has taken a strong customer-centric approach to building their product line. The team being honored, only 5 percent of the total company, has generated 50 percent of the company's overall revenue.

In both cases, the results can be attributed squarely to the people involved, and they should take full credit.

Don't get caught up in any of the hype that is pitched your way. Look inward to identify the primary driver for your success or failure.

If the packaging around defined frameworks, methodologies, or development approaches helps increase awareness and adoption within a group, so much the better, but they are information only, structuring the discipline of effective collaboration. The key factor in successful implementation of these tools is not what is embodied in the content, but how the team deals with the information they have at their disposal, and their openness to the discovery of other information that may fit their needs. The strength lies in how the ideas are embraced, not the ideas themselves.

Similarly, new tools can have all the novel technology in the world, but the manner of adoption will determine the payback. Marketing materials will cite all sorts of statistics about the benefits experienced by other users, but the relevance to your culture and your needs can't be expressed, or is consciously omitted.

Beware also of consultants who come in and suggest that you can't live without them on the team or that they are the driver of their previous clients' success. There is grave danger in dependency on high-priced external consultants who don't focus primarily on building your team's expertise. Prima-donna–based expertise can be a deadly addiction indeed, and merely bringing in the heroes sends a negative message to your group. When the heroes leave, have you lost a core competency? As with everything else, seek investments that strengthen your team, and you will easily stand out in the crowd.

Question any elixir that comes with guarantees of performance and question anything (or anyone) that locks you in before demonstrating value by strengthening your team. External support is merely a means to the end, whether in the form of information, technology, or human capital.

Remember that reasonable execution to success is the responsibility of your team, and that the team should own the credit for success!

Apply credit appropriately, cherish your team, and you will get more of the same in return.

Summary

It takes ongoing effort to end up at the place where we intended to be on our projects. Any bump in the road can set us off course or weaken our resolve to continue on the proper path.

Frameworks and defined approaches can help to provide guidance on how to get the job done. In the end, however, the efforts of the individuals on the team will determine success or failure. Ensure that people on the team are recognized for their contribution to that success. Work with the team as a whole to determine what could have been done better to address any failures.

How Is This Relevant?

Ongoing vigilance. Are you as careful in tending your projects as you are in building the initial plans? Can you reasonably focus on completing your tasks done while retaining focus on the overall goals?

Falling into old habits. Do you find yourself falling back into bad habits after a brief period of care? Have you consciously worked to retain these new habits long enough? Is there enough value in change to maintain the effort?

Proper credit. Do you and your group receive proper credit for a job well done? Do you acknowledge the efforts of others often enough? Are there opportunities today for you to recognize the success of someone you work with?

References

1. J. Stewart Black and Hal B. Gregersen, *Leading Strategic Change* (Prentice Hall, 2003).

PART SEVEN

Appendix

Here is a collection of tools that I have found to be extremely valuable over the years. Most of these have been beneficial in the practice of developing software and running projects, but many have been useful in other aspects of life.

This list of tools you might find useful is not exhaustive. Think of this more as a subset to add to your ever-growing collection. Although some of these tools have been implemented as software solutions, pencil and paper or whiteboard and marker work perfectly fine in most situations.

There are additional tools not listed here, because they are relatively well known and explained in better detail elsewhere. One of these is the Team Contract, described in Chapter 11, "Alignment," another is Leveling and Prioritizing Scope in Chapter 18, "Prioritization." Decision support tools and project retrospectives fall into this category as well.

For each tool, there is a brief description of the tool and benefit, some insights based on my experience in using the tools, and in most cases references to lead you in the best direction for more information.

Core Tools

Consciously Designed Workspaces

Overview

Few of us take the time to consciously manage our work environment, and the cost to our efficiency and effectiveness is enormous.

With care, we can design a physical and electronic environment that will make it easier to work more effectively. Better organization and less clutter allow us to focus on the important things we need to do, and an organization of where we spend our time makes us more efficient.

Core Elements

Have a look at your physical workspace. Can you even identify the color of your desktop? Do you spend a lot of time trying to find things? Is reference material close by? Do you have a system for managing all the information you want to keep, and for getting rid of everything you don't need?

Are you a slave to your e-mail inbox or do you manage to stay ahead of the game. (Is e-mail an effective communication tool, or merely a procrastination tool?) Are all of your planned activities listed in one place or scattered in e-mail, post-its, whiteboard lists, and (worse yet) buried in the corners of your brain? Do you manage your electronic files using the same "system" as your paper files?

When you have a workspace that doesn't deflate your zeal for work on sight, you can focus on other things. Are you generally working on tasks that are important and aligned to appropriate business goals? Are you focused on the perceived urgent things that have just popped into your inbox or have been handed to you with a phrase such as "can I have this by the end of the day?" Do you have the opportunity to carve out large chunks of uninterrupted time to do what you need to do, or do you simply arrive at work to find out today's schedule based on where the loudest screams are coming from? Do you have any idea what the next month has in store for you, and how much control do you have in managing that?

Hints and Caveats

From my experience, and in coaching others in this area, there are a few critical hints:

- **Be conscientious.** Take the time to design your system up front, a system that is consistent across your logical and physical spaces. Ensure you design a system that will accommodate changes reasonably: Starting a new project or gaining a new client shouldn't disrupt your system.

- **Be ruthless.** Especially when it is time to eliminate stuff that has been in your inbox for years or consuming valuable office space, this is not the time to err on the side of caution. If you haven't touched something for a long time (six months or so), the likelihood that you will need it again diminishes rapidly. If you can safely archive it out of your way, off to a server or in a box placed in long-term storage, get rid of it.

- **Stick with it.** Like quitting smoking or dropping a few pounds, this is a change in habits and behaviors. There will be times when you catch yourself falling into your old ways. Do this carefully, however, and you should see some benefits very soon, in a matter of days or weeks. Eventually it becomes your new habits.

- **Deal with your own mess first.** Before you try to tackle organization at the group level, get your own system organized first. There will be fewer opinions about what organization is best (hopefully), and you will understand just how challenging it can be to change behaviors.

Additional Information

Tom DeMarco and Timothy Lister, *Peopleware: Productive Projects and Teams, 2nd Edition* (Dorsett House Publishing, 1999).

David Allen, *Getting Things Done: The Art of Stress-Free Productivity* (Penguin, 2002).

Steve Prentice, *Cool Time: A Hands-on Plan for Managing Work and Balancing Time* (Wiley, 2005).

Mind Maps

Overview

We don't think in a linear fashion, but we have been forced to think that way given the lines on a page and the way words are organized in a book.

Mind maps are a great way to capture and organize information in a nonlinear (but far from random) fashion. The inner covers of this book started as mind maps as a way of capturing the key points of the four stages of teamwork.

Core Elements

Tony Buzan suggests using the following foundation structures for mind mapping:

- Start in the center with an image of the topic, using at least three colors.
- Use images, symbols, codes, and dimensions throughout your mind map.
- Select keywords and print using upper- or lowercase letters.
- Each word/image must be alone and sitting on its own line.
- The lines must be connected, starting from the central image. The central lines are thicker, organic, and flowing, becoming thinner as they radiate out from the centre.
- Make the lines the same length as the word/image.
- Use colors—your own code—throughout the mind map.
- Develop your own personal style of mind mapping.
- Use emphasis and show associations in your mind map.
- Keep the mind map clear by using radial hierarchy, numeric order, or outlines to embrace your branches.

Hints and Caveats

Here are some hints based on my experience:

- **Feel free to use color and pictures.** It is useful to get away from thinking only in words, just as it is useful to get away from thinking in a linear fashion. Colors and pictures can be a great way to express ideas.
- **Software can be useful, but get comfortable with it on paper or whiteboard.** I use software to create mind maps when I'm near a computer. However, whenever I am thinking about a new idea, I grab a piece of paper, drop the main theme in the middle, and start capturing ideas.
- **Useful in meetings.** On a whiteboard or with software and a data projector, mind maps can be great for capturing brainstorms from a group.

Additional Information

Tony Buzan, *The Mind Map Book* (Penguin, 1991).

MindJet/MindManager, at www.mindjet.com (software on both PC and Mac).

Vision Statements

Overview

In most projects, the team is all working frantically to get the product out the door, but there is rarely a single clear expression of exactly what product is being built, for whom, and why. Geoffrey Moore provides a great tool to use as a basis for discussion within the group to get closure on the core elements of any product: the vision statement.

Core Elements

A vision statement is built by completing each of the following statements:

- For [identify the primary customer]
- Who [identify their primary need]
- The [named product or service]
- Is a [categorized product or service]
- Which [identify the key features that address the need described above]
- Unlike [the primary competition]
- Our product [identify the key differentiation]

Hints and Caveats

Here are a few hints based on my experience:

- This works for physical products or service-based solutions.
- Often, there are several classes of competitors. Feel free to branch out for the last two items and to discuss how you differentiate from each of the major competitive classes.
- Chances are, no matter what stage your project is in, using this framework for discussion can generate some very interesting debate.

Additional Information

Karl Wiegers, *Software Requirements, 2nd Edition* (Microsoft Press, 2003). Karl describes the use of a vision statement in the context of software projects.

Conflict Management

Overview

We're conditioned to "come to the table with a solution," but this rarely results in a satisfactory solution for all stakeholders. When we do this, we have no idea whether the solutions we have pre-envisioned are even going to fit the needs of others.

We have to find a way to understand everyone's needs before we can start the solutioning exercise, and this is even more important when the parties are in conflict.

Core Elements

This is a critical succession of events, although we tend to skip steps in our haste to get to closure. We need to accomplish these steps, *in order,* for success:

- Ask yourself whether you are truly ready to learn something, to empathize with the other side. If you are heading into the situation to win, you are not ready.
- Introduce the topic, expressed from your perspective, and ask whether it is okay to discuss the issues.
- Dive into active listening mode, to dig down and truly appreciate the perspective of others. This isn't accomplished until you can paraphrase what their position is, and they can say that you truly understand their position.
- With permission, provide your perspective, again to the point where others can paraphrase your position so that you can say they truly understand.
- From there, identify a common ground, dig deeper if you have to, and formulate a solution from that basis.

Hints and Caveats

- Although this is critical to resolve conflict, this approach can be effective in any situation.
- Practice this first in a neutral environment. You will find yourself jumping past the first few steps, and it is best to do understand this before you dive into a critical situation.
- Without doing this, you won't know whether any of your suggestions are stepping on toes.

Additional Information

Roger Fischer and William Ury, *Getting to Yes: Negotiating Agreement Without Giving In* (Penguin, 1981).

William Ury, *Getting Past No: Negotiating Your Way from Confrontation to Cooperation* (Bantam, 1991).

Guidance for Special Situations

Overview

Most defined approaches focus on the happy path, what to do under normal conditions when things are going as expected. This is the easiest to do, and the natural place to start.

Unfortunately, most of the problems lie in the areas where things are not going according to plan. It is these special situations where guidance would be most appropriate, but is usually absent.

Just as best practices in the area of requirements and design suggest that you focus on the exceptions and error conditions to provide an appropriate and efficient approach for dealing with nonstandard issues, so should it be with defined approaches.

Core Elements

As an example, let's look at a change management process.

Most look very similar, and it is good practice to ensure that everything follows this defined process. Unfortunately, there will be times when the customer calls to say that your product is currently down (and it's costing them a fortune until it is up again). The last thing you want to tell them is to fill in the proper paperwork and that you'll get to it on Tuesday.

A well-defined, robust approach clearly identifies the following:

- What constitutes a reasonable deviation from the standard approach (more than Bob doesn't want to do the paperwork)
- What steps in the defined process can reasonably be shortened or removed to expedite the response
- What steps need to be taken to ensure that the system is brought back to a reasonable level of fidelity as soon as possible (how to clean up the mess)

Hints and Caveats

When involved in setting up a defined approach, always ask what could go wrong and what we should do when that happens.

Index

Q

BOOKS ONLINE

ENABLED

THIS BOOK IS SAFARI ENABLED

INCLUDES FREE 45-DAY ACCESS TO THE ONLINE EDITION

The Safari® Enabled icon on the cover of your favorite technology book means the book is available through Safari Bookshelf. When you buy this book, you get free access to the online edition for 45 days.

Safari Bookshelf is an electronic reference library that lets you easily search thousands of technical books, find code samples, download chapters, and access technical information whenever and wherever you need it.

TO GAIN 45-DAY SAFARI ENABLED ACCESS TO THIS BOOK:

- Go to **http://www.awprofessional.com/safarienabled**

- Complete the brief registration form

- Enter the coupon code found in the front
  of this book on the "Copyright" page

Addison
Wesley

Teams

	11. Alignment	12. Organization	13. Coordination	14. Guidance
Trouble Signs	• People head in conflicting directions • Rules emphasize avoiding the negative • Direction is mandated, not agreed	• Can't easily find the latest versions of documents • The defined approach is not being used • The purchased approach does not fit your culture • Early phases are neglected in the name of speed	• Leaders dwell on details • Documentation is perceived as bad • Outsourcing is not working • Clients are satisfied but there is internal conflict	• The team is told what to do • Process is derived from a single external framework • Shortcuts cause major problems on projects • Some team members are not required to follow the defined approach
Success Indicators	• Team behaviors are aligned • Measures are in place to learn • The team has collaborated to define the rules	• There is a clearly defined structure for information • All stakeholders participate in training • Even for a small team, there is a clearly understood approach	• Leaders facilitate rather than direct • The team works well together • Information is collected and shared as a team effort	• Process is used to facilitate rather than mandate • Elegant solutions are applied to process issues • The process has been tailored for each project
Questions to Ask	• Is team growth managed? • Does the team culture fit the individuals? • How would new team members absorb our behaviors?	• How is information organized on our project? • Do we spend too much time debating which process to follow?	• Do I have a real stake in this project? • Are we controlling our inputs and outputs? • Are we managing information well?	• Would we gain value in a more clearly defined approach? • Do we consistently apply our best practices?
Tools for Support	• Agree on a shared vision • Develop clear rules of conduct • Draft a team contract • Identify early symptoms of trouble • Define an approach appropriate for your group size	• Capture the current process before proceeding • Define the approach with the help of others • Consider the architecture of your process • Drive the definition of your approach as a project • Use insights from failures to feed process evolution	• Share information across the team • Actively participate in decision-making • Ensure information is managed as required • Retain responsibility and control when outsourcing • Use a balanced approach for oversight	• Help others understand the value of proposed changes • Consider and apply all perspectives of process • Include the end users of the process in the initial definition • Explicitly address consistent application of practices